PRAISE FOR
DEAD SERIOUS

"Clever prose and gifted storytelling enliven Eli J. Knapp's *Dead Serious*...diverting descriptions of flora and fauna lead into captivating lessons about biological principles, all of which are embellished with humor. A rousing read."

—*FOREWORD REVIEWS*

"For Emily Dickinson, 'Hope is the thing with feathers.' True in so many ways, but in *Dead Serious*, Eli J. Knapp reminds us that in the face of the ongoing 'sixth extinction,' hope also is the thing with fur, fins, or scales—and at times, even a thing with an upright, bipedal posture and opposable thumbs. Through a mix of personal story and descriptive vignettes of conservation science, Knapp leads us on a fascinating and entertaining journey through the many causes of extinction—and toward the hope that we need to do the hard and at times discouraging work of saving the world we love."

—CHRISTOPHER NORMENT, author of *Relicts of a Beautiful Sea: Survival, Extinction, and Conservation in a Desert World*

"A humorous take on extinction? Although the theme of this book is extinction, and although Eli J. Knapp's charming stories often crack me up, this book is, indeed, dead serious—except where it is heartfelt and funny. Knapp makes extinction relatable to those of us who feel far removed from ivory-billed woodpeckers and tiny arctic flowers growing on high peaks of the Adirondacks. I'm not surprised that always-insightful Knapp has come up with an original take on such a dire and disturbing topic. Heavy-handed, hard-science writings on what is happening to the biosphere are challenging to read and leave one feeling hopeless. This book is the opposite of that: personal, engaging, even hopeful—what a great way to confront such an important, weighty subject."

—DAWN HEWITT, editor of *Bird Watcher's Digest*

"A book about our wild lives teetering on the edge of extinction titled *Dead Serious* that is also dead smart and dead funny could only be written by Eli J. Knapp. Knapp offers himself as companion and guide to lead us toward a hope as wild and inspired as his imagination."

—SUSAN FOX ROGERS, author of
My Reach: A Hudson River Memoir

"In *Dead Serious*, Eli J. Knapp outlines the evolutionary ecology regarding extinction of species—a very serious issue for our time. However, this is not a depressing read, but a highly engaging one, with many intriguing encounters with wildlife."

—TOM WESSELS, author of *Reading the Forested Landscape:*
A Natural History of New England

DEAD SERIOUS

DEAD SERIOUS

Wild Hope Amid the Sixth Extinction

ELI J. KNAPP

TORREY HOUSE PRESS

Salt Lake City • Torrey

First Torrey House Press Edition, September 2021
Copyright © 2021 by Eli J. Knapp

Published by Torrey House Press
Salt Lake City, Utah
www.torreyhouse.org

MIX
Paper from
responsible sources
FSC
www.fsc.org   FSC® C011935

International Standard Book Number: 978-1-948814-40-9
E-book ISBN: 978-1-948814-41-6
Library of Congress Control Number: 2020946735

Cover photo by Dennis Goodman
Cover design by Kathleen Metcalf
Interior design by Rachel Buck-Cockayne
Chapter illustrations by Linda M. Knapp
Distributed to the trade by Consortium Book Sales and Distribution

Torrey House Press offices in Salt Lake City sit on the homelands of Ute, Goshute, Shoshone, and Paiute nations. Offices in Torrey are on homelands of Southern Paiute, Ute, and Navajo nations.

Expert birder Kimberly Kaufman has said that everyone is a birder somewhere deep down inside.

Everybody, that is, except my mother.

Even so, I dedicate this book to Mom and Dad, for the love and ceaseless support you've shown me. I recognize that my life has been for the birds. But what a joy it has been to share it with you.

Hands cupped around a mouth. I had thought sophisticated apps were needed for this. This unflinching, soft-spoken man with dancing eyes was rewriting what being attuned to nature really meant.

Not long after, I stood behind a tree to relieve myself. Suddenly a hand grabbed my shoulder and dragged me through the brush. "Hey!" I protested. "I'm not done!" My abductor cared not. I staggered through the dense brush, pants around my ankles, unable to offer resistance. It was Wilberforce. He stopped abruptly and pointed. I followed his finger and saw it.

Whitish breast, dingy gray back, faint black throat stripe, and a jaunty rufous cap. This one I knew, I'd memorized its field marks— Turner's eremomela. It was a species found in just a few choice locations. At fewer than thirty thousand in number, its existence here a decade from now was as chancy as a dice roll. The bird's toehold on this remnant scrap of forest looked as tenuous as its spaghetti-thin metatarsals. Small, drab, little-regarded. Also: near-threatened, threatened, endangered—depending on which conservation listing you check.

There is nothing exceptional about this bird. I can count the number of times I've discussed it—even with other birders—on one hand. One finger, actually. It's the epitome of a background bird, an unnoticed prop on a cluttered stage set. The show can go on without it. On my hike with Wilberforce, the African blue flycatchers were showier, the red-tailed bristlebills were vocally richer. The common buzzards were easier to pronounce. But while all of Kakamega's birds face myriad threats, the drab little eremomela faces the greatest chance of extinction.

Two valid questions emerge: One, who cares? And two, why is the eremomela facing its doom? Outside of a few East African conservationists, the answer to the first question is, probably no one. Why the bird faces extinction, however, is more interesting. It's more a head than a heart question. You may recognize a slew of foreboding buzzwords implicated in the bird's demise: climate change, habitat loss, and development. While such generalities aren't wrong, they're not enlightening either, just an opaque mass of advancing storm clouds. Often, conversation-killing concepts like that obscure relevant questions. Like: Why isn't another little nondescript forest bird, the rufous-crowned eremomela, practically indistinguishable from Turner's eremomela, also staring down extinction? Why does the rufous-crowned flit winsomely about while Turner's teeters on the edge? Not to mention a host of other little anonymous birds that have been much more persecuted than the Turner's eremomela.

• • • •

I'd prefer to answer questions like these with a sly hagiography that subtly showcases my own wise, Wilberforcian approach to nature. One that conveniently omits head-scratching blind spots, inexcusable hypocrisy, and unsound decision making. So why won't I? Because I already have. Look no further than my first book, *The Delightful Horror of Family Birding: Sharing Nature with the Next Generation.* I didn't set out to appear like the reincarnation of St. Francis, it was merely a byproduct of cherry-picking my favorite stories. Perhaps it's better that way. After all, in that book I was chasing wonder, not extinction.

A smidgeon older, I'm ready to lay more out there. Plus, Michael Pollan wrote that an author's second book is more critical than the first, because it determines an author's trajectory, setting a path that becomes difficult to veer away from. I'm ripening on the vine. My widow's peak is detaching from the mainland, the crow's feet around my eyes look ever more like fossil impressions, and my back often hurts just from riding the mower. Life suddenly seems too short for caring about appearances, in the mirror and on the page. I'll likely alienate a few of you. But that seems better than edging around the brushy tangles.

Besides, if all our elementary school teachers are right, if we really learn best from our mistakes, then shouldn't conservationists and midlife professors admit them too? So that's what this more exposed book is, a plunge into a darker, more jargon-filled thicket with little more than a flickering headlamp and a rusty pair of loppers. The beast we're after is extinction, lumbering about with Sasquatchian stealth claiming victims out from under our noses. Mysterious yet traceable. For all we uncover along the way, I hope finger pointing and condemnation aren't among them. Condemnation kills hope.

Let's lay our guilt on the table and get on with it. Skip this paragraph if you're already heavyhearted. I'm only doing this once; here goes.

Wily housecats squirt out between our legs and annihilate the birds we've lured to our windowsills. The birds that escape collide with our Windex-scrubbed windows and the reflective glass of our skyscrapers, or end up in the grills of our SUVs. We burn fossil fuels 24-7. Our unused lawns exist in a miasma of arrested development and ecological sterility. If a dandelion appears, we blast it with Roundup. We coat the world in asphalt. High-fructose corn syrup powers our lives. Our umbilical cords have been replaced with power cords. We hunch over glowing screens in windowless, climate-controlled cubicles. We've replaced birdsong with ringtones and notification jingles that erode already shriveled attention spans. When our nerves get too frazzled at work, we hit the road for that sacred summer week, plugging in oversized RVs spitting distance from sixty-four others. Our shrink-wrapped meals are consumed under the roar of generators, nixing any chance of hearing an owl. We leave lights on. We let faucets run. We plant nonnative plants. We don't carpool. We consume too much. We throw out too much. Heaven forbid, we eat Pop-Tarts.

There. Done.

How can I find hope and redemption amid such guilt-wracked wreckage? I'm not sure. But despite all this, despite everything we've done to the planet and to ourselves, cool species remain. As you're reading this, a snow leopard pads along a narrow ledge in the Himalayas. A five-foot-long salamander lies hungry and alert in a crystal-clear Japanese headwater. A pod of Amazonian river dolphins picks through a flooded forest in Brazil. Oh, and by the way, they're pink. These creatures live. We should celebrate them. As we should the ones we're more used to—robins, deer, rabbits. Don't all the wild ones that have hung with us this far deserve some passing acclaim?

Academic types like me have an annoying habit of concluding our technical papers with the tired but true line: more research is needed. Yes, it is. And writing it over and over validates our existence and secures us a job. But when it comes to extinction, I don't think we need any more research. We need stories. Meaningful stories that inspire and educate. While stories abound, I've opted here for moldering cherries, overlooked by most, plus stories of my own riddled with personal folly and schadenfreude. "The world cannot be understood without numbers," Hans Rosling writes in his bestseller, *Factfulness*, "and it cannot be understood with numbers alone." Our beast—extinction—has been crunching numbers underfoot for far too long, leaving a wake of statistical, eye-crossing carnage. I'm done with more statistics of decline and doom. In its stead, misadventure. Like when I paraglided into the crowns of acacia trees. Or the night I shot a bear with a bow from my living room window (skip to Chapter 16, if you must).

Nobility won't be found here. Just an incompetent nature snoop letting the natural world captivate as it should. I mean, why not celebrate through story? I've realized my days for staining the back deck are numbered. Maybe you have too. While I knew midlife would make me more aware of my mortality, I didn't expect it to sensitize me to the mortality of the world's other 1.7 million different creatures spinning sixty-seven thousand miles per hour around the sun along with me. I can't articulate why I care about the fate of my fellow flora and fauna, I just do. Mass extinctions of the past intrigue me. But lately, I'm fixated on the one we're in, the one we're creating. Yes, we're smack in the throes of what most scientists call the sixth extinction, in reality a spate of extinctions rivaling anything the earth has endured before.

In such a time, it's easy to feel pessimistic and gloomy. In his book *A Walk Through the Year*, renowned naturalist Edwin Way Teale wrote about a time he watched a squirrel get snatched by a cat. Rather than fight back or try to escape, the squirrel went limp. It laid down on the grass immobilized in shock. I know conservationists who have done the same. I've done the same.

That's why I've written this book: herein is the most hopeful book about extinction you'll ever read. Eighteen anfractuous chapters from now, it'll be clear why a chance encounter with a Turner's eremomela means so much to me. More importantly, you'll learn why so many creatures like it face imminent extinction. Why eighteen chapters? Well, you're busy. Since my first book was designed for bathroom trips, this one is for the golf course. One chapter per hole for your non-golfing spouse. Also, eighteen happens to be the exact number of factors that underpin extinction. In other words, if you understand these eighteen, you understand extinction. Or so says a recently deceased ecological savant named Michael Soulé, unfortunately unknown except in nerdy conservation circles.

• • • •

Too often in life, important events happen without the world noticing. The year 1983 is a case in point. The United States invaded Grenada. A massive famine in Ethiopia claimed four million lives. Microsoft Word emerged along with the world's first mobile phones. If these events didn't capture you, then surely *Return of the Jedi* did. Or the debut of *Super Mario Brothers*, for Nintendo. If you were alive way back then as I was, I'm sure of one thing: you didn't notice a little essay by Michael Soulé.

Like me, Soulé was a college professor who loved wildlife and ecology. Perhaps in a midlife crisis of his own, he grew weary of the endless academic cycle of research, grading, and department meetings. No more. He quit his post at the University of California, San Diego, gravitated to Eastern religions, and plunged into a Zen period, replete with meditation. Fortunately for us, his wandering was more spiritual than intellectual. His interest in conservation held. Sometime during that span—in 1983—Soulé wrote his crowning achievement, a straightforward essay phrased as a question: "What Do We Know about Extinction?" His conclusion: not much. But he did list eighteen things that we need to know, a laundry list as unadorned as a December maple. Here they are:

1. Rarity – Low Density
2. Rarity – Small, Infrequent Patches
3. Limited Dispersal Ability
4. Inbreeding
5. Loss of Heterozygosity
6. Founder Effects
7. Hybridization
8. Successional Loss of Habitat
9. Environmental Variation
10. Long-Term Environmental Trends
11. Catastrophe
12. Extinction of Mutualist Populations
13. Competition
14. Predation
15. Disease
16. Hunting and Collecting
17. Habitat Disturbance
18. Habitat Destruction

If you just skimmed these, you're in good company. Outside of a cadre of like-minded conservationists, nobody noticed Soulé's eighteen points. I wouldn't have noticed either, had I not devoured another conservation masterpiece: David Quammen's *The Song of the Dodo*. Thick enough to knock out a goat, the book explains imperiled species through an underappreciated theory called island biogeography. I'll touch on that, but unlike Quammen, my crosshairs will be on Soulé's eighteen points. We'll take them one by one and cloak the clunkiest terms—heterozygosity and hybridization—in story.

That's what I've done here: shoehorned Soulé's eighteen points into a convenient chrysalis for storytelling. If you're looking to run the river quickly, however, this isn't your best pirogue. Extinction is a multifaceted phenomenon, riddled with oxbows and debris flows. Yes, extinction is forever, but what leads to it can't be squeezed onto a bumper sticker. To see it best, we'll head up tributaries and count on the current to lead us back. I sought personal vignettes wherever possible, but sometimes, I admit, I overreached. So, roll your eyes where you must, judge, and damn me to ecological hell. My Lyme-ridden body can handle it (Chapter 15, if you're wondering). All I ask is that you hang on to the gunwales long enough to let each chapter twist and turn and run its course. By journey's end, I'm betting the grandeur of Soulé's new world will send your eyebrows up like they did mine, and you'll emerge in a dazzling new understanding of ecology, natural history, and most of all, extinction.

It's a tall order. If Protestantism called for ninety-five theses for any sort of reformation, eighteen seems hardly sufficient. It isn't. But it's better than zero. And there's another reason too. Understanding these eighteen points, and doing so without becoming that catatonic squirrel, might do us good. Understanding can lend us hope. Hope can lend us motivation. And motivation may be that final critical ingredient. "The only hope for the species still living," E. O. Wilson wrote, "is a human effort commensurate with the magnitude of the problem." We can't afford to be immobilized out of shock or despair any longer.

To solve a problem, one first has to understand it. This can take a little work. A bit of focus and rolling up of the sleeves. The best part? You can leave your trousers on.

1

No Risk It, No Biscuit

Rarity (Low Density)

"Something in the lone survivor knows that even the ironclad law of Now can be outlasted."
—Richard Powers, *The Overstory*

It may seem odd to begin a book about hope with a bird that is extinct. I agree, it is. But the ivory-billed woodpecker's tale isn't like that of other species that have been scrubbed off the planet; this bird died, resurrected, then died again. Not really, of course. No, the ivorybill didn't go extinct twice. Its numbers merely dropped so low that we failed to find the bird for over fifty years. This reason—extreme rarity—makes the ivorybill ideal for illustrating Michael Soulé's first factor of extinction: rarity due to low density.

Since you're far more likely to encounter a foul pun than a live ivorybill, I'll discuss another woodpecker, too, one you *are* likely to see that's just a few inches less grand—the pileated woodpecker. If you've seen a pileated, you've almost seen an ivorybill. If you haven't seen a pileated, it has a spiky red Mohawk, striped face, smudgy dark bill, and coal-black feathers. Ivorybills had a similar gestalt, though they were bigger and had bold white-on-black feathers. Plus, the reason for their name, those creamy bills.

So we'll crane our necks at two woodpeckers, the presumably extinct ivorybill and the flashy and familiar pileated. Woodpeckers are a good starting point because we already know what they do: they peck wood. They also peck windows, propane tanks, gutters, cacti, and street signs, but let's ignore that. Woodpeckers depend on trees, giving them a clear connection to a distinct resource, which also partially accounts for the ivorybill's demise. While the specifics depend on who you ask, most agree that the bird's rarity and low density played a key part, too. As did everything about the trees they hitched their lives to, their: type, age, health, numbers, range, density, composition, and most importantly, eventual disappearance. But lest we lose the woodpeckers for the wood too soon, the fact that woodpeckers peck wood—and depend on it—is enough for now. Now for something that doesn't depend on wood. Football.

• • • •

"One Mississippi, two Missippi, three Missippi..." Adam counted, subtly subtracting syllables from the state that underpins all childhood backyard football games. Adam was the quintessential neighbor kid, besting me by a year and forty pounds. Ostensibly two-hand touch, every touch was a shove—if not a tackle. The latter risked snapping my sapling frame in two. And in our game bereft of talent and referees, the risk was real. If I wanted to live, I needed to chuck the faded Nerf ball as fast as possible.

Instead I stubbornly held the ball, backpedaling as Adam charged, his unzipped coat doubling his size. "Go DEEEEEEEEP!" I yelled to my little brother, his unlaced boots not helping his ten-year-old galumph downfield. Going deep was stupid. I couldn't throw far and my brother couldn't catch. David, another neighbor kid, stood wide open at the line of scrimmage. He waved his arms, begging me to make a simple, direct pass. I pretended not to see him.

Insistence on throwing the deep ball was just one of many reasons my football career was mercifully short. It's related, in a way, to the Cornell Lab of Ornithology's decision to announce the rediscovery of the greatest woodpecker to ever grace America's forests. It's why I applaud them for doing so.

But before we return to woodpeckers and extinction, note that my pubescent approach to football success had at least one supporter at the highest level. Bruce Arians, longtime NFL coach, has built a living on the deep ball. During his ten years in the league as an offensive coordinator or head coach, his teams threw the ball fifteen-plus yards on 22 percent of their pass attempts, easily the highest in the NFL. So much so that Arians's aggressive style of play assumed the motto, "No risk it, no biscuit." But critics were quick to indict this style. Arians's approach didn't produce a Super Bowl ring for the Arizona Cardinals. Throwing deep, they concluded, doesn't win.

• • • •

Partly for self-preservation, I spent far more time watching birds than playing backyard football. After hopping off the school bus, I'd drop my backpack on the floor, grab a Pop-Tart and my BB gun, and head outside. I spooked deer, caught snakes, reached into holes, stuck feathers in the waistbands of sweatpants, stalked squirrels, and advanced Darwinian selection upon the unwariest rabbits. What I got in return was contentment, perpetual poison ivy, and a nifty unintentional education about a little of everything: tracks, scrapes, scolds, snorts, and songs. I learned what lived in my little woodlot, and, by omission, what didn't.

But decades later, while sitting in the understory of a forest in northern Michigan during a break from a conservation biology course I was teaching, I heard something new. A sound. Rhythmic, reverberant, and difficult to pinpoint. *KEK-KEK-KEK-KEK-KEK-KEK!* A pileated woodpecker sliced by, rending my revelry. With a dip, the bird thrust out its clawed toes, effortlessly grasping the perforated trunk of a long-dead cottonwood a stone's throw from where I stood slackjawed. The tree was as limbless as a telephone pole, its broken crown melting back into the forest floor around me. The deep, reverberating drumming ceased, replaced with high-pitched squealing. My gaze settled just above the pileated, on a clearly chiseled hole thirty feet up. On cue, two scraggly heads popped out, each sporting a strawberry-red tuft. Pencil-necked, colorful, and strident. Little rock stars.

These were the obvious makers of the puzzling sound. They had drummed, I realized, from the inside out, producing a deeper, palpable sound, not the hammer-on-nail pounding I'd grown up hearing. The youngsters hadn't been able to wait, preparing early for lives of ceaseless head-banging.

So cool. A new discovery predicated on being in the right place at the right time. "Beauty and grace are performed whether or not we will or sense them," Annie Dillard wrote. "The least we can do is try to be there." That's all I had done—gone for a walk after class, listened, and been there. Minor yet fulfilling. How many others, I wondered, had heard woodpeckers drumming from the inside of a tree? Had Tecumseh? Thoreau? Meriwether Lewis?

One person might have. Artist Don Eckelberry, armed with pencil, sketchbooks, and a sturdy boat, longed for such a sound. Hastily dispatched in 1944 by Audubon Society president John Baker, Eckelberry paddled his way into Louisiana's Singer Tract, 130,000 acres of old-growth forest owned by the Singer sewing machine company. But Eckelberry wasn't after pileated woodpeckers, he was after their larger, flashier relative, ivorybills. His mission was simple: find them and sketch them.

His haste was due to the fact that the once-flourishing ivorybill had become astonishingly rare. Again, woodpeckers peck wood. At the turn of the twentieth century, ivorybills had precious little to peck—a whopping 98 percent of their native forest had been removed since the time John James Audubon traversed the Southeast over one hundred years earlier. As the removal of trees caused the Lorax to lose his beloved Swomee-Swans, so America lost its beloved ivorybill.

Well, not entirely. Intensive searching in 1944 did turn up one stalwart survivor for Eckelberry to study. A female.

• • • •

The adult pileated woodpecker ratcheted up to its two nestlings. The nestling on top immediately thrust its head into the adult's open bill. The other hatchling stood by, hungry and hopeful. A chance never came. Its greedy sibling's head moved like a sewing machine, quickly exhausting whatever supply the parent had brought. Fledging from the nest was no sure thing. The nestlings had hatched asynchronously, so the first had a sizable lead on the second; it was bigger, stronger, and more voracious. Parents don't spread the wealth, opting instead to feed whatever open maw they see first. Sibling rivalry isn't for the faint of heart; only a bountiful food year would ensure that both would live.

Now empty, the parent pulled its great crested head out of reach of the clamoring nestling, skittered to the side of the nest hole, and launched, the underside of its white wings striking a sharp contrast to the ebony feathers of its body.

Grand as the pileated is, ivorybills were grander. A pale, cream-colored bill lent the bird its name. But those who saw it called it something else. "Lord God!" onlookers exclaimed, as an ivorybill sailed past. The reverential nom de plume stuck, due in part to the massive, mythical old-growth hardwoods the bird flew among. The Lord God bird's power matched its moniker, prompting John James Audubon to write, "The strength of this Woodpecker is such, that I have seen it detach pieces of bark seven or eight inches in length at a single blow of its powerful bill." Audubon's vivid observations make one wish he'd glimpsed Mexico's imperial woodpecker, the largest woodpecker to ever live, a full three inches larger than even the ivorybill. It, too, is no more.

Adult gone, the young pileated woodpeckers retreated back into the cavity. The forest fell silent. An obsessive note-taker, I sat on a toppled white pine and started scribbling. "There is not a sprig of grass that shoots uninteresting to me, nor anything that moves," Thomas Jefferson wrote. While it's often a curse, I share his curiosity. Here was a ripe opportunity to learn more. How often, I wondered, do they feed their young? Twenty-four minutes later, I had my answer. That session at the nest hole turned into many, sucking me like a black hole, too, with my notebook and more questions. Both parents, I realized, were devoted, taking turns with a constant stream of grocery runs. Without fail, the larger sibling stuck its head out first and received most, if not all, of the food. One week later, only one head popped out of the hole.

Never again did I see the smaller sibling. Several weeks later, the lone sibling fledged, the stunted bones of its dead sibling entombed within the tree.

Eckelberry also took notes about the lone ivorybill he tracked. He scribbled "KENT" in his journal, describing his phonetic handle of the ivorybill's call. Other observations record the vegetation and other creatures he found near the female's roosting tree. Sparse but significant, Eckelberry's records are the last ever done on a living ivorybill. You can see them yourself in the Leigh Yawkey Woodson Art Museum, in Wisconsin, where some pages blur the line between science and poetry:

> About 5:30—*KENT*!
> Double rap while walking
> Through small uncut
> area about 1/3 mile from rd.
> Found her immediately.

Eckelberry's last line is darkly ironic. The ivorybill was never found immediately again. Despite a prolonged, intensive search, the bird vanished. For the next five decades nobody conclusively saw another ivorybill. Tragically, the ornithological community concluded, the bird was extinct. But in this case, extinction wasn't for forever.

• • • •

On an overcast day in 2004, Gene Sparling kayaked down the Cache River National Wildlife Refuge near Brinkley, Arkansas. Suddenly, a huge woodpecker flew toward him, landing on a nearby tree. A pileated. The bird hitched around a tree in a "herky-jerky, cartoon-like" manner, making him pause. Sparling studied the bird, memorizing every field mark. When he returned home, he posted his description on an online message board. The observation migrated around the web, eventually winding up on the desk of ivorybill expert Tim Gallagher, then writing a book about the extinct bird. Gallagher contacted Sparling, thinking a follow-up interview might augment his book, or the quarterly magazine he edited for the Cornell Lab of Ornithology, *Living Bird*.

The magazine title was appropriate. A living bird—an extant ivorybill—was exactly what Gallagher needed to confirm or deny. Why not, Gallagher thought. In 2001, he'd embarked on a dangerous trip to ascertain the existence of the imperial woodpecker, which his party hadn't been able to verify. Maybe this trip would be different. Sparling's vivid description sparked Gallagher's imagination. Gallagher contacted another ivorybill fan, Bobby Harrison, who agreed to a trip south. Not long later, the three paddlers—Gallagher, Harrison, and Sparling—had set off down the Cache River, with Sparling in the lead.

I can't help but wonder how Sparling felt that first time Gallagher and Harrison joined him on a paddle down the Cache River. His story—his one brief sighting—had convinced two busy academics and ornithological heavyweights to interrupt their lives and lighten their wallets. On that first day, when no ivorybill appeared, did he question himself? Did he feel his credibility gradually eroding with every passing birdless hour?

• • • •

Maybe. Or maybe he trusted himself, as I had not long ago upon discovering a seldom seen, sleek raptor called a merlin not far from my house. Excited by the rare sighting, I did what many bird enthusiasts do—immediately posted my find on eBird. The small falcon had just caught a nuthatch and sat plucking it on a limb, more interested in breakfast than in me. As the nuthatch feathers drifted down like snowflakes, I did what I did with the pileated woodpecker discovery. I pulled out my notebook and jotted down everything relevant: time, appearance, behavior, even the tree species it perched upon. Nature OCD in action. Which later went on eBird.

The next day an email appeared. It was from our region's system administrator, a widely acknowledged bird guru of western New York. His email was short and polite. But it was also—*gasp!*—skeptical. Instantly, I went from Bruce Banner to the Hulk in *The Avengers*. Where did this guy live? I wanted to show up at his house and smash him over the head with my laptop. How dare he not trust me?! Birdology flowed in my veins. I typed back a hasty, passive-aggressive message detailing the merlin's behavior. I added a few other field marks. Take that, I thought, clicking send.

The guru took it but unfortunately not as proof. A day later he remained unconvinced. I reread his second perfidious message, my temples growing even hotter. This was no longer about the bird; it was about me. I knew my raptors, had studied them since childhood. One of my rare finds across the ocean had appeared in a definitive book about African raptors. I had taught ornithology for a decade. Who was this bloke to question me? How patronizing! I forced myself to breathe. And then, ever so surreptitiously, one niggling doubt scampered by in the shadowy margin of my mind. Was I *sure* it was a merlin? *Absolutely* sure? Then another. Had I *really* looked at it long enough? Had I wanted it to be something it wasn't? Could I, heaven forbid, have mistaken it for a sharp-shinned hawk? Sometime later, thank heavens, a friend sent me an email with photo attachments. He, too, had seen the merlin near where I had. Better yet, he had photos.

● ● ● ●

If only Sparling had taken photos, too. Then, regardless of what they saw, his proof would have been incontrovertible. Instead, he had a growing number of doubts. But, on day two, at 1:15 p.m., a woodpecker flew across the bayou right in front of the three paddlers. Each of them knew instantly—it was an ivorybill. Sparling must have exhaled mightily. Sweet vindication.

That sighting was just the beginning. In a hush-hush operation, others joined the search. By the time all the kayak paddles had dried, thirteen sightings were made, all in 2004. For fourteen months, scientists from the Cornell lab systematically scoured the Cache, still hoping for conclusive audio or visual documentation. But that never came. All the team managed were a few blurry images and inconclusive recordings. Figureheads met, debate ensued, and finally, the lab confirmed:

the ivorybill was alive. A year later, in a controversial move, the world's leading bird lab went public. Their announcement was far too big for a middling ornithological monograph. Only the best, most prestigious journal—*Science*—befitted the resurrection of the Lord God bird. Even a prosaic title—"Ivory-billed Woodpecker (*Campephilus principalis*) Persists in Continental North America"—couldn't deaden the impact. A bird bomb had been dropped.

The bird world went ballistic. This was a true miracle, a triumph of resilience flouting a half-century of sinful exploitation. Every news outlet splashed the story on its front page. Birders salivated for a chance to find the bird themselves. Yet amid the hoopla, one inconvenient datum slowly emerged. With every passing week, month, and year, the rain fell heavier on the parade. No fourteenth sighting occurred. No living ivorybill was ever seen again. Despite amateur birdwatching's meteoric ascent, personal kayaks costing about the same as a nice dinner out, and rewards of $50,000 for evidence, precious little has turned up since. Optimistic field guides remain equivocal. "The ivory-bill is *probably* extinct," admits Cornell's website. I hate to agree—it probably is.

• • • •

The shadow of Michael Soulé's first contributing factor of extinction—rarity and low density—looms over the ivorybill's dispiriting disappearing act. "Ivorybills naturally occur at very low densities," commented Dave Wilcove in *Science*. Wilcove then cited J. Tanner, who completed the ivorybill's only field study just before Eckelberry jotted down his final notes on the lone female. Tanner "estimated the density of ivorybills to be no more than one pair per 16-44 km^2 of suitable habitat," wrote Wilcove. "When coupled with the degraded condition of the current habitat and the paucity of the sightings," he went on, "it suggests that any breeding population must be extremely small, perhaps only a few pairs. Such a tiny population would be highly vulnerable to stochastic extinction processes."

What Wilcove meant was that for however many individuals remained, the survival of the species was down to dumb luck. One stealthy bobcat, a few feisty rat snakes, or a bad storm could close the curtains on ivorybills. I understand his sentiment. For the bird, these were the worst of times. But I couldn't help but wonder, what about the best of times? Before all the degradation and the paucity of sightings? Were they ever easy to see? Or were they always, in Soulé's lingo, a "rare, low-density" bird?

It's a hard question to answer definitively, especially since eBird arrived two centuries too late. So, I turn to the next best source: John James Audubon himself. During the early 1800s, nobody was watching the skies—and the swamps—more carefully than he. When he wasn't watching, shooting, and painting birds, he was commenting on them. The following is his two cents on ivorybills: "Descending the Ohio," he wrote, "we meet this splendid bird for the first time near the confluence of that beautiful river and the Mississippi; after which, following the windings of the latter, either downwards toward the sea, or upwards in the direction of the Missouri, we frequently observe it." He later added: "I found it very abundant along the finely wooded margins of that singular stream, called 'Buffalo Bayou,' in the Texas, where we procured several specimens."

Abundant? All the way to Texas? This strains credulity. But Audubon sharpens his claim in a unique way: with his encounters with Native Americans. "I have seen entire belts of Indian chiefs," he wrote, "closely ornamented with the tufts and bills of this species, and have observed that a great value is frequently put upon them." The oxymoronic nature of Audubon's anecdote supports Wilcove's and Tanner's observations about the bird's density: ivorybills were common enough to adorn entire belts, but rare enough to command a great value.

Rarity is determined by two interlinked factors: the geographical range of a species—its extent of occurrence—and the abundance of that species within any specified area. This allows two ways for a species to be rare. One, if it has a limited geographical range (regardless of abundance). And two, if it's numerically few (regardless of a widespread range). The rarest species are those that are numerically few and geographically limited. Species like this, of course, are in the greatest jeopardy.

In this light, Audubon's remarks reveal a longstanding truth about rarity: it is relative. Relative to both other species and the observer's whereabouts. In Texas's Buffalo Bayou, the ivorybill *seemed* abundant. As it did along the Mississippi. Had Audubon ventured away from the great rivers, the bird would have dropped off. In the context of the United States in the nineteenth century, these unique habitats—towering old-growth cypress trees flanking sinuous watercourses—were limited. They're much more limited today. Although conjecture, I bet the ivorybill seemed abundant there because he hadn't seen them elsewhere. Relative to where he'd previously been, they were suddenly abundant.

Rarity is relative to body size, too. In their chapter "Who is Rare?" from the comprehensive book *The Biology of Rarity*, authors Blackburn and Gaston illustrate this by comparing a bird to an insect. If a bird attained a density of one hundred individuals per square kilometer, most ornithologists would call the bird common, or abundant. But if an insect—a great leopard moth, for example—attained the same density, entomologists would call the moth rare. If there's any dogma in the science of rarity, this is it: large-bodied species tend to be rarer than small-bodied species.

The pileated woodpeckers I watched in Michigan reveal this lucidly. Despite being smaller than ivorybills, they're the seventh-largest woodpecker in the world, outsizing 214 others. At seventeen and a half inches long and weighing over half a pound, they're relative heavyweights, nearly eleven times heavier than America's smallest, the puny downy woodpecker.

Such size demands a constant food supply, especially when they're raising young. One way to achieve that is to defend the fridge. Not once during my month-long vigil under the pileated nest did I see any other pileated approach the nest tree. Or even do a flyby. It wasn't because others weren't around, nor was it my shoddy observational skills. Rather, it was because my pileated pair patrolled their territory diligently, chasing away interlopers on sight. For many birds, private property is paramount, a matter of life or death. Had I seen the world through pileated eyes, bold "no trespassing" signs would have extended out from the nest tree in all directions, nearly two square kilometers large. Intruders were neither trusted nor tolerated. It explains why America's forests don't drip with pileated woodpeckers: their density is dictated—at least partially—by territoriality.

Here's an obvious truism: larger species need more resources than smaller ones. Often that means larger territories. For woodpeckers surviving on the storehouses that dead and decaying trees provide, territory size depends on that all-important variable. Most forests are habitat mosaics, the trees that woodpeckers need scattered slipshod across a landscape. Large fires, in addition to widespread insect and disease outbreaks, can uniformize habitats to a degree. But, especially in the wetter eastern half of the country, trees more often die piecemeal, providing an inconsistent and patchy food source. In such settings, forest free-for-alls won't cut it, especially for a pileated pair trying to meet the demands of their voracious young.

In response, they carve up forests into defensible units, the most vigorous males commanding the best, most food-rich glades. People, of course, do it too. For years I snaked my small truck through the winding roads of Montecito, California, just discerning the terracotta roofs of the well-heeled estates of Oprah and other celebrities. While they had means to carve out luxurious estates defended by high walls, my meager graduate school stipend forced me to rent a single room in a crowded development. While my cavity was perfectly adequate in the short-term, it wouldn't be ideal for raising a family.

Better and larger forests generally, but not always, hold more woodpeckers. Forest quality is in the eye of the beholder. To a lumberjack eyeing efficiency and economic return, a good forest is a monoculture of even-aged, easily harvestable trees. A hiker may prefer a forest without undergrowth and fallen trees to scramble over and around. A woodpecker wants a deathly forest. One with oodles of dead, dying, degenerate trees brimming with luscious insect larvae and pockmarked with roosting and nest holes. Exactly the kind of forest we've been culturally conditioned to condemn.

As America's forests were razed to fuel expansion, so, too, went the woodpeckers. As they've regenerated, the woodpeckers, biding their time in overlooked, less accessible places, have also come back. So, the pileated is back, occasionally making cameos at suet feeders, even. And why not the ivorybill? Why did one return while the other didn't?

Because ivorybills had another all-important need. One that likely was their doom. Crummy, interstitial forests weren't sufficient. Only magisterial, old-growth—and preferably flooded—forests sufficed. Bottomland swamps of bald cypress trees. And for the population to grow, they needed some sizable nearby stands of pines or dying trees to feed in. This wasn't too big a request for the Choctaw and the Natchez people who lived in such places. For centuries, they lived alongside ivorybills just fine. European colonizers didn't make such tolerant neighbors. As the forests went, so went the birds.

• • • •

But as the forests went, some birds did just fine. In late August this past year, I looked out the window and counted eighteen robins hopping across my backyard. And there were likely more in the front. Robins, and other highly adaptable birds like European starlings and house sparrows, have tolerated our spreading cities and suburbs just fine. Obviously, we needn't fret over the city slickers. What we *should* fret over is how they aggressively compete with the rare, low-density birds lurking around them. This is the rationale explaining why rarity and low density appears as Soulé's first extinction factor.

The trends aren't good for some formerly abundant birds. According to the Cornell lab, bobolinks declined 65 percent from 1966 to 2015. During the same period, purple martins dropped 37 percent, and golden-winged warblers dropped 68 percent. Spotted owls plummeted. California condors went on life support. According to a recent report in *Science*, populations are trending downward for 529 bird species. In the United States and Canada, the decline is nearly 30 percent since 1970, stated the study's lead author, conservation scientist Ken Rosenberg.

If the previous paragraph didn't quicken your pulse, you're in good company. Statistics of doom and gloom, which I promised I'd spare you from, don't raise eyebrows anymore. We're desensitized, worn down with conservation fatigue. Chicken Little made it clear: when it comes to losing species, we're utterly clucked.

That's precisely why the Cornell lab's decision to go public with the ivorybill's rediscovery was so important, revolutionary even. It struck a wholly different tune. With one brave announcement, bird fans and nature lovers found a bounce in their step. For the first time in ages, they felt a new emotion—hope. Not just for a nondescript species, but a glorious one. For the conservation community and the ivorybill, the sky was rising.

Media outlets jumped all over the story and the Lord God bird rightly stole the spotlight. But it raised another question, too. Publicizing a sensitive bird's existence—even with its specific location under wraps—risked instant harassment from frenzied birders hellbent on adding the mythical bird to their personal lists. Inaccessible swamp or not, crazy birders would stalk it. Heck, had I been within a day's drive, I would have thrown my kayak on the car roof and headed for the bayou. (This, incidentally, is the sound rationale behind eBird's decision not to reveal specific locations for rare, low-density owls. It keeps bird creeps like me at bay.) Shouldn't the world's best ornithological research center do everything in its power to safeguard such a treasure? Wouldn't prudence call for keeping the mythical bird's existence a secret?

Yes, and yes. Keeping mum about the rediscovery may have been prudent. But I'm unconvinced it would have been better. Hope was in short supply back in 2004. It joyously reemerged with the ivorybill. And like the bird, it's seemingly gone again. Yet hope, I contend, is the one species we can't afford to lose.

How do we conserve hope? With what science writer David Quammen calls "gloriously improbable gambits." Sometimes, what our tinder-dry imaginations need most are simply some sparks.

• • • •

In 1763, not long after the French and Indian War, a group of Ojibwa and Sauk people played a routine, innocent game of stickball just outside the walls of Fort Michilimackinac. The fort was guarded by thirty-five British soldiers, who no longer viewed the Indians as a viable threat. Stickball games were a pleasant diversion from the tedium of daily fort life.

While the games went on, Ojibwa women were working inside, conscripted to help the soldiers with sundry tasks. Mutually acknowledged peace—and convenience—kept the fort gate lightly guarded, if at all.

Unbeknownst to the British, a loose confederation of Native American nations had grown dissatisfied with the string of harsh policies enacted in the Great Lakes region. Outnumbered and outmatched, Chief Pontiac opted for a high-risk enterprise, which included taking Fort Michilimackinac by surprise.

On June 2, a Native American player intentionally hit the ball through the fort's open gate. The players feigned innocence, all rushing after the ball. The unsuspecting British, lulled into complacency, didn't react. Once inside, Ojibwa women handed each warrior a tomahawk they had smuggled in. At close combat and ill-prepared, the British were no match for the Ojibwa. Fifteen to twenty British were killed as the fort quickly changed hands.

High risk combined with clever creativity resulted in a minor victory for a long-suffering people. But the spoils of this victory were richer than most: a story, worthy of future retelling in birchbark longhouses, the ingenuity of it accentuated by the tendrils of smoke searching their way upward, to freedom. A story to ignite the imaginations of the youngest listeners, a story to bestow hope and identity, invaluable in a war facing long odds.

The Cornell lab smashed their own ball into Fort Michilimackinac. Unorthodox but not uncalculated. The team studied the evidence and deliberated. Then, the gambit. Like the British guards, few saw it coming. Critics quickly retaliated, spurring a philosophical bloodbath that spilled over into a slew of technical journals. Some compared the lab's evidence and blurry photos to Nessie-and-Sasquatch-level fodder. Commandeering the media has a cost, they argued, redirecting attention, money, and research from other, more recoverable species. So many other species were desperate for such attention, silently clamoring for reintroduction, relocation, and recovery. Why sabotage them with such a long shot? Especially one that could be hurt by the publicity?

While practicality is essential in conservation, I'm growing leerier of it. Cool, level-headed voices have steered conservation budgets for decades. Instead of emptying our budget out on the red wolf, the thinking goes, let's focus our efforts on species that actually have a chance. Like the Dismal Swamp southeastern shrew and the Furbish's lousewort. Let's stabilize those first, then move on to the Northern Idaho ground squirrel, the southeastern beach mouse, and the lesser slow loris. Five for the price of one.

Yes, more for the money. But most folks want nothing to do with dismal swamps and warty lice. Squirrels, mice, a lesser slow loris? Seriously?

I feel for these creatures. I really do. But I worry that too much budget-conscious decision-making kills hope. While triage is necessary in conservation, so too is imagination.

Certainly, charismatic megafauna is a tired concept and overused, especially in conservation circles. But the animals themselves—Bengal tigers, snow leopards, giant pandas—remain vital and, for now at least, at large. Tigers and leopards quicken our pulse and remind us that other creatures exist that are undeniably faster, stronger, sleeker, and in the case of the panda, far more adorable. They have *it*. That indescribable and oh-so-important quality. Something that, regardless of a botanist's impassioned protestations, the lousewort never will.

Triage is prudent, short-pass thinking. It may win NFL games, but its efficacy in long-range conservation is iffier. According to the Environmental Protection Agency, over 1,300 species are threatened or endangered in the United States alone. In the world, 36,000 species have similar designations, according to the Convention on International Trade in Endangered Species (CITES). A tall order—especially when coupled with the high rates of poverty and habitat loss in equatorial latitudes. Even expertly executed triage, I'm afraid, is unlikely to make a dent.

Gene Sparling knew what he saw. As did ivorybill experts Tim Gallagher and Bobby Harrison. I've spent enough time in nature to know that improbable things do happen. Baby woodpeckers drum on the insides of trees. To hear it, or see them, you just need to be there. Call me a sucker, but I trust their sightings entirely.

The paucity of follow-up sightings has left me less convinced that Sparling's ivorybill is still ratcheting up cypress trees, rending the still morning air with a chorus of staccato cries. But I am convinced that going public with the rediscovery was the right thing to do. In a world of atrophied budgets, cynicism, and dour forecasts, it gave everybody a momentary toehold of hope. Enough, perhaps, to rouse people and change things.

• • • •

Four Mississippi…five Mississippi…Adam charged me, arms outstretched for bludgeoning. He hit me just as I released the ball. It sailed into the overcast November sky like a cheap set of dud fireworks. Up and then down, landing with a dull thud, twenty yards shy of my scowling brother.

I could have thrown it short, of course. But I opted for a miracle, the gloriously improbable gambit. At fourteen years old, I was driven by imagined glory, not completion percentage. Decades later, I still am, even more so. Imagination, and the inspiration it spawns, forge our collective identities. They give us against-all-odds stories, stories we sorely need in the bleak midwinter of the extinction crisis. Sure, the chances of taking Fort Michilimackinac are slim. But if we win some, they give us hope.

Bengal tigers still pad through the mangrove swamps of the Sundarbans. Snow leopards pace castellated Himalayan peaks. Giant pandas sit on their furry fannies munching vegetables. All species are worth it, but these have something else—an innate ability to activate our imagination. To momentarily forget ourselves, tilt our heads in awe, and exclaim, "Lord God!"

If prudent conservation means a slow slog to extinction, then deep-six it. Let's go for the Hail Mary.

2
Goodness Snakes Alive

Rarity
(Small, Infrequent Patches)

"But most of all I love them because they make me feel alive in a way nothing else can."
—Christina Baal, *When Birds Are Near*

"Jen, I gotta go. Eli's being attacked by a rattlesnake!" Dustin pocketed his phone and sprang off the ledge, searching for weapons. I remained fixed on the ledge like a gargoyle, my eyes locked on the snake's triangular head, now inches from my right elbow. Any sudden movement might incite a strike. The snake began rattling, sounds I'd moments earlier assumed were produced by cicadas. Frontal shields on its head lent the unblinking eyes a menacing look. They searched for movement as the forked tongue flickered, tasting the air. Lurid chevrons ran the length of the fat body, turning darker until halted by a half dozen buzzing rattles. The creature seemed too foul for bucolic Pennsylvania.

Ironically, I spent my youth longing for such an encounter. While Eve took the apple, I longed for the snake. I had searched, too, endlessly hoofing across the rolling forested hills of northeastern Pennsylvania. My reference books insisted eastern timber rattlesnakes had a widespread distribution, extending from New Hampshire to Wisconsin and all over the South, from Florida to Texas. I firmly disbelieved them; my boyhood summers spent peering into nooks and crannies had produced not one serpentine scale.

But that was then. Now, during a summer off between grad school semesters, my hand-me-down Huffy with a loose, rusty chain had given way to Dustin's rental car. Hoping for a bit of bracing backcountry camping in a new place, we had chosen Loyalsock State Forest, a hundred-thousand-acre swath of crumbling Appalachian Mountains several hours southwest from my boyhood summer cottage. Since neither of us liked to follow the crowd, we chose our off-the-beaten path intentionally. Loyalsock lacked people but not vistas. A surfeit of south-facing sedimentary ledges afforded marvelous views, one of which flanked our campsite. The ledges soaked up the spring and summer sun with the alacrity of an asphalt parking lot. Pockmarking them were deep recesses, some extending well below the frost line. This unique combination was vital for timber rattlesnakes, lacking internal thermostats. It also explained why I hadn't found them decades earlier; such ledges leveled out further north. Only in special places like this lurked *Crotalus horridus*, loosely translating: something godawful in the hollow of the rocks.

Calling these creatures godawful is fine. Calling them cold-blooded, however, isn't. It oversimplifies the way they regulate their temperatures. Some of the time, like when they're basking on a sunny ledge in July with a belly full of chipmunks, their blood is downright warm. This makes them ectothermic, or that fancier term our fourth-grade teachers couldn't get us to pronounce correctly: poikilothermic.

If you insist on calling them cold-blooded, you better call chipmunks the same. Hyperactive in summer, endothermic chipmunks hibernate in the winter. As warm-blooded as Alvin, Simon, and Theodore appear, their core temperatures drop extremely low—rattlesnake style—during the months they're inactive. Animal physiologists call them, and the scads of bees, moths, reptiles, and marine fishes that also do this, partially endothermic, or heterothermic. Despite their differing internal engines, both predator and prey have hit on the same solution to survive. And both are high performance.

Equatorial habitats don't endure such climatic whimsy. Near the equator, ectothermy offers a greater advantage; vipers and their kin absorb the sun's abundant heat, freeing them from the fetters of continual hunting. While my brother reminds me that life is killing time between meals, I occasionally find taking time to eat interruptive, like when I'm birding or tardily prepping a class. But as a homeothermic slave to constant caloric intake, I must. So, moments before I sheepishly walk into a room to rail against the horrors of the globally destructive prepackaged food industry, I wolf down a Pop-Tart, careful to brush implicating crumbs off my lower lip. If I have a hair longer, I opt for Triscuits and sardines. The sardines are a tradeoff: omega-3s and a shot of protein for severe halitosis and a crimped social life. But as an introvert by nature, I'm fine with warding off a few.

Timber rattlers face tradeoffs, too. Unable to migrate or forage adequately in the cold, they take the winter off. Rather than freeze amid the leaf litter, they enter vast hibernacula—literal snake pits—where they dial back their summer metabolisms. This is one instance where Steven Spielberg got it right. The scene of Indiana Jones peeling snakes off himself in *Raiders of the Lost Ark* is fleetingly plausible. Snakes love caves. They offer refuge from predators, a buffet of bats and rodents, and most importantly, constant—and warmer—temperatures to better outlast winter's icy grip. It is also why eastern timber rattlesnakes illustrate well Michael Soulé's second point about how rarity can lead to extinction: when it comes to real estate, timber rattlesnakes are picky.

So, where *are* they outside of the Appalachians? One answer is: wherever frostline-protected winter refugia Velcroed to summer feeding and breeding grounds exist. Too big a mouthful—I prefer pithiness: hither and yon. And with every new subdivision that goes up, they're found even less hither and yon. Such specific requirements result in a scattered distribution. It makes them exist, in Michael Soulé's words, "in small, infrequent patches." Compared to more cosmopolitan snakes with broader tastes, it also makes them rare. How rare depends on where you live. The only refugia within a half-day's drive for me occurs in Letchworth State Park, a forested park bisected by the Genesee River and seventeen miles of vertiginous sedimentary cliffs that flank it. Without crucial south-facing ledges, rattlesnakes wouldn't be there at all. "The Grand Canyon of the East," we smugly call our nearest park. It's grander to us than to the snakes, however. Despite decent habitat and tens of thousands of annual visitors, only one or two are spotted each summer. Either the snakes are invisible, or they're exceedingly few.

I bet it's a bit of both. They're cryptically masterful, often hidden in plain sight. But we may never know how many exist; timber rattlesnakes aren't easy to census. They chill out (pun intended) in inaccessible places, look like the forest floor, and don't command the conservation dollars of furrier, sexier species. "Snakes," Indiana Jones quipped. "Why does it always have to be snakes?" How big is the population? Nobody knows. But I do know that sober-minded conservationists are worried. Populations that remain are isolated, effectively marooned, never to meet up with wayfaring vagrants without intervention. We know this because in New York State at least 99 percent of them return to the same den sites each fall. When they emerge in April, they rarely stray more than four miles. Going too far risks a high chance of not finding a suitable place to outlast winter. But occasionally these venomous homebodies do slither out for a night on the town. Like the one that recently rattled a guy in Hancock, New York. When the unsuspecting man popped the hood of his car open, the irascible snake was coiled around the engine block.

These snakes seek warmth more effectively than they spread it. They also seek spouses. But handing them a rattlesnake range map won't help them find love. They don't help us much either. For many species, range maps are alarmingly misleading. In the average field guide, they're small, not much bigger than a postage stamp. This limits critical detail. Rattlesnake presence, often indicated by a primary color, extends in most guides across the Northeast. It's true, sort of, tantamount to saying that lakes extend across the Northeast. Yes, lakes do extend across the Northeast; but that doesn't mean we live via houseboat and gondola. While lakes extend across the landscape, many are in different watersheds, utterly disconnected from one another. As are many other distinct habitats like bogs, mountaintops, pine barrens, old-growth forests, and caves. This makes their fauna isolated, too (we'll get to flora in a minute). Isolated fauna suffers from insularity.

It's a shame that insularity is five syllables long and difficult to casually drop into conversation. It's a shame because it's the Jesus nut holding conservation's main rotor to the mast. Insularity can be a single point of failure, and ignoring it can have catastrophic consequences. It's also mystifying that while Soulé talked all about rarity, he never once mentioned insularity.

In a word, insularity is about rootedness. While timber rattlesnakes scoot through forests each summer, they're the ball on a rope in tetherball, that weird summer camp game I've never managed to play without whacking my fist on the metal pole. So affixed, they only move in a small, unsatisfying orbit. Rattlesnake mobility has always been restricted by the proximity of sufficient hibernacula. This hasn't changed. What has changed is the length of their leash, shortened by the inexorable advance of a far more insidious foe: development. Interstates, suburbs, strip malls, cities, and corn. Acre upon acre of corn. While snakes can slither through cornfields unscathed, dodging the gargantuan wheels of twenty-ton combines is orders of magnitude tougher. Even the most intrepid, determined disperser is dissuaded by a Walmart parking lot. Remaining populations are as rooted as an oak tree.

Insularity makes a population vulnerable. Once cut off, the dominoes can be toppled all too easily. Without mixing populations, inbreeding can be the first to fall. This can skew genetics and compromise the immune system. What falls next is a crapshoot. Maybe a disease outbreak. The arrival of a new predator. A bad chipmunk year. A poorly placed highway divider. A hard winter. Whatever falls can cause a positive feedback loop, exacerbating the initial problem. Insularity can set it off, and greater insularity can result, precluding the population's escape and rescue. Insularity isn't a new concept. Pontiac and his Ojibwa community understood it. It is, after all, what allowed them to capture Fort Michilimackinac.

• • • •

The problem with snakes, of course, is that they're snakes. Even the most tenderhearted conservationists have trouble rallying to their cause. But dainty alpine plants, on the other hand, are an entirely different matter. "Flowers are the sweetest things that God ever made and forgot to put a soul into," wrote Henry Ward Beecher. High alpine flowers may be the sweetest of the sweet. It just so happens that they also epitomize insularity. Inch-high and dangerously exposed, they're separated from neighboring populations on other high peaks by miles of inhospitable terrain. I didn't seek this discovery out. In the Adirondack high peaks this past summer, I literally trampled upon it.

I wasn't after rare plants. Rather, I was chasing a lowly, egomaniacal goal: bragging rights. While reading the well-known account of Teddy Roosevelt receiving the news of President McKinley's death while descending the slopes of Mount Marcy, it dawned on me that I'd never stood on my own state's highest point. According to biographer Douglas Brinkley, Roosevelt felt it wrong for a governor of New York not to have climbed the great summit. If Roosevelt felt it wrong, shouldn't I—the governed—feel it wrong, too? After all, I'd made it up the Lower 48's highest peak, Mount Whitney, and even stood on the roof of Africa, Kilimanjaro. How could I ignore Mount Marcy? Roosevelt was in his early forties. In Brinkley's words, he felt "a shadow coming over him like a dark shroud." I was just starting my forties, too. It was now or never; my knees were nearing their expiration date.

Hastily I concocted a plan with two friends, cajoled my son Ezra with visions of glory, and stuffed my pack with—what else? Triscuits and sardines. Tasty in a stuffy college office, they'd be exquisite on a high peak. Everything went swimmingly. With heavy legs and Marcy's peak in sight, I started longing for my fishy reward; this was one lunch I'd make time for.

"Hey Dad, I'm higher than everybody else in the entire state!" Ezra exclaimed, standing on a little knoll above the two dozen other people milling around us. I flashed him a thumbs-up and drove my arm into my sweaty pack, searching out the flattened sardine tin. Just as my fingers encircled it, a twenty-something woman approached. "Do you know you're in a fragile alpine plant zone?" she asked cheerily, her eyes obscured by large, reflective sunglasses. I let go of the sardines.

"Um, yes," I said reflexively. Was this a trick question? I was on an alpine summit and there were some low-growing plants around. Whatever plants they were—I hadn't bothered to look—were likely fragile. Weren't most plants fragile?

Her smile was inscrutable. As she looked down at my boots I noticed an official-looking badge on the sleeve of her teal North Face jacket. Time to change tactics—perhaps admitting ignorance would get me to my sardines faster. "I mean, no, I didn't know I was in a fragile alpine plant zone." I forced a smile. Her return smile was far more genuine. Yes, this was the response she wanted.

"Do you know what diapensia is?" she asked, nudging her sunglasses slightly higher on her nose.

Ugh. Annoyance washed over me. I had just covered 7.2 miles with 3,500 feet of elevation gain and watched Ezra complete his first Adirondack high peak, the tallest one in New York. All I wanted to do was sit down, celebrate, and slide sardines down my esophagus.

"I bet you're about to tell me," I answered, instantly regretting my snarky retort.

"Would you like me to?" she asked, unfazed. She was obviously used to jerks like me. Her question wasn't rhetorical; surely some of the other hiking parties up here on the summit would enjoy her free gift of knowledge with far less sass.

"Okay," I said, my heart softening. "Tell me about dia…dia…what was it?"

"Pensia," she finished, taking off her fluffy knit hat to reveal blond hair pulled into a tight bun. "Diapensia is one of our most beautiful alpine plants, although it's done blooming now. See these dark green cushions all around you? That's it, one of our cushion plants. It's really good at absorbing the sun's heat and creating its own microclimate. It's an arctic plant."

Her mention of the word *arctic* triggered memories of the geology course I'd taught several years before. I'd explained how a billion-year-old dome of metamorphic rock forms the high peaks of the Adirondacks. As tectonic forces pushed the dome up like a geological uppercut, layers of sedimentary rock had eroded off it. Later, a vast glacier, over a mile thick, had pressed down upon the dome ineffectually. The glacier's eventual retreat—just thirteen thousand years ago—left a scarred and scoured landscape. One with similarities to the Arctic.

What I hadn't lectured on, nor knew much about, was how the region's botany had responded to these geological forces. I stared around me at the dark green dollops of diapensia.

"Diapensia and the other alpine specialists are our only remaining arctic plants in New York. We only have 173 acres of alpine habitat, just 85 of which have these plants. It's one of New York's rarest habitats."

"Really?" I asked, my nerd button pressed. I loved ecological curiosities like this. "What other plants are up here?"

"Well, there's mountain sandwort," she said.

"Where?" Again, she looked down at my feet. I followed her gaze. Ezra had capped his Gatorade and wandered over, content to relinquish his perch to other haughty geographical pedants.

"You're standing on it," she said. I rocked back on my heels. Sure enough, a small, barely discernible cushion of green was clinging to what I'd mistaken for bare rock. Right under my size twelves. "The soil is thin and nutrient poor up here," she continued. "Mountain sandwort uses those little gravel patches most hikers don't see."

I groaned. Despite my advanced degree in ecology and decade of collegiate teaching experience, I'd just been lumped in with "most hikers." Right in front of my son. I swallowed. Regardless, this woman's rare combo of knowledge and conviction had won me over. There was something admirable in her dedication to small, sessile plants. She seemed as rare as the plants. I had to know more.

"So, do you hike up here every day?"

"Most days in the summer," she said cheerily. "I'm a summit steward! Though there aren't many of us, we do our best to educate the public and keep them from crushing the plants." Despite endless conversations with hundreds of hikers like me, and exposure to harsh sun, unyielding wind, and sudden storms, her enthusiasm was as resolute as the plants she defended, enduring and growing where most won't. I was exhausted from one hike but she did it daily, enduring public apathy and snark following every ascent. Her presence atop the peak filled me with hope.

Her reward was substantial: purpose. A gift almost as rare as the plants she was protecting, far outweighing whatever meager stipend she received. Heart now soft as putty, I sincerely thanked her. "Plants are worth it!" she said, scanning over my shoulder at an encroaching phalanx of newly arriving hikers. Some of them would surely blunder into diapensia as I had. They needed to know how Soulé's factor worked, too: how when a species is relegated to small and infrequent patches, it's more susceptible to extinction.

• • • •

It's not just Adirondack alpine plants that face possible extinction, of course. Across the country, in the sun-scorched deserts of western Nevada, grows a calico-patterned flower with a Seussian tuft called Tiehm's buckwheat. The little buckwheat exists in six separate subpopulations that have trouble spreading across the arid landscape. The global population grows on just twenty-one acres, hardly enough for a few holes on a golf course.

Tiehm's buckwheat might have gone anonymously to its grave had it not been inconveniently found in the path of a proposed open-pit lithium mine. While the rare plant awaited recognition by the Endangered Species Act, somebody slipped into the area, determined to remove the plant and make way for the mine. In a single dastardly act, the person dug up and destroyed more than seventeen thousand of the plants. The plants were mangled, their taproots cut and then hauled offsite. Not scandalous enough for major news outlets. Just a blip in some local papers. But it's a blip that reinforces an earlier point: insularity breeds vulnerability. Just one person with a shovel and bone to pick can remove 40 percent of a plant's global population in a single, angsty night.

While Tiehm's buckwheat lacked a summit steward, it did have Patrick Donnelly, Nevada State director at the Center for Biological Diversity. Unfortunately, like everybody else, Donnelly discovered the ecocide after the fact. "I was absolutely devastated when I discovered this annihilation of these beautiful little wildflowers," said Donnelly. "But we're not going to let this stop our fight against extinction. We'll fight for every single buckwheat."

• • • •

But will we fight for every single rattlesnake? A lot of sane people would rather we didn't. I learned this early—seventh grade, to be exact. I had just stepped off the school bus when I noticed my neighbor, Mrs. Fielding, frozen on the small concrete steps of her one-story, prefab home. She clutched an empty plastic laundry basket just above her navy rubber boots, which she wore even during prolonged dry spells. As soon as the bus pulled away, she yelled my name. "Eliiiiiiii!"

I dropped my schoolbag. Young as I was, her panic was palpable. "Hi!" I called back.

"Can you see if it's gone?"

"See if what's gone?"

"The snake!" she said, motioning clumsily with her entire basket. Aha. Her dilemma became clear. Mrs. Fielding couldn't get to her clothes, fluttering on the line. A snake lay in her path. I dropped my backpack and trotted across the street, ducking under the white bedsheets. I searched the grass. Nothing. Whatever snake had been present no longer was. Also, it had likely been a harmless little garter snake, the ubiquitous species commonly found across the United States.

"Is it safe?" Mrs. Fielding asked. Her laundry basket was trembling like an aspen leaf.

"I think so," I said, marching unnecessary transect lines around her laundry. Slowly, Mrs. Fielding approached, frowning.

"I hate snakes so much," she blurted, involuntarily shuddering. Although her reaction was incomprehensible, next to her I felt brave and heroic, the greatest of childhood feelings. Plus, a warm plate of

Mrs. Fielding's freshly baked cookies would surely reward my chivalry as it had when we'd shoveled her driveway.

I, on the other hand, didn't fear snakes. Rather, I sought them out. My own sprig of fear didn't emerge until over a decade later, when I started jogging on rural paths in Africa. Just one fateful moment sufficed. It was dusk and I was rounding a bend near a large boulder. Out of the corner of my eye, at the boulder's base, I noticed an unnaturally fat coiled rope. Except it wasn't a rope. It was a large adult puff adder.

"There are times in your life that become touchstones," Jenn Dean wrote, "that define all else that came before and all else that will follow." For me, the puff adder was such a touchstone. For whatever reason, the snake didn't strike. But it changed me, instantly activating an evolutionary instinct that most humanity shares: snake fear. *Homo sapiens* doesn't harbor this fear alone. Our bipedal cousins, the primates, have it coded into their DNA, too. Charles Darwin reported that he once "took a stuffed snake into [a] monkey house and the hair of several species instantly became erect."

People do routinely die from snakebites. But more people die cleaning gutters and stringing up Christmas lights. In the temperate latitudes, fear outweighs fact. And the fact is, snakes want nothing to do with people; they'd love a human-free world. In places like Africa, the trouble traces back to their ectothermic physiology. Paths offer perfect places to capture heat radiating out of the earth on chilly evenings. Many, like the venomous vipers, are ambush predators. Too slow to capture anything in a race, they sit back, save their energy, and let small, hyperactive mammals come to them. If given enough time, they'll flee if they sense danger. Villagers hurrying home with crops, or a clumsy human jogger, don't allow them this option. Too fat and slow to escape, puff adders strike as a last resort, a desperate attempt at self-preservation.

My experience with the puff adder made me jumpy and paranoid. What if I'd stepped on it? Even seven thousand miles away in my adder-free lawn in New York, the fear remained, causing wild, last-second, evasive leaps upon glimpsing my garden hose. So, fraught I remained, the fascination of my youth mingling with the fear of one lone experience. Whichever won out depended heavily upon my mindset.

• • • •

Rattlesnakes are particularly impressive. They are pit vipers, named so because the heat-sensing pits on their heads allow them to strike prey even in total darkness. But like any home-run hitter, even rattlers strike out. Prey is fast and vegetation can block the blow. A quarter of the time, they whiff. But when they succeed and envenomate, the game's over. Consider a bitten chipmunk. After the bite, a slurry of water, enzymes, and peptides seep into the chipmunk's pleural and peritoneal cavities. What happens next is as incredible as it is jargon-heavy. Here's a taste: When a chipmunk is struck, its cell membranes collapse. This spreads the venom, jumpstarts complex polypeptide action, and releases a host of unpleasant things including edema, ecchymosis, macrophage differentiation, neutrophil degranulation, leukocyte migration, interleukin abundance, hypotension, hypovolemic shock, lactic acidosis, and the destruction of vascular basement membranes and perivascular extracellular matrices. That's just the tissue damage. The cardiovascular effects and coagulopathy are equally hard to pronounce, byzantine, and, most of all, destructive.

If you're in shock, rest assured the chipmunk is too. Even more astounding is what happens next, insight I gleaned from Sherman Minton, a herpetologist who worked with white, small-bodied mice. When his mice were bitten in the lab, Minton found high variability between when the strike occurred and when his mice actually keeled over—a few seconds to well over an hour. Let's give our scampering chipmunk, say, five minutes. In that time, and despite massive internal hemorrhaging, the ill-fated chipmunk bounds across four logs, sprints through a brush pile, pirouettes across a rock wall, and then, in a sudden spasm brought on by cardiac arrest, unceremoniously capsizes into the leaf litter.

For visual predators like hawks, an inert chipmunk in the leaf litter is virtually unrecoverable. Not so for the timber rattlesnake. It's built for such tracking. Using its vomeronasal organs and tongue, the snake takes up the scent like a seasoned bloodhound, easily discerning the chipmunk's unique moribund signature. Across the logs, through the brush pile, and up onto the rock wall. Briefly it pauses, confused by the scent's sudden disappearance. Then, an updraft. A waft. The snake slithers off the wall, locates its prey, and prods it a few times with its triangular head. Assured of the chipmunk's incapacitation, it tastes the air anew. So close, the odors differentiate into a kaleidoscope of colorful scent. Distinct odors seep out of the chipmunk's mouth. On cue, the snake curls around and grabs the chipmunk headfirst. Natural selection has developed this critical instinct, which helps prevent the chipmunk's joints from protruding at angles that might hinder digestion. Too big a lump would slow peristalsis and mobility, each vital for helping the snake accomplish its next feat before the oncoming frost: finding a mate.

The window for breeding is short. For sexually mature males, locating a receptive female is a high-stakes treasure hunt. As summer wanes, females release pheromones, which float through the forest like dandelion seeds. For our male resting by a brook with a bellyful of chipmunk, it's a welcome aroma. He stirs, soon following it in dogged pursuit. He navigates over the brook and follows a ridgeline, which brings him to a recently mowed backyard enclosed by a picket fence. Normally the manicured yard's lack of cover would drive him back into the safety of the forest. But hormonal urges spur him on. He slides under the fence, wards off a high-strung, yapping dog, and barely avoids the Goodyear treads of a Dodge Ram hightailing around a street corner. Fortunately, the driver doesn't spot him.

Chances to die are everywhere. But our snake has beat the odds for several years now. It's a good thing, too, because he's a K-selected species, bio-speak for species with long lifespans, late maturation, and low reproductive output. These characteristics make K-selected species inherently more prone to extinction than r-selected species. Unlike r-selected species, which breed almost the minute they're born and bear litters in the thousands, rattlesnakes are reproductively conservative, aging more like fine wine. Other than a lightning-fast strike, their lives are unhurried.

Many years ago, as a vulnerable, pencil-long baby, a nightly parade of raccoons passed our rattlesnake by none the wiser, his intricate pattern perfectly blending with the lichen-covered log he coiled under. Two years later, on a late June night, a possum bumbled into him, eventually deciding the now twenty-inch, belligerent snake wasn't worth the trouble. While crossing a glade, a broad-winged hawk missed him by inches. Since then, he's found just enough food. A bullfrog here, a vole there. Summers have come and gone, and each fall he's found his way back to the sedimentary slab he was born under.

To show how this relates to Soulé's concept of rarity caused by small and infrequent patches, let's put numbers to it. We'll be generous and give ourselves a hypothetical population of thirty-four snakes. Our snake is a male, less critical for ensuring the species' long-term viability. Females are far more important. They need to evade raccoons and car tires for at least six years before they can breed. If a female snake succeeds and produces a litter of four to ten young, she won't breed again for at least three more years. By age twenty, her reproductive output will be finished. If she beats these long odds, that's just five or six litters over her lifetime. In this reptilian lottery, every snake matters.

Of our isolated patch of thirty-four snakes in western New York, let's assume eighteen are male, leaving sixteen female snakes. For these sixteen, eight are immature, two suffer from a fungal disease, and one is twenty-three years old, well past her reproductive years. Of the five viable females, three had litters in the last two years and are yet to reenter estrus. So, this particular summer, we're down to two potentially receptive females for the cadre of horny males. One of these females followed a rat she'd envenomated into a drainage culvert under a two-lane highway. With ceaseless traffic roaring overhead, she hasn't yet found the nerve to emerge. That leaves just one receptive female for our eagerly questing male.

Having cut through the housing development, the male is back in the forest but not out of the woods. Within a hundred yards of the female, two four-wheelers careen by, spitting dirt in their wake. Lucky again, our snake was neither squashed nor spotted. Briefly, he cowers under a protective spicebush. The four-wheelers' exhaust has masked the female's pheromone trail. An hour later, however, the wind shifts. He picks up the trail and resumes following. But now he detects another scent, this one far less pleasant. Another male rattlesnake. It's strong, revealing that the other snake is equally hormonal. Headstrong, he ignores the waiting female and heads for his rival. In a makeshift arena of rusty fallen needles under a white pine, they meet, rising up and rattling fiercely.

The first hour is all intimidation. Posturing and puffing, each hopes the other will turn tail. It's energy well spent—a good bluff can ensure mating rights and avoid a costly, and potentially lethal, end. Our male is younger and smaller. But with just one receptive female about, there's too much at stake to surrender. Females are too rare, this population too isolated. In a game without consolation prizes, his eagerness overrides retreat.

A twisting, tortured combat ensues. Blue jays notice the writhing bodies and scold the combatants. Crows and chickadees join in. For two and a half minutes, pine needles fly as serpentine fury mars the understory. Both snakes tire. Each strike becomes more unwieldy. More daring. Our male lands several but fails to envenomate. Less experienced, he lunges too far, leaving his body momentarily exposed like a splayed hose. His adversary strikes, inserting two hypodermic needles into our male's back. It's only a split second, but it's sufficient. Venom swims into our snake's bloodstream.

It's over. Our snake instinctively backs down. He's defeated but, yet again, lucky. This strike won't kill him. He has one final trick in his bag, natural antibodies that will counteract the venom now wreaking havoc on his exhausted body. But it'll take weeks for his Lazarus-like return, precious weeks that will preclude him from passing on his genes for yet another summer. This defeat will also hamper his ability to hunt and fatten up for winter, throwing his own survival into question. (Since you're now fascinated, too, here's one more herpetological factoid I'm certain you're wondering about: this *isn't* how rattlesnakes avoid dying from the rodents they eat upon envenomating them. Rather, during prey consumption, a snake's stomach acids and digestive enzymes break down the venom, rendering it harmless. Incidentally, this also explains why diabetics have to inject insulin rather than ingest it. If insulin was popped like a pill, digestive enzymes would destroy it. Like snakes, our bodies are magnificently compartmentalized; the deadly cocktail produced by our pancreas would quickly kill us if it entered our bloodstream. Hence why acute pancreatitis requires immediate medical attention.)

To the victor go the spoils. The other male, tired but victorious, soon finds the waiting female. In the blink of an eye, they copulate and go their separate ways. The male goes squirrel hunting. Sensing change, the female moves in the general direction of the ledges, her winter refugia, the fate of the entire population hinging on her ability to make it there intact.

Most serpentine drama happens beyond our gaze with long static interludes punctuated by dramatic, life-or-death moments. For rare species found in small, infrequent patches of suitable habitat, the outcome of such moments can determine the very survival of the species. Lots can go wrong. But when things go right and the species persists, a beautiful layer of ecological complexity remains in our world. Glorious richness whether we witness it or not.

• • • •

Up on a narrow ledge in Loyalsock State Forest, I wasn't merely a witness of the ecological complexity involving rattlesnakes, I was a participant. Decades earlier, I had rescued Mrs. Fielding from a snake at her clothesline. Now, here in Loyalsock, it was Dustin's time to be a hero. After a brief search in the underbrush, he returned with a long, forked stick.

"What are you planning to do?" I asked through clenched teeth, my elbow still only inches away from the snake's head.

"Move it," he said, grinning ear to ear. Dustin was a whitewater kayaker. He relished tense moments.

"To where? Over the cliff?"

"Perhaps," he said, poking the stick toward the snake. Annoyed, the snake rattled harder, its tail sounding like a dozen cicadas. The snake didn't retreat. Unlike every other snake I'd ever encountered, this one remained as unyielding as a defensive lineman. This was her ledge and she wasn't about to give ground to two sunburnt backpackers, forked stick or not.

"If you move it, won't it just come back?" I asked, my eyes still locked on the serpent.

Dustin didn't reply. "I need one more stick," he mumbled, looking around. But before he could find one, the snake slunk back into her rock lair. Once the tail disappeared, I exhaled, leaping to my feet. Dustin and I looked at each other.

Now what? Campsites were sparse on this ridge and darkness was upon us. Our tent was pitched, our bags were unpacked, and our shoulders ached. But was it wise to share a home with a venomous snake? One that had no intention of leaving?

"Hey Dustin, are rattlers nocturnal?" It was a question aimed at gathering info and preserving my ego.

Dustin pulled out his phone. I figured he was researching my question. He wasn't. "*Crotalus horridus*," he said, pocketing his phone. Reciting Latin names was one of his quirks.

"*Horridus*?" I asked, disbelieving him. Dustin smirked. This didn't bode well.

"Do you have the cooking stove?" he asked. Our undemocratic decision had just been made. Wise or not, we would sleep here among the serpents. "Let's clear some brush away," Dustin suggested. "That way we can avoid stepping on it come nightfall." With this I heartily agreed. I hastily scooped up limbs and hauled them away, relieved to be doing something for the sake of self-preservation.

An hour later, we sat around a roaring fire just eight feet from the snake's den. "I wonder how you treat rattlesnake bites," Dustin mused, taking a swig from his Nalgene.

"Me too," I said. "Doesn't it involve elevating the bitten limb? If I get bitten tonight, I expect you to lacerate my limb and suck out the poison," I said, "for picking this campsite." Dustin pulled out his phone again. I peered into the shadows. So far, the rattler had stayed put. I looked back at the fire, savoring the light Appalachian breeze.

A sour-cream moon slowly rose behind us, casting a natural spotlight on our lighthearted banter. Gradually I grew more comfortable with our campsite. With the light of the dancing flames arcing into the indigo sky, the threat of the snake's presence lessened. Then, a gift, bestowing sharpened senses and heightened awareness. Humility, too. Another creature had claimed this cliff and was willing to fight for it. Here I had to acquiesce, defer, give ground to another deserving being.

In the span of a few hours I had changed. From kneejerk repulsion to cautious acceptance. Had the chance of switching campsites existed, had darkness not fallen so soon, I surely would have hightailed it. I would have done everything possible to distance myself from the source of my discomfort.

But I'm glad I lacked that chance. Forced coexistence led to tolerance and respect. Fear, coiled up in my DNA, had subverted such a possibility. For many of the world's most fearsome and wondrous creatures, mere tolerance—however begrudging—is conservation's greatest hurdle. If we can't learn it, neither the most contiguous habitats nor the greatest antibodies in the world can save the timber rattlesnake.

"It says here that you're wrong on both counts," Dustin said all too happily. He looked down at his phone. "If bitten, keep the limb below the heart. And, never attempt to bleed or suck out the venom."

"So how do you treat it then?" I asked, feeling stupid.

"Get the victim immediately to a hospital," Dustin read aloud. We both chuckled at the irony. Fat chance.

The night went as any other night in the backcountry, with one exception: I double-checked the tent zipper. A light drizzle pattered softly on the rainfly. Otherwise it was quiet. No slithering, hissing, or rattling. The next morning was equally snake-free. We cautiously reclaimed the ledge and spread our breakfast supplies out. My eyes scoured the ground, searching for elongated irregularities. Nothing. Only sunlight snaked across the rock.

I was halfway through my oatmeal when I heard it. Rattling. This time, however, was different. It was softer and slower, more like a hello than an expletive. Plus, I didn't jump or flail. My pulse quickened, then slowed again. Hesitantly, the snake emerged. I stepped back slowly, found another seat, and continued eating. But then came something I didn't expect: another rattler emerged from the crevice. Then another. And another. Instead of the previous day's lone snake, four now basked next to us.

The campsite should have felt more dangerous. But it didn't; it actually seemed less so. Perhaps it was the sun warming my back, a good night of sleep, or the tasty wild blueberries I'd just picked and dropped in my oatmeal. But I don't think so. I think it was something deeper, a new perspective. Or more accurately, a return to an old one. I was twelve years old again, back in search of awesomeness. Best of all, I'd found it: four heat-sensing pit vipers with the ability to withstand venom, frost, and small, patchy habitats. Hopefully they'd withstand extinction, too.

Our motivations for seeking out this rocky ledge were the same as the snakes'. They were here because this location offered them a good place to do what rattlers do—kill mice, bask in the sun, grow larger, and lead healthy serpentine lives. We were here to do what we do—eat trail mix, reminisce, refocus, and lead healthy human lives. To do so, we each needed the same thing—refuge.

The snakes sought it from predators, interstates, and a fluctuating climate. We sought it from overpacked schedules, stress, and unending responsibilities. The rattlers knew retreat well, human development forcing them onto ever-smaller reservations. They were rare enough already—victims of insularity—with nowhere else to go. So, here they were, on this precarious south-facing ledge, making their last stand.

We let them make it. The only thing to toss over the ledge was Dustin's forked stick.

The rest of the morning was leisurely. We finished our breakfast, packed up our tent, and set off. Restored, I left with paradox. By granting the rattlesnakes refuge, I found my own.

3
WORMS ON THE PIANO
Limited Dispersal Ability

"In the West, time is like gold. You save it, you lose it, you waste it, or you don't have enough of it. In the Barasana language there is no word for time."
—Stephen Hugh-Jones

There's never a right time nor place to flip a tortoise onto its back. But on a crisp June morning before a full day of research in Serengeti National Park, I thought otherwise.

"Eli, what is that?" Linda asked as we ate our last remaining—and much treasured—packets of Quaker Instant Oatmeal. We sat across from each other at a wobbly metal foldout table placed in front of our open kitchen window. Chain-link covered the opening instead of a screen, making us feel like inmates. But if it kept out lions and baboons, we were happy.

"What is what?" I asked, looking deep into my bowl.

"Why is that poor turtle on its back?" she asked, leaning forward in her camp chair for a better look.

"It's not a turtle," I said, still not looking up.

"Yes, it is."

"Tortoise. Not turtle."

"How did it...*you* did that!"

Shoot. The ruse was up; I had hoped Linda wouldn't notice. How naïve. If something was suffering within a ten-mile radius, Linda noticed.

"Is it *roose* or *rews*?" I asked, hoping to buy time with a distracting non sequitur.

"What?"

"R-U-S-E. How do you pronounce it?"

"Like *news*," she said. "Now go help that turtle!"

This was an order. Time to play my final card.

"Just give me one minute. I'm doing an experiment."

"An experiment?" she asked, searching my eyes. I avoided eye contact by staring out at the tortoise. The reptile pawed the air, feebly trying to use its head as a fifth leg, a fulcrum to help it flip over. Assuming the tortoise would try this, I'd placed it on a flat-topped, granite boulder to thwart the technique. Sure enough, the boulder wasn't allowing much purchase. I glanced at my watch. One minute, thirty-six seconds and counting. I—well, the tortoise—needed a little more time. Coming clean might afford what I needed and perhaps redirect Linda's empathy toward me. How could a sensitive spouse not acquiesce to a budding scientist's drive for formalized curiosity?

"I need to see if leopard tortoises can right themselves in the wild," I said.

"You *need* to?"

"Okay, want to," I conceded.

"Why?"

Linda had me here. Tortoises were about as relevant to my dissertation as high heels to a garden snail.

"Surely tortoises find themselves on their backs sometimes," I said. "I mean, given enough tortoises and enough boulders, statistically, it has to happen."

"Why would a tortoise climb a boulder?"

"Well, what if they lost their footing and rolled down a hill?"

Linda eyed me skeptically. The fact that most of Serengeti National Park's topography resembled a parking lot didn't bolster my case. I tried again: "What if a hyena flips one over trying to eat it?" Linda rolled her eyes. The real reason for my experiment, we both knew, was that my insatiable curiosity was too often tangled up with insanity.

It helped that other historical figures shared my condition. Charles Darwin kept a glass jar of worms on his living room piano so he could study their reactions to sound vibrations. Ben Franklin electroshocked a chicken and then revived it with mouth-to-beak resuscitation. And one mustn't forget Soviet physician Sergei Brukhonenko, who kept the severed head of a dog alive with a primitive heart-lung machine he invented. Detached though the head was, Sergei managed to feed it a lump of cheese (which promptly popped out of the unhooked esophagus). Some wacky experiments bear real fruit. Others are just demented. The trouble is, it's not always easy to discern the two. There's legitimate tension in the scientific method; many great discoveries necessitate a willingness to be questioned and criticized, even ostracized. Being thought a little loony is getting off easy. Great discoveries require great curiosity. This I had. The trouble is, they also require a great mind. This I lacked. Along with adequate empathy for tortoises.

Linda pushed her chair back. "If you're not going to help the turtle, then *I* will," she said.

"Tortoise," I said, sighing. "Whatever. I'll go flip it back over."

This was not turning out to be the morning for a great leap in tortoise science. Maybe next week. That'd give me time to correct my study's only glaring flaw: reposition it away from Linda's all-seeing, empathetic eyes.

• • • •

The truth is, I've always had an obsession with tortoises. My great chain of beings ranks like this: deer, birds, tortoises. Not just tortoises, though; all chelonians—turtles and terrapins, too. Chelonians warrant third-tier obsession for a host of reasons: They're 220-million-year-old relics, little changed from the Jurassic, live in fuel-efficient motorhomes, regularly outlive us (a Galápagos tortoise lived 170 years in captivity), procreate hysterically, are easy for a slow-footed biped to catch, and hang out in the slow lane. Chelonians stop to smell—and taste—the flowers. Even the terminology is cool. The shell: a plastron.

The undercarriage: a carapace. And those exquisite geometric designs along the plastron that look like carefully laid mosaic are scutes.

But one thing is far less agreeable. More than half of the 360 living chelonians are threatened with extinction. Of our fellow vertebrates, they have the unhappy distinction of being one of the most likely to blink out.

It's well worth hanging out with these virtuous animals, reorienting, in fact. They're patient. I've finished reading entire book chapters waiting—sometimes fruitlessly—for a tortoise to pop its head out. When they do, they exhibit Houdini-level escapism. While I fiddle with camera lenses during photo shoots, they sprout legs and—poof—vanish into the underbrush. Liminality allows them to move between worlds as effortlessly as Loki: from water to terra firma and back again. Come winter, they seemingly dissipate. Unlike many birds that undergo the madness of migration, chelonians just plop into a mucky pond and burrow into the bottom. Such fetid frigidity is a fine trade for three months of uninterrupted sleep.

When I encounter a chelonian on the road, sometimes I do the right thing. Pull over, help it across, and drive on smiling in my rearview mirror. Just as often I don't. If other cars aren't around, I grab the surprised reptile, lob it in my trunk, and speed off with my booty like a zealous pirate. It's a justified heist; chelonians *are* zoological gold. They're affordable, low-maintenance pets my kids adore. Upon arrival home, we scramble to ready the dusty aquarium, transforming it in minutes into a ten-gallon vivarium. I do it because each turtle represents a possible point of attachment, another chance for my kids to draw one step closer to the natural world. Interrupt this one turtle's life for the future untold lives of others; ends over means thinking.

It's a lie though. The real reason is simpler: I do it for myself. I just want a few more hours with an omnivorous tetrapod that predated T. rex by one hundred million years, back when Pangaea was still a thing. I fear I'm an outlier; chelonian love is hardly a given among our species. Some, in fact, seem offended by the creature's glacially slow approach to life. A precocious lad named Nathan Weaver, then an undergraduate at Clemson, demonstrated this when he placed a realistic rubber eastern box turtle in the middle of the street near campus. Weaver concealed himself nearby to record how motorists reacted. What he saw revealed humanity's multilayered relationship with turtles. Over the next hour, seven drivers swerved out of their lane to deliberately run the turtle over. Many others tried but missed.

"Sometimes humans feel a need to prove they are the dominant species on the planet," psychology professor Hal Herzog wrote in his book *Some We Love, Some We Hate, Some We Eat*. We do this "by taking a two-ton metal vehicle and squishing a defenseless creature under the tires. They aren't thinking, really. It is not something people think about," he added.

Our primeval urge to express our dominance over turtles is odd indeed. Venomous snakes can kill us. Heck, some are big enough to wrap us up and swallow us like a multivitamin. With snake fear encoded in our DNA, I get the desire of some folks to scrub them off the planet. But turtles?

Perhaps chelonians are like climate change. Just too slow for us to care about. Out of sight and out of mind. If so, then chelonian accommodation—wetland preservation, habitat restoration, creation of highway underpasses, fencing—won't ever be in the cards for them. Everything about them is slow. They eat slowly, move slowly, and they're slow to reach sexual maturity—five to eight years for Weaver's eastern box turtles. Such profound slowness greatly limits them. It limits their ability to find mates, reach good habitat, cross roads, and escape disaster. For our purposes here, it limits their dispersal ability. Limited dispersal ability, as Michael Soulé wrote, is a key factor in extinction.

Imperial woodpeckers could disperse but simply ran out of places to go. Timber rattlesnakes can disperse, but their small, infrequent patches of suitable hibernacula, especially in the north, isolate them. Box turtles? There are plenty of places to go. They're just really, really bad at getting there. Feeling frisky is risky. Back roads and side streets are gambles. Anything else, like main streets, highways, and interstates, are certain death. In summer, the eastern box turtle travels an average of fifty meters a day. *A day*! Fifty meters hardly gets them across a four-lane highway.

It's ironic that we laud the tortoise in fables. Because our words for slowness—sluggardly, snail-like, and sloth—are all pejorative. And in real life we punish them, too. Why? Because culture in the western hemisphere isn't at all tortoise-like. We live fast. Speed is the name of the game. Assembly lines. Automation. Multiple screens and multitasking. When our efficiency flounders, we reach for an energy drink. We hurry out the door. We hurry through our work. And if the coast is clear of cops, we hurry on home, focused more on the next task than ubiquitous speed-limit signs. In Aesop's fable, we're the hare.

Hares, of course, face little threat of extinction. Though they live fast and die often, they make up for it through profligate breeding. An eastern cottontail reaches sexual maturity in six months. She can produce a dozen babies per litter every month thereafter. In a perfect world, one without disease, predators, or food limitations, one pair of rabbits can exponentially become 3,745,000 after four years.

One pair. Almost four million.

If you don't know what to be grateful for during these uncertain days, disease, predators, and food limitations—for rabbits—is as good a start as any. Praise God for checks and balances.

• • • •

But I've sold my beloved chelonians short. Just because tortoises can't cross roads doesn't mean they can't disperse. Au contraire! The Galápagos Islands, in fact, are named for them: *galapago*, Spanish for tortoise. Why would a remote oceanic island archipelago harbor seven native tortoises? Because the otherwise landlubbers swam there.

"Swam there" is a bit generous. Really, they got there using the bobbing Coke bottle approach, a fine method for traversing six hundred miles of open ocean. Perseverance, not skill, was their trick. We know this because the Galápagos didn't split off of South America loaded down with chelonian cargo; they're volcanic, having arisen from the ocean floor like a carpet that's been bunched together. DNA studies confirm this, revealing that all the tortoises on the Galápagos Islands evolved from common ancestors that arrived from mainland South America. So, how did those South American tortoises do it? With buoyancy, a periscope-like neck, ability to survive for months without food and water, and the goodwill of the Humboldt Current.

Once there, they grew. Really grew, the largest nearing one thousand pounds. With bountiful food and few predators, the islands offered a bonanza. How the population grew, however, is conjecture. Perhaps a breeding pair washed up simultaneously. More likely, a lone pregnant female made the trek, culminating her lucky crossing with opportunistic will. She needed soil substrate to bury her eggs and an optimal temperature for her eggs to hatch. Hatchlings then needed time to grow and willingness to breed with each other. That lone female already had a large straight. To win—to colonize—she needed a Yahtzee.

Small odds indeed. But endowed with insane perseverance, buoyancy, and time, tortoise colonization gradually changed from unlikely to probable. Like always, the tortoises took their time. They had five million years to play with after Española and San Cristobal Islands first peeked above the cold, Pacific waters. It turned out to be plenty. But tortoise takeover wasn't finished. From these two islands, mitochondrial evidence reveals that the nascent population took to the seas again and again, in a stepping stone fashion, controlled entirely by the predictable local currents. This likely safeguarded against inbreeding, too.

Lest you give the Galápagos tortoises too much credit, realize their great sea journeys were likely born more of clumsiness rather than an intrepid spirit. One scenario may have gone like this: In South America, a happy-go-lucky tortoise extends her neck on a ridgeline, reaching for a tasty-looking succulent. She loses her balance on the unstable scree and starts rolling, her domed plastron accelerating her descent like a bowling ball. Splash! From there, the startled tortoise slips into the Humboldt Current, which takes her—predictably—to the Galápagos. The other islands likely got their castaways much the same way.

Some all the way from South America. Others from nearby islands in the archipelago. Arriving like this, all the Galápagos tortoises should be related, resembling one another.

Though they're related, not all of them look alike. In 2002, two researchers from Yale discovered five tortoises on Wolf, the northernmost island in the archipelago, that looked nothing like the others. One resembled those on San Cristobal while the other four were Española lookalikes. They obviously hadn't interbred much. So, how did these oddball fugitives arrive? It didn't take the researchers long to sniff out a culprit, one that lies behind far too many biogeographical puzzles: humans.

Although lacking a smoking gun, they gleaned valuable clues from an unlikely source: a naval captain's journal, some letters, and a twelve-year-old's diary. The clues concern a bizarre, way-out-of-the-way skirmish from the War of 1812. Unlike other distasteful historical accounts that make me squirm in my American skin, this one is delightful, prompting me to raise my head up high, like a floating tortoise. It displays a current of courage and savvy in my ancestral stock. Coincidentally, it also involves bobbing tortoises.

· · · ·

The skirmish started over a dispute over maritime law. On April 29, 1813, Captain David Porter was patrolling Galápagos waters in the US frigate *Essex* when he spotted two British whalers, the *Georgiana* and the *Policy*, off the bow. Together, the two enemy whaling boats had sixty-one men and sixteen large guns, easily enough to take down Porter's *Essex*. But they lacked the derring-do of the American captain who was, as he later recorded in his *Journal of a Cruise*, "determined to have them at all hazards." Rather than turn tail, Porter attacked, launching a small fleet of rowboats full of musket-wielding men. Armed or not, Porter's fleet of leaky rowboats reeked of cocksure, an improbable gambit with longer odds of success than a tortoise surviving a six-hundred-mile oceanic journey. But Porter knew something crucial about rowboats that I didn't—they're hard to hit.

The British, like those attacked at Fort Michilimackinac, were gobsmacked. Such chutzpah! Porter's Lilliputian armada resolutely advanced over the calm seas. The wind was dead. Escape wouldn't be possible. The British whalers turned to their little-used, inaccurate artillery. The guns were a joke, like shooting cannons at hummingbirds. So, the British had two strikes against them in this out-of-the-way dustup. But their third strike even Captain Porter couldn't have foreseen. They had too many tortoises aboard.

The whalers had just raided San Cristobal, one of the islands in the Galápagos. There, they'd grabbed chelonians like I do, loading them onto the deck like freight pallets. Rationale was sound. Giant tortoises were an easily transportable feast that, if alive, didn't require refrigeration. Perfect for long voyages and a lovely complement to the monotony of fish. The trouble was, the foodstuffs were strong-willed. And though they had feet, they didn't move on command, or much at all. With guns going off, they hunkered down, dozens of unwieldy, five-hundred-pound boulders glued to the deck. Squeezed between the ticked-off tortoises, the British had trouble maneuvering. As a last-ditch effort to free up sorely needed space, they lowered their shoulders and rolled them overboard.

There's a lot I wonder about when I read historical accounts. Like why was Teddy climbing Mount Marcy, considering that the president hadn't fully recovered from his gunshot wounds? Or why was twelve-year-old David Farragut aboard one of the attacking rowboats instead of remaining on the *Essex*? Whatever the reason, there he was, absorbing the rollicking assault as only a boy can. Thankfully, he scrawled his impressions down in his diary.

"The appearance of these [land] turtles in the water was very singular," Farragut penned. "They floated as light as corks, stretching their long necks as high as possible, for fear of drowning. They were the first we had ever seen, and excited much curiosity as we pushed them aside."

Captain Porter, aided by giant tortoises in the unlikeliest of places, picked up Farragut's account. "None of the cannons hit their mark," he wrote in a letter back to his superiors. The boats "rowed up beneath the muzzles of the guns and took their stations for attacking the first ship." The British aboard the *Georgiana* waved a white flag and surrendered. The *Policy*, equally hampered by inaccuracy and a chelonian-cluttered deck, followed suit. "Thus were two fine British ships surrendered," Captain Porter wrote proudly, "without the slightest resistance, to seven small open boats, with 50 men, armed only with muskets, pistols, boarding-axes and cutlasses!" Porter couldn't resist a final vainglorious flourish: "Britons have either learned to respect the courage of the Americans, or they are not so courageous themselves as they would wish us believe."

Regardless of courage, the Britons knew the value of tortoises, at least as durable foodstuffs. The Americans soon learned a few days later. Upon securing the captured British boats, they passed through a sizable swell of jettisoned tortoises, not far from where they'd been heaved overboard. The poor creatures were "incapable of any exertion in that element," Captain Porter wrote, "except that of stretching out their long necks." Seeing this, the Americans hauled in all they could find. Not for the sake of conservation, of course. In the coming months, cooked chelonian became a relished American delicacy.

The Yale researchers speculated that some of the tortoises weren't recovered by Captain Porter's men. The lucky flotsam, they posit, could have floated their way to Wolf. The two researchers didn't underestimate their dispersal abilities and sheer doggedness in overcoming long odds. Their conclusions impart ironic hope, too. A tortoise—inextricably bound to life on dry land—may today face a greater challenge walking across a terrestrial landscape than bobbing across the high seas. We can steal these zoological holdovers, eat them, and push them overboard, in addition to many other possible depredations. Giant tortoises are down from 250,000 in the sixteenth century to 3,000 today, and with populations already extinct on three of their namesake islands, their fate in the Galápagos is hardly secure. But if we give them a fighter's chance, they can shock us with their resilience, too.

• • • •

In the 1960s, two prominent biologists didn't discount dispersal abilities either. One, E. O. Wilson, was a myrmecologist (one who studies ants, not mermaids, as some of my students have assumed). The other, Robert MacArthur, was a gifted mathematician with a soft spot for nature, too. Both converged on a little-known field called island biogeography, a fledgling branch of biology that focuses on zoological and botanical distributions. But it's more than just where the wild things are; it's also where they aren't. Like every good field of inquiry, it also asks why.

Why, for example, do those wide-eyed, lovable lemurs only swing through Madagascar's forests? Why do dumpy little kiwi birds only scamper—mammal-like—through the New Zealand night? Why do egg-laying, milk-providing monotremes—platypuses and echidnas—only inhabit Australia and New Guinea? Why are there no penguins in the Arctic? Why are there no polar bears in the Antarctic? Why does Alaska buzz with mosquitoes but Iceland doesn't? And why, for the love of all that is sacred, do South American monkey nostrils point upward while all African and Asian monkey nostrils point downward?

If the orientation of monkey nostrils is your jam, island biogeography is for you. It's also for anybody who likes to ask simple but important questions. The kind our self-consciousness tends to erase as we age, in our unending efforts to conceal our ignorance. Perhaps Wilson and MacArthur's intellectual chops—both Ivy League stars with countless publications—gave them confidence we mere mortals lack. Whatever the case, question they did. To figure out why things are where they are, they first asked *how* they arrived. In biogeography, arrival is contingent on dispersal.

Michael Soulé was so focused on dispersal because it shares a bed with extinction. To keep from going extinct, animals must disperse. It allows breeding, gene flow, and habitat procurement. It maintains populations. Plus, if a population is threatened in one place—say, by a new strip mall—it can theoretically disperse to another. It's an escape hatch. In biology, plants and animals have two main forms of dispersal ability: breeding dispersal and natal dispersal. Breeding dispersal involves traveling from one breeding site to another, while natal dispersal is the movement from a birthing site to a breeding site. Each phase of these two forms—departure, transfer, and settlement—is hazardous.

Travel always carries risk. That's why we wear seatbelts and are ceaselessly reminded that our seat cushions double as personal flotation devices in the event of a water landing. Colonization is risky, too, as any one of the starving, sickly colonists at Jamestown would have attested. But if you're interested in avoiding extinction and sticking around for the long haul, like tortoises, staying put can be just as risky. Effective means of dispersal and colonization safeguard populations against extinction. If one subpopulation gets snuffed out in a certain habitat, a brave band of dispersers can recolonize it. Examples are legion: prothonotary warblers winging into a newly flooded forest, headstrong wolves loping out of Yellowstone's Lamar Valley for the forests of Idaho, monarch butterflies fluttering into a new patch of milkweed, hunter-gatherers crossing a land bridge to Beringia, and even—cough, cough—seasick, germ-laden colonists stepping off the *Mayflower*. All animals disperse and many don't survive the journey. But the lucky few can accomplish a lot. Rescue a moribund population from extinction. Or, like our clumsy tortoises that slipped off a Chilean cliff, kickstart a new one.

Wilson and MacArthur kickstarted something, too: a whole new way of viewing dispersal—in Soulé's phrase, dispersal limitations. Wilson, the obsessive natural historian, fed reams of ecological data to mathematical MacArthur, who transferred it into eye-crossing algorithms. Together, the two published technical papers in a mélange of journals. Then, in 1967, they synthesized them in a book. The title, *The Theory of Island Biogeography*, was as unadorned as the mustard-yellow cover. This figure-laden work wasn't fluffy beach reading. An austere, passive voice narrated the army of equations. Each of the two hundred pages contributed to a culminating argument, punctuated by a few simple graphs with curved and intersecting lines.

The idea was that islands—all land masses, really—can only hold so many species. Since resources are finite, the species compete for food and space. Eventually, they reach an equilibrium. A high school basketball team makes a good analogy. While the roster may change over time, the number of players on the roster doesn't. Competition to make the team may cause the players to specialize—some become good at shooting while others become expert rebounders. If they're not good enough, or can't carve out a role, they get cut. Maybe they can play JV, or in a rec league. Back on islands, those that get cut disperse elsewhere. Or they go extinct. Resources mandate a given number of species—an equilibrium.

Their other point, relevant to our drifting tortoises, depicted which islands the dispersers were likely to land on. Like many synthesizing ideas viewed in hindsight, this one seems painfully obvious. In short: living things that disperse from a mainland are more likely to reach large islands that are close by than they are to reach small islands that are far away. This explains why, for example, Columbus ran into the larger, closer island of San Salvador instead of the smaller, further islands of Conception and Rum Cay, after sailing the ocean blue back in 1492. Granted, it was more probable Columbus would hit a continent. Of the possible islands, however, he hit the one island biogeography predicted he would. Columbus, of course, was nine thousand miles off in his calculations. But Wilson and MacArthur were spot-on, their theory buttressed by the prospect of clear-eyed prediction.

It was the long-lost puzzle piece, fitting snugly with other emerging revelations regarding plate tectonics and continental drift. Not only was biogeography now on the map, it made zoological maps make sense, giving scientists what they crave most: coherence. Now biogeographers could address all those questions about kiwis and penguins and monkey nostril anatomy. It helped them understand how tortoises dispersed to the Galápagos. And it helped me understand how a dainty, four-petaled flower was the first to colonize a sinking island in the Atlantic.

• • • •

Unsurprisingly, the first real island biogeography work was done on islands. They make fabulous natural laboratories. Due to their insularity, they're easy places to record dispersal, colonization, and, for our purposes, extinction. Upon the publication of Wilson and MacArthur's book, scientists flocked to various islands to gather data to either support or falsify the finer points of the Wilson-MacArthur theory. The Florida Keys, Indian Ocean atolls, Krakatoa, the list is long. My favorite place the scientists went is a tidbit of terra firma well off Iceland's southern shore. Its name, Surtsey, seems more appropriate for an old milk cow than the Norse god of fire—Surtur—it was named after.

My intellectual romance with Surtsey is borne out of the deep-seated human tendency to crave the unattainable. However much I'd love a long walk on its beach, I never will; Surtsey is off-limits to all but a few blessed biogeographers. It's a long-running natural experiment, one of humanity's all-too-few expressions of scientific opportunism and laudable self-restraint. But I'm okay. After all, I've been closer than most, seeing it through a curtain of tears at forty mph in a banana-yellow speedboat. The tears—and rivulets of snot—were caused by the wind and the salt. But maybe not. Ezra was by my side, Imagine Dragons was blasting out of the boat's speakers, and thousands of pearly white northern gannets soared overhead like an angelic host. The mere sight of that chunk of lava-born basalt, like a tortoise's plastron above the sea, was enough.

Surtsey is a geological infant. It emerged from the earth's womb as a submarine volcano, rising above the Atlantic in 1963. It steadily grew for four years, eventually covering over a square mile. But then it stopped, passing the baton to erosion, which is now indefatigably running the final leg. Like all good things, it won't last. Scientists predict it'll dip below the sea again within the next century. Yes indeed, Galápagos tortoises—*tortoises*—can outlive islands. Researchers watched colonization on this bare, newly exposed habitat in real time.

The first to arrive was sea rocket. The plant's seeds washed up on Surtsey even before the lava had cooled. It found a crevice in the porous rock and sent out a long taproot. Anchor set, the plant lifted its head off the beachhead, buffeting the harsh Atlantic winds with its succulent structure. When the seeds of other plants tried to do the same, sea rocket welcomed them with an allelopathic brew of noxious chemicals it released in the sand. Entrepreneurial, ambitious, and murderous—sea rocket is the perfect disperser.

A parade of other dispersers soon followed, most hailing from the Icelandic mainland fifteen miles away. Some floated in like sea rocket, while others rode the wind or hitched rides. Any mode of transport sufficed: feet, feathers, even inside the guts of gulls busy making colonies of their own. For the botanical pioneers, the island's habitability improved every time a gull pooped, vomited, or simply discarded something inedible. Nutrients built up. So nourished, so did the colonists. A team of four authors at the Icelandic Institute of Natural History recorded twenty-three species of vascular plants that had become established by 1986. Twenty-seven years later, Surtsey boasted sixty-nine plants, not to mention a few hundred obstreperous gulls.

This may have been the island's botanical magic number—the locale's equilibrium Wilson and MacArthur discussed. We'll never know. For one thing, ecology tends to be too dynamic, the only constant being change. For another, Surtur withdrew his hand as suddenly as he'd extended it; Surtsey started shrinking. As of today, half of the one-square-mile island has slipped back under the sea, erosion—incessantly pounding surf—having pulled the freshly formed basalt back under. The crowded remnant is squeezing the colonists more tightly.

More real estate equals more species, this a basic thread of Wilson and MacArthur's theory. I know, stifle your gasp. Rest assured this straight-line graph was besmeared in flummoxing equations and given a no-nonsense name: the species-area relationship. The growth of Surtsey illustrated this in real time. As the island grew over time, more species colonized it. As it shrank like a calving glacier, they dropped away. Since 2007, the loss on Surtsey has been a steady drip. The remaining homesteaders better enjoy their solitude. By 2100, there's a good chance there won't be any rock left to stand on. Surtsey, and my hapless dreams of dispersing there myself, will be hopelessly sunk.

• • • •

Surtsey is a microcosm. From the perspective of outer space, we're all packed on a little blue island, running our very own biogeographical experiment. Daily, we're increasing our population and aggressively competing with other species. Every new housing development and big-box store that goes up, every new highway and parking lot, decreases their chance to live alongside us. It's an erosion of sorts, not only of our habitats but also of our minds. This revelation didn't come from tortoise experimentation nor travelogues of little-known maritime battles. Rather, I picked this up from Ötzi, one of my favorite dispersers, who unfortunately never reached where he was going. He lacked the perseverance of a Galápagos tortoise and the pioneering savvy of sea rocket. Ötzi had what Soulé would call limited dispersal abilities.

His story unfolds like this: In 1991, German hikers discovered the upper torso of a corpse sticking out of the ice in the Swiss Alps. The body was so well-preserved that the hikers assumed he was the recent victim of a mountaineering accident. Not so. The body turned out to be a Neolithic man from the Stone Age, whom the press christened Ötzi. His trek through the Alps predated Hannibal's by 5,100 years. That makes his incredible corpse older than both the pyramids and Stonehenge. Think about this: when Ötzi was living, mastodons were still stomping around the planet! Forensic recovery teams successfully extracted him along with what Captain Jack Sparrow would call his effects.

His effects have me spellbound. A copper axe, a bearskin cap, a quiver, string, shoes, a leather bag, and my personal favorite, a necklace strung with pieces of birch polypore. These clues tell us that Ötzi and his clansmen were shooting bears with rustic bows and obtaining metals, and some were avantgarde enough to carry a man purse. The birch polypore fungus is especially intriguing. It's a common fungus that decomposes dead and dying trees throughout the northern hemisphere. So common, in fact, that I've often found it growing in nearby woodlots. For some, the fungus's tan top and creamy underside reminds them of a meringue. I side with others who see a horse's hoof, another common name for it. Obviously, we don't know what Ötzi called it. But we do know it wasn't merely a fashion accessory. Quite literally, it was his medicine chest. Scientists think Ötzi used it to treat intestinal parasites, of which the forensic team found evidence of many.

Herein lies my fascination. I see a demure little fungus clinging to a birch tree and rarely think anything other than, "sweet, kinda looks like a horse's hoof." Not Ötzi. He knew their actual uses, and better yet, *how* to use them. Perhaps he thought, "I remember Uncle Wog using that to mollify his aching innards. Think I'll do the same."

There is no definitive list of the number of fungi in my home state of New York. Cornell's Plant Pathology Herbarium boasts a cool three hundred thousand mostly local specimens, so that's a clue. Despite a decade of effort using cameras and guidebooks, I can identify maybe a dozen, the largest ones with the fanciest fruiting bodies. I know their names. That's it. I have no idea what they do. Primitive, hirsute, Stone Age Ötzi, on the other hand, was stringing them around his neck and eking out every antiparasitic, antibacterial, antiviral, anti-inflammatory, and antioxidant property possible. I'll never come close to his easy command of natural history. And here's the crux: the more habitat and species we lose, the less likely I'll have the chance.

Ötzi certainly needed to know his plants. The poor guy was a mess, forty-five years old going on ninety. In addition to his load of intestinal parasites, he had hardened arteries, worn joints, gallstones, advanced gum disease, tooth decay, Lyme disease, and high levels of arsenic in his blood. Not to mention a nasty growth on his little toe. Such a high degree of pain was likely his impetus for the fifty-odd tattoos besmearing his skin. Notwithstanding the fact that he looked fit for a Seattle grunge band, Ötzi's tattoos—lacerations filled with charcoal—were unlikely meant for adornment. They were a form of acupuncture aimed to numb his constant pain.

Unfortunately, all the acupuncture and birch polypore in the world wasn't going to help him. Ötzi was living on borrowed time. The only real question was what ailment would nail him first. It's a trick question. None of his ailments doled the final blow. More alarmingly, and perhaps another bleak reminder of humanity's nature, it was his own species's doing.

Remember, traveling is risky. Ötzi was on the move, dispersing. Here's what forensics revealed: two hours before he died, he downed a meager meal of ibex meat and grains he had procured en route. While he ate, or perhaps just after, somebody with a bow and a bone to pick crept up on him. We don't know if Ötzi detected his assailant or not. Either way, he was shot with an arrow in the shoulder. Perhaps he tried to grab his own bow. Or maybe he fled. For better or worse, his attacker wasn't finished. Shortly after taking the arrow, Ötzi was clubbed in the head. His forty-five years on earth—and his vast accumulation of Indigenous knowledge—was erased in an instant.

Another microcosm. A metaphor. Ötzi represents our fellow endangered species worn down by habitat loss and fragmentation. Humanity—endlessly expanding economies—the assailant. Our fellow creatures have limited dispersal abilities. They're trying to reach breeding and natal grounds in efforts to colonize and rescue foundering populations from extinction. We've wounded them already. Can we refrain from striking a final blow?

• • • •

Slowing down may be the first step to take. And, like my wife, show a little more empathy. In Serengeti National Park, I hadn't yet discovered that. Not long after my first tortoise-on-the-back experiment was thwarted, another opportunity arose with another unsuspecting chelonian. My wife was napping and the only onlooker was a listless, young baboon. Like before, I found a slab of granite and placed the tortoise upside down upon it. I stepped back, started my stopwatch, and watched. Three minutes and forty-six seconds later, through a comical blend of leg flails and neck lunges, the tortoise flipped over. It looked at me smugly. Then, slowly and deliberately, it sauntered off.

Leopard tortoises, it turns out, can right themselves.

I can't help but wonder if we can too.

4
THE GREEN FIRE
Inbreeding

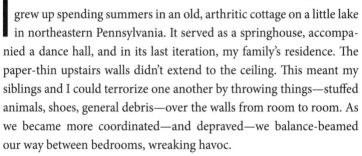

*"There are no hopeless cases, only
people without hope and expensive cases."*
—Michael Soulé

I grew up spending summers in an old, arthritic cottage on a little lake in northeastern Pennsylvania. It served as a springhouse, accompanied a dance hall, and in its last iteration, my family's residence. The paper-thin upstairs walls didn't extend to the ceiling. This meant my siblings and I could terrorize one another by throwing things—stuffed animals, shoes, general debris—over the walls from room to room. As we became more coordinated—and depraved—we balance-beamed our way between bedrooms, wreaking havoc.

The porous cottage was creaky, capacious, and on nights that I stayed there alone in my twenties, terrifying. Traced drawings of prize fish adorned the cobwebbed walls, mouse corpses splayed out in the closets, bats hung from the ceiling, and hundreds of tacked-up cutout Sunday comics layered the bathroom walls. The rough-hewn, tinder-dry, hemlock walls were speckled with knots, like leering eyes. My sister's room boasted a random trapdoor, windows were opened with antiquated pulleys, and an endless supply of clutter-filled corners beckoned the intrepid antique collector. All this to say, the cottage was perfect. Especially for an adventurous kid with an overactive imagination and disregard for basic hygiene.

It proved imperfect, however, for arsonists.

One summer night just before bedtime, my dad called my siblings into the living room, saying he had something to show us. He slid a rocker over a few feet and then lifted the corner of our thick, grimy rug. Wooden floorboards lay underneath. My jaw dropped. A section not much bigger than a welcome mat was blackened and charred. I looked at my dad. "Probably some local kids were messing around while we were gone one winter," he said matter-of-factly. "Or, it was an arson attempt. That's why I don't let you use candles. This cottage is a tinderbox." He dropped the rug back down. "The amazing thing is," he paused, looking back down at the floor, "that they failed."

● ● ● ●

I'm no longer amazed the arsonists failed. While some people are pyromaniacs, others are pyro-morons. I'm firmly in this latter group. A few years ago, while reading Gary Paulsen's *Hatchet* to my son, I became enamored with the idea of flint and steel. The book's protagonist, Brian, staved off death in northern Canada with it, after all.

So, during a sabbatical out west, I bought a simple flint and steel fire-starter kit and headed for a night of solitude in Lava Beds National Monument in northeastern California. Where better to turn sparks to flames, I reasoned, than a place born of liquid fire? I carefully made a nest of dry tinder as a bold kangaroo rat eyed me skeptically. I'd bought a package of jumbo hot dogs at a grocery en route. Intentionally, I hadn't bought backup matches. Or a lighter. If pain-riddled Ötzi could do it 5,300 years ago with his modest effects, I could do it with industrial-grade flint and steel.

Except I couldn't.

Despite everything at my disposal—time, tinder, a windless night—I couldn't start a fire. I even had experience—in Africa, I'd watched Masai pastoralists and Hadzabe hunter-gatherers light fires by rapidly rotating one stick into the thumb-sized depression of another. Here in Lava Beds, with a headlamp for light, I struck and struck, my weakening parade of sparks too feeble to ignite the tinder nest. Both my zeal and my arms flagged. Incipient blisters formed on my hands.

"Stupid flint!" I shouted, flinging my kit into the sagebrush. The kangaroo rat scuttled for cover.

I glared at the uncooked hot dogs and stood, deflated as a two-week-old party balloon. My identity had just sprung a leak. My boyhood diet of survival books had failed. *I* had failed. Reality dawned: I wasn't Daniel Boone. Not even close. Just another inept, coddled tourist. The kind Edward Abbey maligned as needing the shrink-wrapped services of "syphilization."

I faced a choice. Crawl into my tent in self-loathing, or grovel for help. Hunger versus humility. The thought of cheddar-stuffed, nitrate-laden, overprocessed hot dogs won out. My psyche and my stomach growling, I set off widdershins along the looping campground road.

Solitude, I soon discovered, can still be found in the West. A lot of it, in fact, if you visit northeastern California on a random weeknight in October. On the far side of the campground, I spied the monument's only other human, a guy sitting outside an RV next to a roaring fire. The flames mocked me as I approached; hospital surgeries could be performed in the light they threw off. I waved my flashlight so as not to surprise him. "So sorry to bother you!" I yelled over his humming generator.

"No worries," he said, unfolding out of his collapsible lawn chair. A fleece beanie topped his ruddy face, manicured stubble below lively eyes. Lit up by the fire, his hiking boots showed hardly a scuff. Unabashed glamper, he made no pretense of shunning modern convenience. How relaxing, I thought, to camp with nothing to prove.

"I, uh, forgot my matches," I said. A lie. I wasn't ready to share my identity crisis with a stranger.

"Well you're in luck," he said, handing me a six-inch-tall lighter. Like so much in western society, it was supersized.

"Do you want me to…?"

"Just keep it," he said. "It came in a three-pack."

I thanked him profusely and returned to my campsite, cradling the lighter like gold. An hour later, a fourth hot dog down the hatch, I stared hard at the glowing coals and thought back to the blackened floorboards in my family's cottage. What if whoever had broken in had lit a window curtain? Would the cottage have burned down? Would we still have spent our summers there?

More to the point, what if the other camper hadn't come to Lava Beds that night? Was it chance my belly was now topped up with assorted pig parts? Just a bit of dumb luck? Or was it fate, maybe even providence? Whatever the word, the world's limitless vagary dawned on me. Not all epiphanies in nature are profound. This one sure wasn't. I merely realized anew the line between success and failure. And as I caught a glint of my fire-starter kit from under the sage bush, I realized just how thin it is.

• • • •

The heroes who dedicated over a decade of their lives to restoring the eastern population of whooping cranes realized how thin the line was between success and failure, too. They fully understood the precarious fate of the stately white bird that stood taller than the average fifth-grader. Whooping cranes, like ivory-billed woodpeckers, were never widespread or abundant. At the start of the Civil War, about 1,400 flew between their breeding grounds in Wisconsin and their wintering grounds in Texas and Florida. The population was never much higher than that. Florida's cranes disappeared quickly in the plume-hunting craze of the late 1800s. Texas's withstood the siege but dropped to just fifteen birds by 1941.

Fifteen. As we learned with timber rattlesnakes, a total population of fifteen quickly drops to maybe half that when we consider the cranes that actually have the ability to breed. For the Texas population, whoopers historically wintered along the coast and bred across wetlands dotting the northern states and Canada. Important side note: growing economies don't like wetlands; they're thorns in the side of agricultural conglomerates and the monocultures they seek. They weigh down economies of scale.

With little thought to the birds, enterprising farmers drained as many wetlands as they could. The resilient flock of fifteen cranes kept flying, bypassing their old haunts—now oceans of corn—for one last undrained paradise: Wood Buffalo National Park, which straddles Canada's Alberta and Northwest Territories. In the relative safety of the park, they raised as many young as they could. With one to two wide-eyed fledglings in tow and winter coming, the vulnerable flock took to the skies for Aransas National Wildlife Refuge, 2,500 miles south along the quickly developing Texas coast. The flock's mission was brave: to breed themselves out of a bottleneck.

Conservation biologists with a mind for genetics are terrified by bottlenecks. Genes get squeezed in a bottle's neck, and often a boatload of genetic diversity gets lost. To illustrate the concept, textbooks fill their bottles with all sorts of items—marbles, coins, beads. My favorite? Legos. Unless, of course, you step on one in the dark.

Take a standard seventy-dollar Lego set—a cute little Star Wars porg—break it apart, and drop all 811 pieces into a narrow-necked bottle. Shake it up and tip the bottle upside down for a few seconds. Let's say 100 pieces slide out. Now, keep duplicating those 100 until you again have 811. Try as you might, you won't be able to build the porg. A few key pieces—an eye, wing, foot—will be missing. That's what bottlenecks do to populations. Something happens, like a hurricane or a fashion-driven plume craze, and the population gets squeezed. The survivors, those that drop out of the bottle, rarely represent the original population. When the population tries to rebuild, it may be missing key pieces, like a gene encoding for migratory instinct or resistance for a virulent strain of bird flu.

But the whooping cranes beat the odds; they squeezed out okay and recovered. Under the watchful eye of a few farsighted conservation organizations, they rebounded from fifteen to over three hundred. Far better than fifteen, but still one hurricane or poaching spree away from total annihilation. Insurance, in the form of a separate Florida-based population, was needed.

Enter Operation Migration. If Cornell's lab threw a deep ball by announcing the rediscovery of the ivorybill, this pass was headed to the upper deck. It was a much larger venture than a mere multiday canoe trip. When the dust settled, Operation Migration involved ultralight aircraft, indefatigable handlers, crane Halloween costumes, infinite patience, exquisitely painted crane puppets, and stifling bureaucratic red tape. Oh, and some money. The ten million dollars at the outset turned out to be just a drop in the bucket.

While the process was elaborate, the goal was simple: establish an eastern population of whooping cranes. Just dumping a handful into Florida wouldn't work. Cranes are highly evolved birds that can live twenty-five years in the wild. Local extinction—the fancier word is *extirpation*—had erased their migratory memories and tampered with their instincts. Each spring, the frisky birds felt the urge to go north but couldn't quite remember the route. But ornithologists did. So they hired dedicated pilots and ultralight aircraft. It wasn't unprecedented. Pilots had succeeded with Canada geese and trumpeter swans. Why not teach whoopers how to fly from Florida to Wisconsin and back again?

The ingredients for a Hollywood ending were all in place. A vexing problem, harrowing odds, a captivating solution, and elegant, endearing protagonists. For eleven years, a handful of nonprofit organizations threw all their creative energy and financial resources at the cranes. The hurdles were many: multiple daily feedings, incessant monitoring, and cross-continental flights involving storms, private-property problems, and powerlines that crossed like a game of cat's cradle. One larger problem arose above all the others, however. Though the captive-reared cranes could relearn their migratory pathway, they couldn't figure out how to be good parents. Unlike their doting handlers, they treated their young with apathy and neglect. All too frequently their nests were untended. While they'd overcome the obstacle of migration and followed the ultralights, a seemingly simple challenge—parenthood—proved too formidable.

After years of failure, the US Fish and Wildlife Service reluctantly pulled the plug. Only ten chicks had fledged and survived to adulthood. The population—and the financial expenditure—had proven unsustainable. This was wet and wooded Wisconsin, not Hollywood. Here, the line between success and failure was too thin.

Alongside Operation Migration, 289 cranes had been released in hopes of establishing a resident flock in Florida. Without the perils that accompany migration, the hope was that here the parents would be dutiful and the flock would become a stronghold. It didn't happen. While the parents did better, predation and powerlines headlined the pitfalls. By 2010, the population had whittled down to 30 birds.

Eight years later, the population had halved. Only fourteen cranes remained. While visiting my parents in Melbourne, Florida, I received word a pair had just been spotted ambling about a pasture two hours away in Polk County. Far but doable. I woke early, left my folks a note on the table, and commandeered their minivan. I sailed down I-95 enshrouded in ethereal fog. Like it, Florida's whoopers were soon to dissipate into nothingness. Too many grand species were disappearing. These, doggonit, I would see in the flesh.

It wasn't hard. Unlike secretive rails, the oversized, snow-white whoopers were cake. Halfway along Backbone Road, I spied them, gleaming like pearls against the dusty backdrop of brown, mono-chrome cattle. I needn't have pulled over on the little-trafficked road. But I did so anyway, eager to settle in and watch. I lowered my window and raised my binoculars. The cranes were clearly used to public scrutiny. Each had an ankle bedecked in multicolored bands, evidence they lived well-monitored lives. Even though these two were free, I couldn't shake the feeling of inmates on parole. One false move, or too close a scrape, and they'd be rounded up, returned to prescriptive lives of captivity. The cranes seemed less contemplative. One picked lazily at the earth. The other preened, oblivious to its singular importance in the iconic plight of its species.

Juxtaposition with the cattle could not have been starker. So dissimilar yet each a tenacious survivor of one of the most severe bottlenecks in our planet's history. Sixty-six million years ago, a 7.5-mile-wide rock rapidly closed in on Earth. Large fronds of tree ferns swayed in a gentle, late Cretaceous breeze. A tyrannosaurus tended a clutch of eggs while a heedful triceratops grazed nearby. Other animals viscerally sensed calamity. Small, weasel-like mammals scurried into burrows. A pod of hadrosaurs stopped feeding and tensed up. The asteroid ripped through the atmosphere and buried into the Yucatán Peninsula. Instantly a chain of environmental disasters rippled over Earth. The North American plate heaved, jumpstarting volcanoes all along its margins. Ash from the impact site and volcanic explosions formed opaque, suffocating clouds, soon circling the globe and strangling photosynthesis. Without the sun, billions of plants died and temperatures plummeted. An unforeseen global winter had begun, a cataclysmic plot twist for all the world's creatures.

With little food to eat, the Cretaceous titans succumbed in a geological blink. But here's the relevant part for us: an anonymous few didn't. This scrappy lot, with smaller needs and a greater tolerance to change, inherited the mangled Earth. Some of these Dinosauria, winged lizards boasting both scales and feathers, ramified into the ten thousand birds we see today, whooping cranes included. And those primitive mammals that had dodged the feet of the giant sauropods and fled to their burrows? They became cynodonts, diverging into five thousand different species, represented today by the cattle.

The cranes, with their scaled tarsi and scythe-like bills, looked prehistoric indeed. The cattle grazing around them, brainless artificially bred slabs of barely animate beef, not so much. It's uncertain just how these varied limbs from the tree of life survived the asteroid's devastation to sprout anew off the phylogenetic trunk. The bottleneck was severe, the survivors were few. So how the incipient Cenozoic—the Age of Mammals—unfurled is conjectural, an evolutionary black box rife with scientific quibbling. But even in the nerdiest ivory towers and dustiest museum wings, most agree on one point: a lot of inbreeding was involved.

● ● ● ●

Inbreeding makes small populations vulnerable to extinction. This is why Michael Soulé cared so much about it. After emerging from a bottleneck, harmful alleles—versions of genes—can become fixed in a population, insidiously reducing a population's fitness over time.

A simple recipe for a distasteful result—inbreeding depression. But paradoxically, inbreeding isn't *always* bad. It can also speed up the loss of harmful alleles. Say, for example, a crane inherits two harmful (usually recessive) alleles that make it more susceptible to bird flu. The bird's quick death at its first exposure to the disease is a severe mercy to the population. The harmful alleles accompany the bird to the grave, safeguarding the survivors from a similar fate. Why? Because dead birds can't pass on genes. Most survivors of the Cretaceous extinction—and the long-term survivors of all bottlenecks— owe their feathered or furry lives to this paradox. Cows, cranes, and my personal favorite, cheetahs. The big cats may have outrun extinction, but a common cliché has proven harder to evade. Yes indeed, cheetahs never prosper.

My tale of the cheetah is wound up with a baboon. The two tales, and tails, intertwine. First, the baboon. In case it has been a while since your last nature documentary or trip to the zoo, a walking baboon holds its tail aloft. When a baboon walks, its slightly kinked tail assumes the shape of a question mark. This isn't the baboon's only questionable trait.

Every journey through grad school is different. Mine was marked by adventure, anxiety, a startling lack of guidance, and baboons. My two-room, concrete bunker research house in Serengeti National Park lacked water and electricity. It didn't lack the presence of a pride of lions, the occasional cheetah, and baboons. Without electricity, the only way I could connect to the outside world was to drive to the desolate park headquarters and hope that one of the other forlorn researchers hadn't commandeered the park's only public ethernet cord or that a curious hyrax hadn't nibbled through the wires. Academic loneliness had darkened my spirit of adventure. I hadn't heard from my advisor in months. In the sink-or-swim world of doctoral research, I felt twenty thousand leagues under the sea.

The austere room at park headquarters seemed more set up for interrogation than email. One table bolted to the middle of the floor. One creaky wooden chair. One cable—upon which all my hopes pinned—snaking from the one dusty outlet to the table. Without windows, the room was a sauna. Lest I die of heatstroke before the dialup connected, I propped the door open. Mistake.

No sooner had I taken my ancient laptop out of its bag when a hateful, hopeful, hirsute head appeared in the doorway. Gray, shaggy hair, doglike snout, and two beady eyes shaded by a heavy Cro-Magnon brow. A large male baboon, its eyes laser-focused on my half-open computer bag, which I'd dumped on the floor. The thief was experienced. Bags meant food. After a morning of insipid seeds and mole crickets, a pinched can of Pringles would be heavenly, a perfect prelude to a midafternoon nap in the crotch of his favorite acacia. The beast wanted my bag. So did I. Without it, my laptop wouldn't stand a chance on Serengeti's washboard roads.

The baboon lunged for it. I jumped, knees hitting the table, chair clattering over backward. The baboon braked. I kicked my bag, which slid across the floor like a hockey puck, slamming against the far wall. Second mistake. Now the only thing between the baboon and my bag was my gangly, defenseless body. The baboon slipped around to the right, intent on the bag. Now it was well away from the door, the room's only exit. I seized the chair and swung it around, lion-tamer style. Third mistake. Now the baboon felt threatened. He turned toward me baring inch-long, conical canines. Then he sprang. I screamed, turning the chair into a shield.

My scream was prolonged and—thank heavens—heard. Two rangers, clad in forest-green uniforms and black berets, appeared at the door. Neither seemed prepared for what they saw. Two wild-eyed primates pirouetting about a room, one swinging a wooden chair like a confused member of the color guard.

To this day, I don't forgive the rangers for what they did next: they laughed. Doubled-over, knee-slapping, utterly humiliating laughter. Worse, they blocked the door. Exit gone and outnumbered, the baboon went berserk, twisting and shrieking and lunging. When it blitzed the nearest ranger, he sidestepped, wielding his rifle like a bayonet. The other ranger, still guffawing, retreated out the door. Daylight. The baboon galloped out the door, this time his tail looking more like an exclamation mark.

• • • •

Baboons terrorize more than just the odd researcher. I've also seen them, for example, go after a big cat. Grad school in the rearview mirror, I recently took my own students to East Africa, to Kenya's Maasai Mara National Reserve, the northern part of the great ecosystem in which I'd done my studies. On an early March morning, as the chilly savanna welcomed the day's first golden sunbeams, our Land Cruiser chanced upon a lone cheetah trotting across the plains.

We drove up, cut the engine, and popped our heads out of the adjustable top like curious prairie dogs. It wasn't hard to see why cheetah are depicted throughout Egyptian tombs. Elegant, sleek, so obviously fast. Zero to sixty miles per hour in three strides.

The cheetah padded toward us. In midstride it froze, hair rising on its gently sloping back. The cat looked past us, focusing on something we couldn't detect. Then it bounded off. Was a lion around? A leopard? Only another big cat could cause the world's fastest land animal to retreat, right?

Wrong. Just behind us, angrily galloping toward the cheetah, was a large, male baboon. This one wasn't interested in computer bags. It had one thing on its mind: annihilate the cheetah. Cheetah and baboon, the fast and the furious. The race was hopelessly lopsided. Determined though the baboon was, its bulky body was no match for a feline Ferrari. Not more than fifty yards in, the baboon gave up, scowling.

Our day concluded with one more cheetah encounter, a mom and her cub. A three-cheetah day—a good haul for any safari goer. First-timers to Africa, my students wrongly assumed it was normal. I knew better. Over the years I'd logged in the park, I chanced upon cheetahs rarely. Not because their cryptic, sun-dappled spots helped them blend in. No, the reason was more disconcerting: there simply weren't many of them.

In 1900, more than one hundred thousand cheetahs roamed from

Africa all the way to the shores of the Indian subcontinent. Today fewer than ten thousand remain worldwide, limited to a few pockets of Africa, excepting a few dozen gaunt Asiatic cheetahs eking out a living in Iran's mountainous central plateau. Everywhere else they've been crowded out by farms, villages, towns, cattle, and even other big cats. As you know, few cats play nicely. The Serengeti-Mara is a lion redoubt, with roughly three thousand calling the place home. Some one thousand leopards slink spitefully around them. Cheetahs? Just three hundred or so. All three species hate each other and will kill each other's cubs if the opportunity arises. Cheetahs, the weakest of the three with their aerodynamic physiques, are the most vulnerable. Adult cheetahs can run from most of their problems. Cubs not so much.

Our cub sighting was my first in nearly two decades of fairly regular safari going. Mesmerized, I drank in the details. Smallish ears, oversized paws, and a blond mullet down its back. Long shaggy hair, found only on cubs, lends the cat the latter half of its scientific name, *jubatus*, from the Latin *juba*, mane. While some suggest it helps them blend in with the long grass of the plains, I prefer another possibility, Batesian mimicry. Just as the perfectly palatable viceroy butterfly dons the garb of the distasteful monarch to fool would-be predators, cheetah cubs may be trying to look like honey badgers.

Not a bad choice. Because honey badgers, as viral video clips remind us, don't care. A friend and mentor of mine told me how a honey badger attacked him when he discovered it raiding his pantry. More distressing is where the badger aimed its assault: his nether regions. A documentary, *Killers of the Kalahari*, shows a honey badger attack a highly venomous puff adder (the species that activated my snake fear). With lightning speed and ferocity, the badger dispatched the snake. But in the midst of the scuffle, the badger gets bitten. It convulses and collapses next to the dead puff adder. There it remained, the filmmakers tell us, for two hours, as inert as a noble gas.

Again, honey badgers don't care. Because suddenly, Lazarus-like, it sprang back to life. While we don't know what Lazarus did just after his resurrection, we do know what the honey badger did. It's right there in the film. Right away, it starts eating the puff adder, which did not spring back to life. No wobbling off to look for water or lick its wounds. Living, dying, and living again is just what honey badgers do.

"The supernatural," Elbert Hubbard said, "is the natural not yet understood." I disagree. Scientists understand how the antivenin in honey badger blood lends them resistance to puff adder bites. To me, however, it's this understanding that makes them supernatural. Here is a creature that regularly stands down snakes, bee swarms, and ticked-off leopards. While the honey badger may not defy the laws of science, it defies my imagination, making me all in for cheetah Batesian mimicry. Honey badger resemblance can't be a coincidence. Whatever the case, this much is clear: in a place chock-full of hungry predators, it certainly beats looking like a knobby-kneed newborn wildebeest.

But as any country star will concur, success takes more than a mullet. Cheetah cub mortality is north of 90 percent. Dens get raided. Diseases pop up. Mothers fail to find enough prey. It isn't easy living in a land of lions, leopards, eagles, and pythons—not to mention black-souled baboons.

Two minibuses pulled up behind ours. Eager full-brimmed heads popped up and cameras clicked like machine guns. The mother and cub didn't flinch; it was the price of charisma. Plus, compared to what they were used to, three cars of paparazzi weren't bad. Sometimes, there were upwards of twenty. On those crowded days, Serengeti-Mara cheetahs drank diesel and dust, utterly engulfed by the adoring masses.

To visit these great places is to be part of the problem. Few things rival watching a playful cub gambol about in real time, batting its mother's ears and somersaulting over her body. However brief, it bonds the observer to the observed, some spectators taking away newfound concern for the species in addition to maxed-out memory cards. But to watch cheetahs, of course, is to crowd them. Too many watchers can constrict them, eliminating chances to encounter prey.

Yet another tension in conservation. Cheetahs need advocates. They also need, at least occasionally, to be left alone. Can another generation of conservationists arise without intimate wild encounters?

Where will concern spring from if not through direct experience? Is it merely a matter of limiting the number of safari cars? If so, how many? Should safari costs increase to limit the number of onlookers? If so, how high should they be? Would such a price hike preclude my students from visiting? None of these questions are easily answered. So, I sit in the Land Cruiser with my students, gnawing my fingernails, gambling at least one will become a conservationist as compensation for our fawning.

The mother cheetah was patient. Her cub stood on hind legs, swiping her flicking ears. Distracted by her tail, it sprang over her head to knock it down. Success. It seized the tail and shook it. But a second later, the tail slipped out of its jaws. The cub's momentary satisfaction changed to bewilderment.

• • • •

I've been bewildered by cheetah tails, too. Normal tails are spotted down the length with four concentric black rings near the end and topped with a tuft of white. Like a vanilla-chocolate twist with a splotch of whipped cream. Before me was exactly that, a cheetah with a normal tail. It was the first I'd seen. All of the tails I'd seen before had been kinked, oddly patterned, or discolored. My experience wasn't unique. In Namibia, for example, data from the Cheetah Conservation Fund reveals a kinked tail in 19 percent of wild cheetahs.

Considering the major issues concerning endangered species, kinked, off-colored tails hardly seem important. But to understand how inbreeding can lead to extinction, it's terribly important. Baboons are not at all endangered. Next to humans, they're the most successful primate—smart, adaptive, and when trapped in a small room, utterly foul. Their genome is sound, the kink in their tails intentional. It helps them transport young and balance at night in their arboreal roosts.

A kink in a cheetah's tail, on the other hand, doesn't help with anything. It's defective, evidence of an unsound genome. Just like whooping cranes, cheetahs became inbred. Not interbred, if you're reading fast. *Inbred*. Not because they lack a sense of decorum, but because there hasn't been a choice. Cheetahs are few. Regardless of the species in question, when things get hot, the flesh gets weak. So rather than forgo mating altogether, cheetah siblings, or offspring with parents, have shacked up. When other options don't exist, hormonal urgings trump instinctual safeguards.

I know. It's gross. But it's not their fault. If you need a scapegoat, blame the latest ice age. It was the Pleistocene, about twelve thousand years ago, that first sent the cheetah roller coaster off the rails. According to a recent study by cheetah expert Stephen O'Brien in the *Journal of Heredity*, cheetah populations were severely squeezed the world over in a global bottleneck. Many populations in Europe, Asia, and America blinked out. In Africa, they barely held on, just a handful managing to sprint their way out of the bottleneck. Subsequent genomic diversity shrank considerably. Evidence for the bottleneck is plain to see in every survivor. The ten thousand cheetahs alive today are remarkably—or distressingly—similar. So similar, in fact, that any old cheetah can accept a skin graft from any other.

Skin grafts? Who exactly is performing cheetah skin grafts? Cheetah researchers, that's who. And although it sounds wacky, the fact that cheetahs can freely exchange skin grafts is significant precisely because you and I can't. Our immune systems are highly specific. Skin from other people, even our own siblings, isn't recognized—it's considered foreign and immediately attacked. Cheetah immune systems, however, don't recognize strangers. Distant relatives don't seem distant for a simple reason: they're not distant at all.

Like the kinked tail, a welcoming immune system hardly seems noteworthy. In and of itself, it's not. Unfortunately, these traits are linked with a host of other abnormalities all too common in cheetahs. Crowded lower incisors, focal palatine erosion, congenital birth defects, undescended testicles, and abnormal sperm are just as upsetting as they sound. And while I've come to terms with my own crowded lower incisors, all the other maladies I've just listed would push me to the doctor.

The host of cheetah defects is the result of a process called unmasking. Lest the genetic jargon get too thick, I'll start with a number, albeit a massive one: 37.2 trillion. You're forgiven for assuming it's the national debt. No, it's something far more wondrous—the number of cells in your body. It's more impressive this way: 37,200,000,000,000. If your jaw isn't already on the floor, consider this: each of these 37.2 trillion is jam-packed with critical components.

Let's ignore mitochondria, vacuoles, cytoplasm—all those terms you've worked hard to forget from high school biology. Genes will suffice. Genes are the instruction manuals for the 37.2 trillion, like those necessary for building the Lego porg. We inherit one copy of each gene from each parent, giving us two versions—called alleles—for each gene. One is dominant, the other recessive. All these instruction manuals account for why we tend to look like our parents, where our eye color, hair color, facial structure, and height come from. But because our alleles combine randomly, we differ from our parents, too.

Even meticulously written instruction manuals can have the odd typo. In the language of genetics, mistakes are called mutations. Unless you're a six-fingered man with Inigo Montoya after you, mutations are hardly worth losing sleep over. They rarely manifest in large and varied populations. They're usually recessive and overruled by the healthy dominant allele. But not always.

In small, bottlenecked populations, when siblings are mating with siblings and offspring with parents, the chances for somebody to get two copies of the same gene go up. If the gene is healthy and sound, it's no biggie. But if it's a trifle wonky—a mutation—the result can be problematic. When two versions of a harmful recessive allele are inherited, it becomes unmasked.

This is the sad tale of the cheetah's tail. The kinked, oddly patterned manifestation is just a minor sign of a more severe problem. Sometimes it's much worse. Just ask the folks from Namibia's Cheetah Conservation Fund who recorded six-legged and two-headed cheetahs trying to make a go of things. Sad defects due entirely to unmasking.

● ● ● ●

Eight billion people on the planet. Just ten thousand screwed-up cheetahs. Vegas bookies wouldn't like these odds. So, is this remnant doomed? Even if we figure out how to coexist, will the cheetah's own troubled genome wield the coup de grace? Maybe. But maybe not. History suggests the cheetah has a puncher's chance. Plenty of species have overcome severe genetic bottlenecks and inbreeding. Elephant seals spiraled down to fewer than 100 and now, thanks to strict protections and a renewed robust genome, number over 150,000. Bison, slaughtered to fewer than five hundred, now number close to half a million. Amur tigers dropped to an effective population size of thirty and yet remain genetically sound. And though the eastern population of whooping cranes hasn't relearned how to migrate yet, the Texas population is clearly rebounding.

If cranes and cheetahs continue living depends largely on our willingness to let them. And willingness can depend on perspective, which can come unexpectedly. For the great conservationist Aldo Leopold, it came after pumping lead into a wolf pack in Arizona:

> We reached the old wolf in time to watch a fierce green fire dying in her eyes. I realized then, and have known ever since, that there was something new to me in those eyes—something known only to her and to the mountain. I was young and full of trigger-itch; I thought that because fewer wolves meant more deer, that no wolves would mean hunters' paradise. But after seeing the green fire die, I sensed that neither wolf nor mountain agreed with such a view.

● ● ● ○

For Leopold it came down to restraint. Restraint that thinks like a mountain. For the ever-plundering, ever-producing human race, restraint is our Achilles' heel. But we need it now more than ever, because there's an important addendum to the inbreeding dilemma: a bottleneck is only worth coming out of if there's somewhere to go, a larger space to inhabit. For the green fire to burn in all species, restraint says this: move over and make room. For wolves, woodpeckers, rattle-snakes, diapensia, buckwheat, tortoises, cranes, and cheetahs.

My epiphany didn't come as dramatically or lyrically as Leopold's. It seeped in slowly over the years, beginning with those blackened floorboards in our creaky old cottage. It revisited me that night in Lava Beds, when the wind snuffed out the feeble sparks from my flint and steel. Meanwhile, fires uncontrollably rage across the West each fall, their initial spark often unknown, leaving little more than ash in their wake. Fire, green or otherwise, is fickle. It ignites, burns, and succumbs unpredictably.

Inbred populations behave similarly. The line between success and failure is thin; whether they burn on or burn up depends upon the fortitude of those little alleles dividing and combining in the dark. One thing is clear: every plant's and animal's fire deserves a chance to keep burning. It's not about whether or not we can light each fire, but rather the irreplaceable glow cast by the species here among us.

5

MONA-SHA-SHA
Loss of Heterozygosity

"In nature the only absolute truths are life and death, eat or die, pass your genes on into the future ordisappear from the evolutionary landscape."
—J. Drew Lanham, *The Home Place*

Some people count sheep to fall asleep. I count deer to stay awake. Growing up, my hourlong bus ride to school took me past old farms, new subdivisions, and everything in between. It was typical small-town America: a mosaic of yards, woodlots, fields, and swamps. Tiny habitat fragments ran into each other like bumper cars and where they collided—edges and ecotones. The term for such an arrangement is habitat fragmentation. My term for it, as I ceaselessly wiped the foggy school bus window, was perfection. Habitat fragmentation makes edges and edges make deer. Nothing at school could rival the splendor of a morning bus ride of deer counting. Perhaps I'd best my record.

I can't recall what first sparked my ungulate intrigue. Perhaps it was when, during the opening day of deer season, a wounded, ten-point buck dragged his nonfunctioning hindquarters across the road in front of our bus, causing a rain of expletives from Gail, our otherwise stoical driver. Perhaps it was when a panicked, dog-chased deer leapt through the first-story window of the first-grade classroom next to mine (it was empty at the time, thank heavens). Throughout that day, we walked goggle-eyed past the cervine crime scene, police tape draped across the open doorway, while custodians cleaned up the shattered glass and splattered gore.

Deer were everywhere. Yet even then, something about their ubiquity didn't seem right.

Turns out, something *isn't* right with deer. Our choppy relationship with deer started in earnest with European settlement. Whatever pre-Columbian balance existed suddenly went haywire and signs of the wonkiness remain. In my neck of the woods in western New York, it's on full display in Letchworth State Park (the same place, incidentally, with the small population of timber rattlesnakes).

Everybody needs a playground nearby; Letchworth is mine. Thirty-five miles of wooded splendor, featuring trails to hike, waterfalls to explore, and warblers to seek. For a flexibly scheduled professor, the pull is too often my peril. I neglect my gutters and my inbox, both endlessly filling with detritus. I grab my binoculars and start the engine, and my truck does the rest, finding its way to a beckoning trailhead. In the rearview mirror, my quotidian duties are always closer than they appear. But I leave them nonetheless. I won't remember that faculty meeting, I reason, but I'll never forget these crisp autumn leaves. I rarely leave without a lagniappe—a roaring waterfall, soaring bald eagle, or the streak of a peregrine falcon. "I never for a moment thought of giving up God's big show for a mere professorship," John Muir wrote. Wanting—needing—the big show, too, I hit up Letchworth. Whom I see depends on the trail I choose. With one exception—deer.

Deer are everywhere. Every autumn, deer cram inside the park like Walmart shoppers on Black Friday. Hunting is limited and carefully regulated. Relatively safe inside their bunker, they relax while guns blaze just outside the boundaries. Strolling down a trail, I watch them nibble everything their incisors can scissor off—an average of seven pounds of woody plant material—on a typical winter day.

For a deer lover, the graceful forms of deer animate my hikes. I enjoy them. I also enjoy the clean forest understory, as uncluttered as an art museum. The dearth of shrubbery and saplings makes detours easy. But while I smile as a hiker, I cringe as an ecologist. Forests aren't supposed to be one-tiered. "You're in a great forest if you cannot pick out a straight-line path through fallen limbs and trunks," writes David Haskell in *The Forest Unseen*. "A bare forest floor is a sign of ill health." Many species, like hooded warblers and ruffed grouse, need shrubbery for nests, food sources, and cover. A stunning place like Letchworth, with little besides mature canopy, is as useless to them as a parking lot. It's even problematic for the old, giant trees themselves. Deer herbivory has created an alarming age gap, like a nursing home with plenty of old folks but nobody to assist them.

Irony abounds. William Pryor Letchworth, whose donation of land in 1907 forms the heart of the park, never saw a deer. Not an antler, hoof, or even a flash of that wonderful white tail. There weren't any about. They had been, of course. The Seneca people, who inhabited the region long before Europeans, saw scads. Arrowheads, routinely found by those with an eye for them, testify to the Seneca's dependence on deer. "Hunting and fishing was not just sport to the Indians," wrote Seneca historian Arch Merrill. "They built brush fences to round up whole herds of deer and sometimes took 100 in a single kill." Deer were a vital source of calories to help the Seneca people withstand the environmental whimsy of western New York winters.

The first Europeans around Letchworth liked deer, too. But a combination of commercial hunting and short-term thinking quickly led to the deer's demise. "In the nineteenth century," writes Haskell, "we stripped more trees from the land than the ice age accomplished in one hundred thousand years." Before European settlement, America was home to an estimated thirty-five million whitetails. "There is such infinite herds," European settler Thomas Ashe penned back in 1682, "that the whole country seems but one continued park." The ungulate reign was not to last. Just a century or so later, they plummeted to fewer than a hundred thousand. In Letchworth and much of the East, they were extirpated entirely.

Times were bleak for some of America's iconic species. Bison, grizzlies, and elk endured hemorrhaging losses. Others, like passenger pigeons and Carolina parakeets, went up in smoke altogether. The ivorybill assumed ethereality. Wolves and mountain lions slunk away, lurking anywhere rapacious settlers weren't, into swamps and mountains, and north into Canada. Deer wisely followed suit.

Unlike other species that dwindled severely, deer had an ace up their sleeve. Compared to the other species we've discussed, they laugh in the face of Soulé's extinction factors. Unlike ivorybills, rattlesnakes, tortoises, cranes, and cheetahs, white-tailed deer thrive on the margins. Deer are generalists thriving in habitat margins. They love life on the edge.

At first, Europeans even deprived them that, so extensively cleared were America's forests. But ever so slowly, feelings of waywardness caught up with the greedy saw. As with the Grinch, a conscience developed. As the nineteenth century concluded, important personalities, organizations, and legislation at last saw the error in unregulated exploitation. John Muir, John Burroughs, Teddy Roosevelt, Gifford Pinchot, the Audubon Society, the Sierra Club, the Lacey Act, the Migratory Bird Treaty Act, Pelican Island, Yellowstone National Park—from these titanic forces sprang a hopeful but uncertain sapling: ecological awareness. Now the gap could be filled. New growth had finally arrived.

Apocalypse over, conditions for the second coming of deer were ripe. Cultural forbearance evolved in step with the small family farm. So long-deprived of deer, slashed forests regenerated quickly. Hedgerows, fields, and woodlots popped up. A habitat mosaic—edges—returned and not far behind were deer.

Just before World War II, somebody finally spied a deer nervously tiptoeing past Letchworth. The event made all the local papers. Spectators flocked, hoping to catch a glimpse of the rare creature. Compared to the late 1800s, the United States had developed better regulation. The Northeast in particular became a DMZ, as state and federal agencies set up regulated hunting seasons and quotas. For deer, rules and regenerating forests were a boon. Even better, they could feed in peace; gone were their longtime nemeses, wolves and mountain lions.

The carefree deer fed and bred. Soon they had rebounded back to thirty million, where they hover today. Life on the edge has never been better, and every patch is well-populated: cemeteries, backyards, golf courses, used-car lots, highway medians, city parks, and roadsides. Roadsides often lead to roadways, answering the proverbial question of why the deer—not the chicken—crossed the road. In the last two years, Linda and I have hit three. My mother, who has had her share of ungulate collisions, shifts the blame, claiming they hit her, as if deer are bounding down the highway at fifty-five mph while she's trying to cross in her minivan. Regardless of culpability, Americans annually collide with 1.3 million, a whopping number that has led to backlash against the animal's resurgence.

"A forest without large herbivores is an orchestra without violins," writes Haskell. He's right, except now it seems the violins are drowning out the symphony. Where I live, a twilight grocery run feels like a cervine slalom course. The upside? There's plenty to count—my record standing at 109 in a four-mile stretch.

● ● ● ●

Today I wasn't interested in counting deer. Commonplace deer, that is. I was after the mystical variety. Justifying my escape as experiential learning, I dodged a slew of meetings for a Cold War–era munitions depot, two hours down the deer-laden interstate. Upon arrival, I'd parked and boarded a short yellow school bus, determined to put visuals on a concept I'd long taught about in my conservation courses—heterozygosity loss. I had caught wind of the depot's white deer from a friend, and was antsy to learn about them firsthand. Childlike enthusiasm suppressed thoughts of my colleagues back on campus, undoubtedly doing the right thing—meeting with students, grading papers, building rapport. Meh, I muttered. I was back on the bus about to perform my favorite pastime. Except this time, the deer I counted would be snow white.

"If you see anything, just shout!" Heather said, gripping the bus's intercom with one hand while bracing herself on the seatback to face us. "I'll be your guide today and if you have any questions while I'm talking, feel free to interrupt."

Despite Heather's encouragement, nobody seemed to be looking. Nor was Heather. From her standing position, she couldn't see out the bus windows, which may as well have been opaque. Most of my dozen fellow passengers were silver-haired and chatty, the afternoon trip likely a lighthearted diversion from the routine of retired life. Two rows diagonally ahead sat a younger guy; all I could see of him was his mop of greasy black hair and tattoos that crawled up his left arm like a swarm of tarantulas as he bore holes into his smartphone. I hoped he wasn't mapping out the depot for ill ends.

Perhaps I looked suspicious, too. My bazooka-long camera lens, diagram-heavy journal, and overtly serious demeanor suggested something untoward, despite my pure intentions. Moreover, I definitely *was* mapping out the depot. Genetically, at least. Michael Soulé's "loss of heterozygosity," a key factor in the extinction of species, had brought me here. While deer obviously aren't in any danger of extinction, they were once. And now, the story of the depot's white deer offered a marvelous example of how genetics and insular environments affected rarity. Questions swirled like the barn swallows winging past the windows. Were the depot's white deer merely a genetic anomaly? Or had this population been manipulated by Cold War military men with too much time on their hands?

Heather read my mind. "You may be wondering why white deer are here," she said, pausing to take a swig from her Nalgene covered in national park stickers. "The depot covers ten thousand acres. A chain-link fence topped with double strands of barbed wire encircles it. The reason, of course, is that the depot once harbored one of the largest stockpiles of nuclear munitions in the US."

Wait, one of the largest stockpiles of nuclear munitions had been protected by a flimsy chain-link fence? One that could be compromised with a simple pair of wire cutters? But I shelved my incredulity. I was here for heterozygosity, not homeland security.

"One unforeseen result of the fence," Heather explained, "was that whatever deer were inside the depot upon completion in 1941 became trapped. They were inmates, cut off from the larger population. Without options, the deer started inbreeding."

Inbreeding. Here it was again, the reason behind the cheetah's kinkiness and partly why the crane's Operation Migration had failed. If an animal seemed aberrant, inbreeding was usually involved.

"Original base commanders noticed a few white deer in the depot," Heather continued. They liked them. So, while they regularly culled the deer population to prevent it from exploding, they never shot the white ones. Although leadership changed, subsequent commanders continued to protect them. The proportion of white deer grew, the population reaching a high of three hundred.

Whoa. We hadn't even seen a white deer and I was already spellbound. First, a questionably guarded depot. Now, a bored squadron of snipers picking off brown deer amid a backdrop of earth-shattering explosives. World War II history books suddenly seemed so incomplete.

I knew why the depot officers were smitten with sour-cream deer. For the same reason I was, and why I'd paid for the privilege of glimpsing one from a bus. People have always been smitten with white deer. Celtic, Hungarian, and Japanese mythology is rife with accounts of such deer. They're mentioned in the forests around King Arthur's court and appear in many Native American narratives, including those of the Seneca, Roanoke, Algonquin, Nanticoke, and Pocomoke people. The Lenape are a case in point, associating the resurgence of all Indigenous peoples with the time when two white deer were seen together.

Some narratives can be more beautiful than the deer. In nearby Letchworth, precious few white deer have been seen among the earth-toned throngs. According to the Seneca, the deer is the spirit of Mona-sha-sha, a beautiful young Seneca bride. Mona-sha-sha lived with her husband and young child near the park's much-photographed middle falls, where the Genesee River plunges one hundred feet onto table-sized pieces of jagged sandstone below. One evening, her husband, Joninedah, returned home after a bad day of hunting. With no food to offer, he couldn't bear to look at her. Mona-sha-sha feared he no longer loved her. Once Joninedah was asleep, she stole away with their child and paddled out into the river in a birch-bark canoe just above the middle falls. When Joninedah awoke the next morning, he followed her trail. Upon finding the canoe gone, he saw two white deer—a mother and a fawn—step out from the forest. When he stepped toward them, they melted away. Grief-stricken, he plunged a knife into his heart to join his wife and child in death.

Hopeless romantic that I am, I can't shake the ethereal legend of Mona-sha-sha. Its elements move me: beautiful bride, a simple misunderstanding, and most of all, a glimpse of pure white deer that dissolve into nothingness. So, I walk the trails of Letchworth, one eye cocked on dark tangles and shadowy groves.

White deer are beautiful, but they're also aberrant. Aberrance, the condition of being abnormal, moves us differently. While it caused Joninedah to take his life, it moved World War II munitions officers to compassion. Five states—Wisconsin, Iowa, Illinois, Montana, and Tennessee—have followed the officers' lead, protecting white deer during hunting season. But they're fair game in the forty-five other states. Even in Wisconsin where the deer are protected, the fine print is bizarre. Full albinos are off-limits but piebalds—partially leucistic deer—aren't.

In a book about extinction, why digress about the varying coat colors of a wildly abundant animal? Well, conservation hinges on how we treat the least of these, the rarest, and sometimes, the most aberrant. But really, it's the easiest way I've found to explain how a loss of heterozygosity can affect small, isolated populations.

• • • •

This story begins on the shoulder of Route 481. It was my birthday and I'd chosen to go to the Rosamond Gifford Zoo in Syracuse with my dad. On the way home, he suddenly pulled over. Mumbling something about coffee thermoses, he popped the trunk and got out. When he slid back in his seat, he grinned and put a heavy gift in my lap, shoddily wrapped in newspaper, his trademark.

I tore it open, practically levitating with delight. *The Deer of North America*, 462 pages of straight, unadulterated deer talk. The author, Leonard Lee Rue III, smiled out from behind a big beard on the jacket. Here was a man who shared my obsession; his existence—this book— validated mine. Finally, I could marinate in antler development and estrus cycles to my heart's content.

That very evening, I set to work committing *The Deer of North America* to memory, while well-adjusted kids read Marvel comics. I flew through the chapters on cud chewing, botflies, and brain worms, pausing only to occasionally sneak outside in homemade camo. There, crawling on all fours, I sailed blowgun darts over the heads of rabbits obliviously munching blackberry stems.

Back inside with the book, I stopped in my tracks. Halfway in, Rue broached the subject of white deer, complete with accompanying photos. White deer? Such a thing existed? I was mesmerized. Despite his dry, encyclopedic prose, Rue's opinion was clear: white deer are bad; they're genetically inferior. *The Deer of North America* lay by my bedside for years, moving from shelf to shelf, surviving puberty, cross-continental trips, and a half dozen moves. Even today, when I need comfort, or merely to brush up on the sequence of stomachs in a deer's gut, I continue to reach for it. So naturally, on the subject of white deer, again I reached for my trusty book.

"When the wildlife population was controlled by natural predators," Rue wrote, "any deer that had the deficient genes to result in a white coat would have been killed because it was so easily seen. Ordinarily," he went on to add, "the other deer will shun the mutations, even going so far as to drive them away." Rue wasn't a man of nuance. To him, protecting white deer was insane. It prevents natural selection from scrubbing out mutation. Therefore, it degrades the herd.

Others share Rue's assessment. Jeannine Fleegle, a biologist with the Pennsylvania Game Commission Management Team, doesn't feel white deer warrant special protection either. "After thousands of years," she wrote, "Mother Nature has weeded out all the inferior deer. I trust her selection."

I understand such sentiment. But I'm a deer-loving romantic, unhindered by the historical trammels of wildlife management protocol. And so, I dissent. Yes, Mother Nature weeds out white deer. That's why they're so rare. At the same time, she tosses them breadcrumbs; white deer keep reappearing. So, when they show up, and if they stir our imaginations, why not protect them? When did variety cease to be the spice of life?

• • • •

Happy-go-lucky Heather shed light on my mental kaleidoscope as we bumped along the munition depot's potholed roads. She grabbed her mic and launched into a monologue. Well, tried to. Her silver-haired audience had finally awoken. "The three hundred white deer we have are one of the largest populations of white deer anywhere in the…"

"Are they albinos?" interrupted a lady in a white sombrero.

"Good question! Actually, they're *not* albinos. They're leucistic."

"Leu…what?" the same lady asked, chuckling.

"LeuCISTIC," Heather said, emphasizing the last two syllables. She sensed her audience's confusion. "I know. It's a weird word. Let me back up a bit."

"Guess you better!" the lady said.

"Your question boils down to one little thing: melanin. Melanin protects the skin and eyes from the sun's harmful ultraviolet radiation. We have it. Deer have it. Most every mammal has it. The question is: How do we get it?"

Silence. Now we were cooking. This is what I'd come for. I pulled out my notebook.

"From our parents, right?" offered a man just in front of me, wiping the lenses of his binoculars, which he still hadn't used, for the umpteenth time.

"Indeed," Heather said, smiling. "Our skin color is determined by a gene that contains the information for producing melanin. But, there's a defective, nonfunctioning version of this gene, too. Sometimes the bad gene also gets passed down family lines. If you inherit two copies of this defective gene, you'll be an albino."

"Never seen one," the man in front of me said. "Are they rare?"

"Indeed," Heather said. "In people…and deer."

"Why?"

"Because the defective gene is recessive. When accompanied by a functional gene, it recedes, fading into the background. You may carry it, but won't express it, so, no harm done. It's simple really: an albino has two defective genes while a carrier just has one."

"Simple for you!" the sombrero lady said, adding another annoying chuckle.

Heather smiled, obviously accustomed to fatuous quips. She looked at us, gauging our interest. The sombrero lady pulled out hot pink lipstick, the lens-cleaning man kept wiping, and the greasy-haired guy was now asleep. Not me. I paused taking notes and flashed Heather my sincerest smile. I was sucked in, desperate for her to continue the genetics lesson. As she lowered her mic, I couldn't resist. "You said these deer aren't albinos, right?"

"Right," she said, happy somebody cared.

"Can you explain the difference between albino and leucistic deer?" I wanted to see if Heather had memorized *The Deer of North America*, as I had.

"Sure thing. Albino and leucistic deer both have defective melanin genes. But leucistic deer only have messed-up melanin. Albino deer have messed-up everything—all their skin pigments are screwed up, not just melanin. While albinism and leucism both turn a deer white, they stem from different mutations."

Wow. Heather was good.

A portly guy with a cane and a black-and-yellow Vietnam vet hat spoke up. He wanted the real thing. "Will we ever see 'em?" Several heads nodded, not hiding their ebbing patience.

"I sure hope so," Heather said, bending to look out the window.

I attempted to defuse the building tension. "If we do, can we tell the two kinds apart?"

"Quite easily," she replied. "If you see them up close. Albino deer have white hooves, pink eyes, and poor vision. The deer in this depot have dark noses, dark hooves, and normal vision. That's how we know they're leucistic."

"Wait, how many genes do they get from each parent?" asked a man who looked uncannily like Fred Rogers. Heather launched in anew. Since the deer were scarce, it was just as well. As a fellow teacher, I wished I could give her what she really needed—a chalkboard. Because now, as genetic lessons so often go, she was talking about Punnett squares.

I turned to the window to search for deer. Punnett squares I knew. Mendel, pea plants, and mind-numbing memories of counting corn kernels. Cute little squares broken into four equally sized quadrants. Across the top were letters, A over one column and a over the other. The capital letters represented dominant traits while the lowercase letters stood for recessive. Similar notation went down the outside left of the square. Filling in the quadrants, I'd learned, was analogous to two critters having sex, which my textbooks prosaically called "a fertilization event." Each resulting quadrant had two letters, thus allowing the prediction of any particular trait in the offspring. If the Punnett square had been coded for eye color, for example, a prediction could be made. Three quarters of the time, dominant "normal" traits were expressed. But one quarter of the time, in the bottom right quadrant, two lowercase letters would pair up, a recessive trait.

A Punnett square for leucism

As a blue-eyed child with two brown-eyed parents, I knew I'd won Reginald C. Punnett's namesake lottery. To do it, both of my parents were blue-eyed carriers, making them heterozygous. They'd given me a roughly 20 percent chance. In reality, eye color doesn't exhibit a simple dominant-recessive inheritance, but it makes the point nonetheless. Not only had I beaten the odds, my older brother had, too. Eye color isn't a big deal. But knowing I'd beaten the odds made me feel special—my brother and I were the family's white deer.

It's a bigger deal with diseases, like Tay-Sachs or hemophilia. Sufferers of these diseases inherit them the same way I had my blue eyes, making them homozygous recessive. Manifesting the disease represented a loss of heterozygosity.

Soulé listed a loss of heterozygosity as a critical factor affecting extinction because it loads the dice, heightening chances for bad traits to pop up. It makes animals less resistant to pathogens and parasites along with a host of other depressing maladies. Recessive genes cross with recessive genes, spreading them more widely, as was the case with the whooping crane and the cheetah. It was the case of the Florida panther, too.

Stuck between the urban centers of Miami and Naples, the Florida panther, a subspecies of mountain lion (*Puma concolor coryi*), was as marooned as the white deer of the munition depot. In the late nineties, habitat loss and hunting decreased their population to fewer than thirty. Calling the survivors lucky wasn't right; they suffered all the problems Africa's cheetahs did—poor immune systems, undescended testicles, low sperm counts, and of course, the kinked tail. With extinction imminent, eight healthy, female mountain lions were brought in from Texas in 1995. It worked. Within fifteen years, the population had increased threefold. The cat's survival and fitness measures improved, and all the yucky inbreeding correlates declined significantly.

Hidden among the positive results was that seven-syllable word—heterozygosity. It doubled. The eight Texas females had infused a flush of new, healthy genes. The newcomers had saved the Florida subspecies from itself.

Sometimes, species can curb heterozygosity loss on their own. Now, however, we've sliced the salami. Cut off, populations are harder pressed to rescue one another. To keep them around, they may need an assist. Without help, heterozygosity loss is inevitable, like the hemophilia that plagued Europe's nobility.

• • • •

Heather never mentioned heterozygosity, hemophilia, Florida panthers, or extinction. Nor did she tell us how our fates are irrevocably tied to Punnett squares. Nonetheless, she wrapped up her lesson and lowered her mic. She may as well have dropped it. Because right then, we saw a real live white deer. A doe. Mona-sha-sha.

Finally, I was looking at something I'd longed to see since my eighth birthday. And after all that buildup, I was most struck by, well, how utterly *normal* it looked. Other than its eggshell coat, it was identical to the brown doe feeding next to it. Just a regular doe. Doe Six-Pack.

Face pressed against the window, it suddenly occurred to me that *The Deer of North America*—big-bearded Leonard Lee Rue III, my lifelong zoological mentor—was dead wrong. Rue claimed brown deer disliked the white ones, that they drove them away. Not these two. They seemed amiable, BFFs even. Oh Leonard, how could you have led me astray?

The bus stopped and Heather raised her mic. "It's our lucky day! For how many of you is this your first white deer?" All hands went up, mine included. Now awake, the greasy-haired guy was madly trying to take a selfie with the white deer through the bus window. Maybe I'd misjudged him.

We crowded to the windows, cameras jostling. The white deer momentarily stopped chewing and stared back at us. Its large, inky eyes held little concern. The white tail, its namesake beacon of alarm, twitched but remained down. In our minute-long vigil of mutual acknowledgment, I made just one other observation: this aberrant deer felt safe.

• • • •

Across the world in Tanzania, this reality doesn't exist. There, the aberrant subject is a small population of people, not deer. The unfortunate few suffer from albinism, not the leucism of the depot's deer. Along the equator, albinism is a formidable foe indeed. Sufferers are extremely vulnerable to sunburn and often have highly compromised vision. While the sun's unrelenting rays are fierce, other people—namely Tanzanians involved with witchcraft—are the real enemy.

Some cultural beliefs die all too slowly. Albinism in Tanzania is a case in point. A stubborn, lingering belief is that albino people have evil spirits. They're associated with witchcraft and persecuted horrifically: beaten, assaulted, and sometimes even chopped up, their body parts used grotesquely. In the monochromatic, dark-skinned sea of East Africa, people with albinism stand out. People stare. Try as I might not to, I'm guilty, too, my eye evolutionarily honed to notice—and fixate—on difference.

Like the white deer of the depot, Tanzanians with albinism know they are being watched. But unlike the deer, they never return a gaze. When forced into public spaces, they flit nervously about, ducking into shop stalls whenever possible, desperate to avoid unnecessary attention. Susceptible to ultraviolet, they live life in the shadows. They're forced there as much by other people as by the sun. With commodified body parts, they know they aren't protected. They're the deer of the nineteenth century, a hunted species in an open season.

Why do people around the world treat aberrance so schizophrenically? Why do we celebrate the rare and different in an old munitions depot yet viciously attack it in Tanzania? Obviously, Tanzania isn't the only place where a minority is slighted. We all react erratically to aberrance. Attracted to it here. Threatened by it there.

● ● ● ●

Perhaps nobody understands this as well as Clemson biologist J. Drew Lanham. A few autumns ago, three colleagues and I jumped in a minivan and drove to a nearby university to hear Dr. Lanham discuss his new book, *The Home Place*. It was a book about Lanham's love of nature, something we all loved as well. But there was a bigger reason we wanted to listen to him, too.

"I am the rare bird, the oddity," Lanham wrote, "appreciated by some for my different perspective and discounted by others as an unnecessary nuisance, an unusually colored fish out of water."

Lanham's hour-long talk felt like minutes. I was spellbound. I had certainly felt odd for my interest in deer and my obsession with counting them, but never for my skin color. Nor had my oddness been discounted as an unnecessary nuisance.

"I am as much a scientist as I am a black man," Lanham wrote in his book's introduction. "My skin defines me no more than my heart does." Judging from the line of people stretching out the door to get a book signed, I wasn't the only one to have recognized his big heart.

• • • •

With the exception of asexual species, we're all products of Punnett squares. While not a slight to hard work, some of us have had a huge head start, not earning half as much as we'd like to think. Rather, we privileged few—born at an optimal time and place with an arbitrary set of favored cultural characteristics—are winners of life's most fundamental and perverse lottery, surfing a tsunami of advantaged birth. Being a certain shape and color at a certain point in history determines so much. All the better if we lack genetically transmitted diseases, too. What's the prize for life's lottery winners? Health and wealth aside, the biggest dividend is the ability to blend in, avoid stigma, and just be considered normal.

It's not a lot to ask.

Few societies are judged by how the lucky few fared. No matter the issue—leucistic deer, albinism in Tanzania, race in America, or rare Florida panthers teetering on the brink of extinction—it's not the winners we need to be concerned about. It's how we value—and treat— those who haven't been so lucky.

6
DUCK, DUCK, GOOSE
Founder Effects

"You lost today, kid.
But that doesn't mean you have to like it."
—Indiana Jones and the Last Crusade

've always liked Mary Oliver's poetry. In case you're unfamiliar, here are the last few lines of "Wild Geese," one of her well-known poems:

> Meanwhile the wild geese, high in the clean blue air,
> are heading home again.
> Whoever you are, no matter how lonely,
> the world offers itself to your imagination,
> calls to you like the wild geese, harsh and exciting—
> over and over announcing your place
> in the family of things.

Poetical genius aside, when skeins of wild geese fly over me each fall, I don't feel belonging; I feel jealous. Whenever I hear them, I put my hands on my hips and lean back, instantly wishing to trade my cumbersome, earthbound body for a lighter, aerodynamic one. A body that would allow me to pump my forelimbs and lift off, watching the forests and fields and cities and cars fade into insignificance below. When I see wild geese, I want to fly.

Mary Oliver was not, and is not, describing Hawaiian geese. First the geese. Later, I'll spiral back down and describe why my desire for flight has been seriously tempered. Plus, I'll lay out the founder effect and why it factors into extinction. Until then, make sure your seatback is in the upright and locked position.

• • • •

If you've never seen a Hawaiian goose, just picture a Canada goose. Both species sport chunky, earth-toned bodies topped with longish necks and black-and-white heads. Also, both graze like cattle and poop on golf courses. That is where their similarities stop. Unlike their Canadian cousins, Hawaiian geese are waterfowl that find water foul. They dislike it, the reduced webbing on their toes evidence of that.

Hawaiian geese also dislike flight. Even though they once flew across thousands of miles of open ocean no worse for the wear, they'd never repeat the journey. In Hawaii, they're homebodies, far more content to waddle upon knife-edged lava rock than fly the friendly skies. Odd proclivities indeed for a creature with perfectly good, highly functional wings.

Rather than through Wikipedia, I learned about Hawaiian geese when I stumbled upon a kindly pair in the flesh. Two decades ago, in a half-mad craze to see endangered honeycreepers, I flew to Maui, hitchhiked around the island, and hiked up the southern flank of Haleakalā Volcano. I had researched my sought-after honeycreepers in depth. I knew their colors, bill lengths, habitat preferences, you name it. Everything else, not so much. Unexpectedly greeting me on Haleakalā was a blazing sun, spiky silversword plants that bloom once a century, and the ghosts of a legendary troop of bighearted Boy Scouts.

Hawaiian geese greeted me, too. They materialized out of the moonscape, two blithe birds with far more curiosity than fear. They didn't explode into the air upon my approach. Nor did they hiss and posture like irascible golf-course geese. They just waddled about, as placid as the dormant volcano they tread upon, the reduced webbing between their toes molding easily to the loose lava rock.

The honeycreepers would wait. I sat down on a slab of rhyolite, dripped water over my head, and pulled out a package of Twizzlers.

Downing a few, I offered one to the gander who was probing the bag with his bill. He politely declined with a soothing *NE-NE-NE-NE*. This was how, I learned later, Hawaii's state bird—the nene—got its name. Perhaps it's also how Hawaii's state fish—the humuhumunukunuku-apua'a—got its name, too, though how that sounds underwater is anybody's guess. I'll leave etymological speculation for the linguists. I will, however, speculate on the goose's preference for waddling.

• • • •

The nene didn't always dislike flight. They liked it enough at one point to fly across the ocean and land on the Hawaiian Islands. Like Iceland's Surtsey, the Hawaiian Islands are volcanic. Like a line of mosquito bites on your arm, the islands swelled out of the sea as the Pacific Plate dragged across a subterranean hotspot. The nene's wings were the only ticket. A few bats arrived this way, too. Before boatloads of other stowaways arrived with people, apart from bats the islands were entirely mammal-less and reptile-less. Even seafaring giant tortoises never floated that far, regardless of how favorable a current there was. Three thousand miles from the nearest mainland is simply too far.

Nene were happy with a mammal-free abode. It meant few predators, little competition, and a perpetual banquet. What could be better? Those original nene, whether they were blown off course, or intrepid explorers, were founders, the avian equivalent of Neil Armstrong planting a flag on the moon.

Michael Soulé cared a lot about founding populations like nene. Anybody who cares about extinction should. If populations successfully disperse, which all conservationists insist they must, they land somewhere and set up shop. If lots of dispersers arrive, it's no biggie, the founding population likely resembles the one they left behind. But if just a few dispersers arrive, things get interesting. A mere handful of founders, like a small flock of nene, is a nonrandom sample, lacking some versions of genes—alleles—that the larger population had. If the population stays put and begins breeding, the only genes they can pass around are from those few individuals that made the trip. In situations like this, fixation can happen, a condition whereby some alleles rise greatly in frequency. Because fewer birds are breeding, the chances for weirder genes to be expressed increase. The dice are loaded from the outset. So, the chances of landing in that lower right quadrant of the Punnett square—the one that can code for a host of maladies—increases.

I have a hunch you're finding it hard to care about a handful of hypothetical Hawaiian goose genes. Let's switch to something we all care about—M&M's. Tip a large bag of M&M's on its side and shake a few out to your three kids. Each kid gets four. Sally gets orange, green, and two blues. Gertrude gets three greens and one orange. Distraught three-year-old Sam gets all yellows. Each kid has less variation than what is in the bag.

The bag, of course, is the original population of geese, the one on whatever mainland they dispersed from. Each child's hand of M&M's is a founding population. Sally's hand has the most diversity, the most representative—and healthy—genome. Gertrude's is second best while Sam's—with just yellow—is the worst. Compared to the bagful of M&M's, their samples are all impoverished, so to speak. If these founding populations went on to breed, the resulting offspring wouldn't represent the original bag. They'd be skewed, able to express only what they started with. Each founding population would differ; they'd all be less diverse than the original. Over time, they'd drift.

Genetic drift is intimately tied to the founder effect. Genetic drift happens whenever allele frequencies change over generations due to chance. Its effects are the strongest in small populations, which happens whenever a small group splits off the main population to found a colony. Or when animals emerge from population bottlenecks. So, to get it straight, the founder effect leads to genetic drift, which ultimately can lead to extinction. The founder effect and genetic drift have formed the backbone of our tale of the Galápagos tortoise, the whooping crane, the cheetah, the Florida panther, and even the rare white deer that found themselves trapped in the depot. On the Hawaiian Islands, it's the nene's tale, too.

Soulé knew the founder effect isn't just an amusing ecological quiddity. Its effects can be serious. People aren't shielded from it, either. It was the cause of a startlingly high number of Tay-Sachs cases in Eastern European Jews, abnormally high cystic fibrosis among Northern Europeans, and for the Afrikaners in South Africa, a spike of Huntington's disease. For this latter group of Afrikaners, for example, the original Dutch colonists composed a nonrandom sample; they happened to carry the Huntington's gene with a high frequency. Without chances to dilute—mask—the bad gene through outbreeding, the population skewed. It drifted. All the result of a founder effect, the equivalent of getting a handful of yellow M&M's.

● ● ● ●

If yellow M&M's coded for the desire to fly, then I must have gotten an entire bagful of them. I've savored opportunities to stare down at the world through airplane windows and the odd trip over teeming herds of wildebeest from the basket of a hot-air balloon. In my mid-twenties, the desire metastasized. Just once I wanted to fly as geese flew, liberated from a bulky Boeing's confines or the infernal roar of hot air. A friend of a friend led me to a Dutch guy named Per. Sandy-haired and affable, Per offered to take me paragliding. Since it was my twenty-fifth birthday, he'd give me a discount. Stupidly ignoring the jagged scars snaking down his wrists and forearms, I immediately accepted.

Truth is I didn't even know what paragliding was. Had I known it involved running off a cliff strapped to another man's chest, I would have politely declined. But taciturn Per said little. He simply drove us up the backside of a lightly wooded hill in northern Tanzania and started untangling a jumble of ropes. The hill dropped off on one side, an ocean of thorny acacia trees lying below.

"Do you see that grassy island out there?" Per asked, pointing below us.

"Um, I think so," I said, lying.

"That's where we'll land," he said, handing me an ill-fitting skateboarding helmet. So, this was it. Like nene, we'd launch off with a parachute and a prayer, hoping to make landfall on an island I couldn't yet discern. Clenched teeth replaced my smile. Nervous sweat trickled down my temples. Up here on this hill, my desire for flight had just flown away.

"When I say run, run," Per said, smiling. I was strapped in front of him, his weather-beaten face just inches from mine. Personal space and doubles paragliding don't go together. "We'll just wait a moment for a nice updraft," he added.

I nodded, though I had no idea what constituted "a nice updraft." I'm not sure Per knew either. But here I was, paying for the privilege to be Per's personal airbag.

"How do we steer?" I asked, hoping my voice wouldn't crack.

"With these thingies here," Per replied, motioning to the levers in his hands. "Just relax," he added. "I'll do the steering. You can just enjoy the …" Per never finished his sentence. Like an impromptu game of duck, duck, goose, he just slapped my helmet and started running. Strapped to the front of him, I did too.

Our cumbersome galumph was mercifully short-lived. Like Wile E. Coyote, off the cliff we went.

Per yanked on the levers. The sail, which had dragged behind us as we ran, caught an updraft. We were airborne. Sort of. "Smaller gust than I thought!" Per shouted from behind me. Ominous words. For a few seconds, we sailed above the savanna, the treetops tiny green islands dappling the umber earth below. We were gliding. But just as quickly we weren't. We dropped, paragliding morphing into para-plummeting. Per yanked harder on the cords, mumbled something, and leaned way back. The treetops grew bigger, bigger, until *WHAM*! We were in them.

My khaki cargo-panted legs raked through acacia crowns. "Sorry mate!" Per yelled, as we tore through the arboreal gauntlet. One tree, two, and then—finally—Per's pint-sized island of grass. We landed in an unceremonious pile, Per's two-hundred-pound torso covering my mangled frame like a heavy horse blanket. He peeled himself off, pulled me up, and put his hand up for a high five.

For a moment I stood there shakily, staring hard at his heavily calloused palm. A glaring lack of judgment had turned me into a pincushion. Why should I reward a kamikaze pilot with a high five? But behind it lay an irrepressible Danish grin. Ignoring my broken body, I slapped his hand. "Not the landing I was hoping for," Per said, bending to gather up the sail.

"You don't say," I muttered, sarcasm doing little to assuage the searing pain shooting down my legs.

"Guess we'll have to hoof it back," he said, handing me an armload of ropes. Hoofing it back hurt even worse than the crash landing. My pantlegs were ripped and blood had soaked through in places. Every step sent pain shooting through my quickly swelling, barely functional knees.

That night, I plucked four thorns from my knees. Two others, embedded too deeply, broke off and remained. Stubborn and prideful, I carried on with my research, waddling the next two months around the Serengeti. Like the nene, I'd stick to land from now on.

• • • •

Nene aren't the only birds that have opted for ground-based lives despite wings and a perfectly good sky above them. More than fifty species can't fly, most having smaller wings, fewer or fused wing bones, and a greatly reduced keel, or breastbone. When we think about flightless birds, most of us get no further than ostriches and penguins. But the list includes over a dozen agile and skinny rails, a handful of ducks and geese, two grebes, a cormorant, and even a nocturnal parrot called the kakapo.

Reasons for giving up flight coalesce around an absence of predators; abundant, easily accessible food; and a climate that doesn't necessitate migration. Often, conditions like this are found on mammal-free islands, New Zealand boasting the highest concentration of flightless birds. For millennia, island-adapted, flightless birds enjoyed their own personal Margaritavilles. All that changed when humans turned a collective eye to the high seas and quickly colonized far-flung locales with a stable of stowaways. Birds like New Zealand's giant moas, Jamaican ibis, Hawaiian rail, great auk, and the dumpy dodo went extinct not long after, unable to adapt to the onslaught of predation. Fifty percent of the world's flightless birds are endangered or threatened.

But it's not just the flightless that are imperiled. On islands, many others, like the nene, retained the ability to fly but gave up the desire for it, analogous to ex-NASCAR drivers who now prefer bicycles. Even though wings could dull their headaches, these stubborn species refuse, scurrying about the ground like mice. And some of them have skirted extinction by barely a whisker…er…feather.

New Zealand's black robin, found only in the Chatham Islands, is a case in point. In 1980, the world's black robin population was reduced to a grand total of five birds. Of those, just one, christened Old Blue by anxious researchers, was a mature female that could reproduce.

One!

Reproductively speaking, Old Blue was New Zealand's equivalent of Martha, the last remaining passenger pigeon, who died a tragically lonesome death in a cage in the Cincinnati Zoo in 1914. Any day now, she'd fall off a perch as pathetically as Martha had.

But Old Blue was buoyed by Old Yellow, the only male interested in knowing her more intimately. While Old Blue and Old Yellow mated, a juvenile female—Old Green—matured. Regardless of the fact that Old Green should have been named Young Green, she also mated with two-timing Old Yellow. Both Old Blue and Old Green soon fledged a chick. But the rescue team's exhale was short-lived; both chicks died, Old Green's nabbed by an introduced predator. Handwringing, hope, then more handwringing—the statistics of small numbers proving a roller-coaster, heart-wrenching affair. Sadly, the New Zealand robin population followed the pattern of haiku: five-seven-five.

Fortunately, conservationists were just as stubborn as the never-say-die birds they wanted to save. Rather than wave a white flag, they captured all five birds and moved them to another island, one lacking rapacious, bird-eating predators that people had myopically released.

Amid the ordeal, the conservation team noticed something: whenever Old Green lost a chick, she immediately renested. Could they, they wondered, coax additional eggs from these two females? Risky indeed but worth a shot.

Here's why there's hope amid the sixth extinction: this quorum of dedicated biologists boarded dinky dinghies and braved bashing waves. They swiped the robin duo's eggs and then compounded their well-intended duplicity by sneaking them under the breasts of brooding Chatham Island warblers. For a few suspenseful weeks, the chicanery succeeded swimmingly. Until it didn't. At eleven days old, the foster chicks inexplicably died. Dire indeed, the fate of the robin appeared to hang on the biologists' next move. They opted for another round of warbler foster care, which again failed.

But Old Blue and Old Green didn't. Even though eggs kept disappearing from under them, they kept laying and brooding. Each fledged two chicks. The population grew to nine. At this point, debate arose among the team. Should they stop with their failed foster care program? They resolved one last attempt, choosing the rotund little tomtit for incubation duties rather than the more discerning warbler. The gamble paid off. Tomtits proved providential, attentive parents. More importantly, they were easily duped.

But Operation Tomtit wasn't foolproof. Not all the foster chicks survived. When one went suddenly limp, the bighearted biologist on hand lifted it up to her pursed lips and, with the tenderest of gestures, tried mouth-to-beak resuscitation. It worked, demonstrating yet again why giving up should never be an option. As long as insanely empathetic people are blowing into the beaks of twenty-five-gram birds, wild hope burns on.

Regardless of their heroics, other problems persisted. A lack of outbreeding options led parents to mate with their offspring. Other males, perhaps addled by adverse effects related to the Punnett square, couldn't be cajoled to mate. Fortunately, none of it mattered much. The Chatham Island population mushroomed to 250, with every bird tracing its roots to Old Blue, the original eight-year-old female, and either

Old Green or Old Yellow. Birds with names that could be mistaken for M&M's. But unlike the famous chocolates, the population refused to melt. Neither in the hand nor in the mouth.

• • • •

Back on the Hawaiian Islands, nene faced a similar degree of peril. Their *la vida loca* lifestyle vanished as the first wide-eyed bipeds stepped ashore. Empty-stomached Polynesians, avaricious Europeans, and boatload upon boatload of rats. Havoc followed in the wake of every landfall. Europeans encountered the fearless nene much the way I had: friendly, approachable, and with a well-placed kick, easily dispatchable. For four decades they hunted them relentlessly and excessively. Every goose was taken, eggs too.

Rats, however, posed an even greater threat. The insatiable stowaways took to the Hawaiian Islands like I take to untended dessert tables. Everything edible was eaten, especially eggs and defenseless fledglings. The native pantry bare, the rats turned to the vast sugarcane plantations. Frustrated, settlers countered by releasing an equally insatiable predator—the Indian mongoose—to control the rats.

Sure, Indian mongooses ate the odd, oblivious rat. But compared to the naïve, starry-eyed native birds, rats were clever escape artists. So the mongooses did what all animals do—they took the easy route, opting for Hawaii's defenseless birds. Any bird that survived the rat-mongoose duo soon faced other foes: dogs, cats, pigs, and—perhaps most insidiously—mosquitoes. Even the hardiest honeycreepers couldn't withstand the whine of mosquitoes, who spread avian malaria like wildfire. Survivors were few. Those that did survive lived up on the highest slopes, like Haleakalā Volcano, where they could escape unnoticed from the predatory onslaught.

This explains why I was halfway up Haleakalā when I met the pair of friendly nene. I was after the world's sole remaining honeycreepers, the resilient few who'd flown the gauntlet of travails. Originally, nene had populated all the Hawaiian Islands. The Big Island harbored twenty-five thousand before Captain James Cook's arrival in 1778. By

1951, that population had shrunk to fewer than thirty. On Maui they'd died out entirely.

• • • •

But wait. Like I said, I was on Haleakalā—in Maui—when I met two nene. Had survivors found the gumption to spread their wings and strike out again? Had they come from the Big Island? Had they founded the island anew?

Yes and no. Nene didn't fly in; they were flown in.

In the summer of 1962, thirty-five nene were raised in England and flown across the world to Maui. Upon arrival, the wide-eyed geese were tucked into boxes. Holes were cut out of the tops so the birds could extend their ebony necks and look around. Straps were affixed and given to a troop of dedicated Boy Scouts. With geese on their backs, the troop hiked up Haleakalā's slope just the way I had, flanked by a few pack mules. "I carried three birds," Carl Eldridge remembered, age seventeen at the time. "We struggled, but we all helped each other. It was a fun thing for us. We knew the importance of the bird."

Ten miles up from the volcano's base, at a place called Paliku within the volcanic crater, the scouts took off their packs. There they released the geese into an open-top pen where they could acclimate back to their ancestral locale. As with the black robin's rescue attempts, not everything went smoothly. Over time, more nene were released—five hundred total—and just one hundred survived. Indian mongoose, rats, and feral pigs still roamed, all of them salivating for goose omelets. Reintroduction wasn't enough. Aggressive predator control was needed, too. When the two methods were finally paired, the tide turned and Maui's nene population grew. Nearly three hundred birds now waddle about Maui, three thousand among all the islands, uttering their sonorous *NE-NE-NE-NE* to whoever is lucky enough to sit among them.

Sit among them is all I'll ever do with geese, Hawaiian or otherwise. Yes, I'll always be jealous of creatures that effortlessly soar above me. But flight, I've concluded, is solely for the birds. Most of them, that is.

7
A New Dog in Town
Hybridization

"The only thing smarter than a coyote is God."
—Dan Flores, *Coyote America*

ootfalls. Light, deliberate, barely discernible. A sound I wouldn't have heard if not for the thin layer of crunchy snow blanketing the ground. A deer approaching the frigid, three-legged stool I'd wedged at the base of a large oak. I eased my gun barrel off my lap and turned toward the sound, my pulse quickening. Finally, after two pitiful, deer-less seasons, I'd stock the freezer with venison.

Or not. This wasn't a deer at all; it was a coyote.

The cautious canid circled upwind of me, sniffing the earth, its ears rotating like radar dishes. Had the perceptive animal been able to see, hear, or smell me, it never would have approached so near. Abruptly it stopped, stiffening. Somehow, with a preternatural sixth sense, it intuited my presence. Seven feet away and broadside, perfectly positioned for an easy shot. The coyote's thick fur shimmered, accented by recently fallen, coruscating snow crystals. Tendrils of quickly condensing air—life-giving breath—snaked around the glistening muzzle.

Slight wind shift. Shockwave of panic. The coyote's back arched, hackles rising. Immediately it looked up, scanning several tree trunks that loomed above.

A clear exhibition of cunning, a behavior I'd disbelieve had I not witnessed it. The coyote knew well the season and the predatory behavior of people. Not only did it associate late autumn with hunters, it understood that for a few consecutive weeks, the clumsy biped took to the trees and sat statuesque. Rifle reports had multiple meanings. A wounded deer, a nutritious gut pile, or—most ominously—their own death from a deerless hunter eager for a consolation prize. A hunter just like me.

The trees revealed nothing. Nostrils flaring, the coyote's gaze lowered and its head turned my way. We locked eyes. Finger on the trigger, I could have rent the stillness and ended its life. But I didn't.

● ● ● ●

My life has been marked by collecting. If it's natural, detachable, and rammable into a pocket or camera bag, home it comes. Rocks, pelts, feathers, fungi, antlers, beetles, seedpods, shells, skulls, tusks, nests, and driftwood. Recently I even managed to secure a few molars from a giant forest hog. The best artifacts claim shelves, the others uncatalogued boxes and trunks. Animal mounts would surely augment my disheveled museum. But so far, all I've managed are a handful of dusty birds rescued from the science building dumpster. They're faded, bug-eyed, and suffering from severe alopecia. I could use a nice, fresh coyote mount in the corner of my office, leering up at me as I sip my coffee.

So why didn't I shoot that late November morning?

I'm still not sure. Such forbearance was uncalculated and sadly uncharacteristic. Three possible explanations account for it. One, the moment's charged beauty overwhelmed me, preventing me from meddling with a masterpiece. Two, I've already collected a coyote, so to speak. And three, the coyote appeared more like a pilgrim than prey, manifesting a long and complicated evolutionary journey. More on the latter two shortly.

I do know this: the animal certainly appeared larger than a mere coyote, more than the sum of its parts. It looked like a wolf.

● ● ● ●

A modest dip into the literature explains the wolfish appearance.

The coyote looked like a wolf because it was, at least partially, a wolf. Canine geneticist Javier Monzón investigated 427 coyotes in northeastern North America and Canada. Coyotes, he discovered, are only 65 percent coyote. Ten percent of their genome has been donated by *Canis familiaris*, the domestic dog. The rest, a full quarter of Monzón's coyotes, comes from those howling creatures that loped through the dreams of my childhood—wolves. As you travel south, the percentages shift toward more dog and less wolf. Monzón's conclusion is clear: coyotes, the wolf's long-maligned little brother, are mutts, genetic amalgams that comprise three species. This makes coyotes, for good or ill, a hybrid.

When the public caught wind of such studies, hyperbolic headlines sporting colloquial nomenclature sprang up like spring crocuses. "Coydogs Roaming the East," ran one headline. "Coywolves the New Dog in Town," claimed another. And then my favorite portmanteau: "The Rise of the Woyote." Most media sources errantly claimed these hybrids were new species. They weren't. Nor did the names—coywolf, coydog, woyote—capture the complexity. Though "coywolfdog" is technically better, it would have muddled the puddle even more.

At the heart of the coywolfdog conundrum—excusing this alliteration—is a contentious concept that has confounded biologists for well over a century: species. What makes a species? How do we tell one from another? Where does one species stop and another begin? Distinguishing elephants from giraffes is easy enough. But what about distinguishing savanna elephants from forest elephants? Or making sense of the nine subpopulations of giraffes striding across the African continent? Some zoologists see one giraffe species. Others see nine.

Technical journals have been the primary battleground for the species concept, registering many distinct definitions and subtle variations of the term. Philosopher of science John Wilkens counted twenty-six. It's a protracted bloodbath with no end in sight. Weary, most folks default to Ernst Mayr's biological species concept, the idea that a species is a population of organisms that can—and do—interbreed. Sounds simple enough. So why so much infighting and head scratching? For this, let's follow Wile E. and hope he doesn't lead us off a cliff.

• • • •

Coyotes and wolves are mortal enemies. Where they coexist, as in Yellowstone, wolves would happily watch the wily canids self-destruct. Plus, like Roadrunner, they'll readily pitch in. In nature, such little-brother aversion isn't unusual. Over in Africa, for example, the big cats share similar dispositions.

While monitoring Serengeti lion prides, Craig Packer once spied an adult male cheetah approach his Land Rover. Always one to seize opportunity, Packer slyly dropped a toy lion cub out his car window. When the cheetah noticed the unattended cub, it sprang over, swiped it a few times, and chomped down on its neck. With the cub in its jaws, the cheetah walked a few hundred yards before dropping it, finally satisfied it was dead.

Why such coldhearted brutality between lions and cheetahs? Packer speculated competition between the two cats lay at its heart; since lions regularly steal cheetah kills, fewer lions means fewer meals get stolen. "Or maybe," Packer wrote, "cheetahs hate lions because lions hate cheetahs, each locked in an eternal cycle of mutual recrimination: one killing the other because the other kills them."

What makes enmity between wolves and coyotes different from the big cats of Africa is that their hatred gets interrupted by the occasional howling one-night stand. In other words, wolves and coyotes can overcome their differences long enough for what a blushing ethologist would call intromission. Such illicit liaisons never happen between lions and cheetahs. Heaven forbid! Unless they find a defenseless cub to dispatch, cheetahs always run from the other big cats. They're not after a roaring good time.

Cats, we all know, are persnickety. So why aren't dogs? Why do wolves and coyotes sometimes search out wayward love connections? For the same reason some lonely people do—desperation. Remember how European colonists scrubbed the eastern forests clean? How the only survivors were those that hid in less accessible places, like the vast forests of northern Minnesota, Wisconsin, and Canada? As the forests and the deer finally returned, opportunistic coyotes did too. Much of America, they serendipitously discovered, was wolf-free.

But not entirely. The recolonizing coyote females seasonally came into heat. The same happened for the few lucky wolves that survived the mass lupine extermination. What resulted was a landscape spread thin with suitors. A few lovesick coyotes and even fewer horny wolves bereft of eligible bachelors or bachelorettes. Estrus is a key ingredient in hybridization. In the absence of other wolves, such a situation could only be culminated—consummated—with a coyote, preferably a coquettish one. Willing or not, I feel for those bewildered coyotes, sudden love objects of a longtime foe. Approached by larger, fiercer wolves, no amount of suggestive eye batting could erase the simple calculus: mate or die. I can't help but wonder: Were they lovestruck or dumbstruck?

Neither size nor personal feelings mattered, however. Chromosomes did. Wolves and coyotes are canids, both members of the family Canidae. Shared ancestry means each species has seventy-eight chromosomes, allowing viability for any bastard offspring. Usually, chromosomal discrepancies keep species apart. While trysts are viable, offspring aren't.

My source? A horse, of course. Horses have sixty-four pairs of chromosomes, donkeys have sixty-two. Horses and donkeys, as we all learned during elementary school fieldtrips to the local farm, produce a mule. But mules cannot reproduce. What we may not have learned is why. It's because mules end up with sixty-three chromosomes, a hopeless harbinger of sterility.

· · · ·

One would be a fool to pule about a rule for the mule. Nature is rarely so straitjacketed. This truth I discovered in one of the unlikeliest of places: Mongolia. While in grad school, my benevolent advisor procured a grant to study various forms of pastoralism. Eastern

Africa we knew. Eastern Asia not so much. To get a feel, we took a two-week trip to the country of yaks, yurts, and bloodcurdling vodka. At one point, we jumped in a tour bus for Hustai National Park, a windswept grassland with a star attraction that I still struggle to pronounce: Przewalski's horse.

If you're not Polish, don't even try to pronounce it, at least not in public. "Shuh-VAL-skee" is what my dictionaries tell me. Some call it a "P-horse," which makes the poor equid sound like it has an enlarged prostate. I prefer the Mongolian name for the horse, "takhi," which mercifully excludes both urine trouble and an armload of misleading letters.

A joyful sufferer of what E. O. Wilson calls biophilia, I naturally smooshed my face against a bus window as we rumbled through Hustai. Used to spying on deer, I relished this chance to search out the world's only surviving wild horse. Glimpsing one in the wild stoked my biophilia—love of life—for years to come.

The takhi's history is as rich as its black, spiky mane. Mitochondrial studies reveal that they first split from horses 160,000 years ago, where they took a liking to the Central Asian steppe. There they flourished until humans—here we go again—began hunting them. Takhi adults grew wily and shy, running at the first sight of people. But the foals were catchable. Takhi numbers plummeted, their decline hastened by a string of harsh winters and an overzealous German merchant who captured them for zoos. The last takhi was seen in 1969. Then, kaput. The steppe had been swept bare.

The zoo population, meanwhile, was hardly flourishing. Compared to the expansive plains they preferred, zoos were stuffy closets. Takhi dropped like dominoes. By the mid-twentieth century, just a dozen survived in captivity. Not quite as bad as Old Blue's odds but nerve-racking nonetheless. While bird lovers rose up to rally Old Blue, horse lovers did the same for the takhi. Where one German brought them down, another brought them up. A zoologist stepped in and, with a scrutinizing eye and a studbook, he monitored every horse. Gradually, with meticulous meddling and pampering, the population recovered.

By 1990, the twelve multiplied like the gospel's loaves and fishes, swelling to 961, spread across 33 countries and 129 institutions. Not long after, captive-reared takhi were reintroduced to Hustai National Park, where the herd steadily grew.

Today, Hustai boasts over 350 horses. But in the early 2000s, when I was scanning the grassy, windswept steppe, there were fewer. Upon boarding the bus, we'd been told our chances of seeing one were low. Two hours in, we still hadn't. The only creatures we'd seen included a handful of marmots, some streaky rock pipits, and a glowering cinereous vulture. The afternoon's vodka dousing had knocked out our party of seven, all in various poses of somnolence. My advisor was slumped forward, head leaning on the seatback in front of her. Any takhi sighting would depend on me or our stone-faced driver. Dusk was settling. Odds were long indeed. "Mongolia is not Mongolia without horses," a Mongolian conservationist once wrote. I knew he was right. Hence my growing despair.

Not that we hadn't seen horses; we had. Plenty of them. The same short, stocky breed that Genghis Khan had ridden upon when he conquered half of Eastern Europe. But those horses were domestic. Insipid *Equus ferus* (subspecies: *caballos*, according to some taxonomies) with flaccid manes and a penchant for people. I craved the untamable takhi, *Equus przewalski*, the special species sporting Mohawks and macchiato-colored coats. They had flirted with death and overcome it, helped along by a German horse-whisperer and their own wild spirit. *Takhi* means "spirit" in Mongolian. For centuries the Mongols had revered them. I wanted the chance to do the same.

Takhi epitomized the wild even more than my mustangs back home did. For all the taut-muscled, freedom-epitomizing, ethnocentric glory that mustangs represent to American horse lovers and visitors to the East Coast's Assateague Island, they're not truly wild. Just domesticated horses gone feral. Tantamount to the wild-eyed tomcat that slips under your porch.

Takhi wildness is evident in their chromosome count. Domestic horses have sixty-four pairs; takhi have sixty-six. When takhi and domestic horses do the wild thing—pun intended—their offspring get sixty-five, akin to the sixty-three that result from horse and donkey crossings. But unlike the mule, the offspring of a horse and takhi can usually reproduce. Using Mayr's biological species concept, this technically makes them the same species, *Equus ferus*, or at least a subspecies—*Equus ferus przewalski*. The same species? A subspecies? Or distinct enough to be a separate species? Apparently, it's all in the eye of the beholder.

On that twilight drive through Hustai, my eye suddenly beheld something far grander than a jumbled species concept. There, on a verdant hill, while my advisor snoozed, was a herd of eight takhi.

"Takhi!" I shouted. Heads snapped up. The minibus screeched to a halt, a cloud of dust momentarily blurring our view. I stood up, pointing, heedless of proper tourist decorum. The other passengers stood up, too, lurching over to my side of the bus. My advisor gave me a groggy smirk as she rummaged in her pack for her camera. She was proud of me, however unfinished my dissertation remained. The mere sight of such a rare herd of wild Mongolian horses trotting across the steppe filled us with awe and lifted me out of my little cluttered life.

The takhi didn't give us long. In less than a minute they trotted over a rocky hill and dissolved into the gloaming. But those precious seconds took the wild horse from an idea to a reality, proving that large, charismatic animals—not just isolated nene and songbirds—can successfully come off life support, captivating imaginations anew.

• • • ◦

Takhi reveal how messy hybridization really is. Their ability to hybridize with feral horses worries conservationists. If they do it too often, they may lose their unique look and heritage, becoming, in a sense, a coywolf.

By definition, hybridization involves the mating of genetically differentiated individuals. It crosses lines, not within species but across them. This adds variety, which, as the cliché suggests, is the spice of life. Ultimately variation is good. It allows adaptation to a changing world through time-honored natural selection. We've learned about the dangers of small populations, bottlenecks, and inbreeding. We know how critical mixing genes is to ward off extinction. So, if it's good to mix within a species, wouldn't it be even better across species?

The answer, unfortunately, is no, which is why Soulé listed hybridization as an extinction factor. Most hybrids are poorly adapted compared to their time-tested predecessors. Often, they're weaker and more ill-suited to their habitat than their parents, or, like the mule, sterile. For species teetering on the edge of extinction, hybridization can provide the final shove. There's another, more subtle threat, too. When different species mate, their offspring effectively merge into one. Biodiversity drops. While isolated populations may speciate over time, like Galápagos tortoises, hybridization often does the opposite, melting them together.

• • • •

But sometimes not. Sometimes, in fact, hybrids are stronger and more capable than their parents. Bigger, faster, smarter, and more adaptable. In such rare instances, hybridization can create novelty, critical in the context of an ever-changing earth. Climates, habitats, and circumstances change. When coyotes returned to a wolf-less, deer-filled America in the twentieth century, they were still too small—thirty pounds—for taking adult deer. Not for long, however.

Wolf genes trickled in from the north, as lone wolves made inroads into the coyotes' world, mating with them when the moment called. Feral dogs did too. A cup of wolf and a teaspoon of dog were added to the coyote batter. What emerged was a robust animal, one with a stronger bite and more cognizant of the perks of pack hunting. Better for tackling deer and better, perhaps, for making a go on a human-dominated planet.

Not just because of their newfound hunting prowess. Coyotes have always coexisted better with people than their larger wolf cousins have. Their dietary needs aren't as great and they're better at living among us in scraps of habitat. Plus, they're not the bloodthirsty antagonist in

The Three Little Pigs and *Little Red Riding Hood*. Adaptable and thieving perhaps. But not nearly so loathed and feared.

Hybridization has only improved their lot. The canine smoothie blended the coyote's cunning, the wolf's power, and the dog's adaptability to humans. But lest we condemn the process for forming the perfect, shadowy predator, realize hybridization likely helped humans take over the planet, too. Buried within our genome, as unmistakable as white deer in a dark forest, lurk the tough, adaptable genes of other early hominids—Neanderthals and Denisovans.

• • • •

I may lack a heavy brow, but my caveman instincts rear up often. A few years back, while speeding along a backcountry road in mid-December, I noticed a dead dog lying on the shoulder. My day's first class started in seven minutes. I tapped the brakes, craning my neck. Hold on a minute.

My small gray pickup's momentum took me past the carcass, bald tires sliding as I hit the brakes harder. Something seemed different about the dog. I threw my truck in reverse and drew alongside it, rolling down my window. My hunch was right. Not a dog at all—this was a coyote. Inert yet in perfect condition, as if it had just tired and lain down. Up close, the coyote was stunningly beautiful. Luxurious salt-and-pepper fur draped over a sleek, leggy body. Far too beautiful to just leave behind.

Ever so gingerly I stepped out, studying the animal's sides for any hint of motion. Nothing. I knew coyotes were famously hard to kill. After being impaled by a car, one coyote remained glued to its grill. Six hundred miles and several pitstops later, the car came to rest. When it did, the resilient canid peeled itself off and stumbled away, disoriented but otherwise not much worse for the wear. I was happy to take a dead coyote to work. A live one would prove more problematic.

Time didn't allow taking the coyote's vitals or even poking it with a stick. So I grabbed it by all four paws, marveled at its heaviness, and heaved it into the back of my truck, praying it'd stay dead. Then I tore off, unwilling to check my rearview mirror for fear another set of eyes would meet my own.

The class was the worst I'd ever taught: disorganized, disjointed, and monologue-heavy. My preoccupation with the body in my truck was clear. I nervously eyed the window as the sun drew higher. Icicles dripped. Due to the camper shell on the back, my truck would soon turn into an oven, trapping heat and cooking the coyote. I pictured tomorrow's headline: "Coyote Cooked by Half-Baked Professor." With a packed schedule, I had little time to deal with the carcass. Akin to Karen's plight in *Frosty the Snowman*, I had to keep it cold.

But where?

I could commandeer a biology lab freezer. But that would risk raising eyebrows, not to mention rearranging trays of beakers and flasks. No, lab freezers were fiercely guarded turf, fiefdoms I'd rather not stir up. I needed a natural freezer. One that wouldn't draw attention. I slipped out to my truck and drummed my fingers on the dash. That's it! Behind the college gymnasium.

Decision made, I looped the campus, reconnoitering. It was a typical day, students scurrying to and fro and our college president's head bent low over her desk in concentration, unaware one of her charges was stashing roadkill behind college property. The coast clear, I parked behind the gym and dumped the coyote on top of a pile of plowed snow. Then I covered it in dead knotweed, waving innocently at two students I'd somehow missed. They halfheartedly waved back, then returned to their phones. Phew—a rare perk of today's student: an inability to notice anything not on a screen.

The rest of the workday crawled by. When the last student had finally left my office, I drove back to the gym and reloaded the coyote into my truck. Now what? The pelt would be perfect for warming my toes on cold winter mornings. But how would I preserve it? I'd never skinned anything larger than a rabbit.

On the drive home, I noticed the tidy farm of our Amish neighbors, Ben and Rhoda. Half a dozen well-tended buildings horseshoed several buggies in the driveway. Though dusk had settled, white and blue laundry remained on the line. We'd shared dinners and picnics, slowly forging a steadfast friendship.

I'd especially clicked with one of their five sons, John. On a whim, I swung into John's driveway, just across the road from his folks. If anybody could help me, or at least decline in the politest way possible, it was John. I'd long envied him, retaining life skills I'd forfeited in my fast-paced, abstract life.

"Hi, John," I said after he opened the door. Sauna-like heat radiated from behind him. "I've got an odd problem." Characteristically, John didn't interrupt. "I want to skin a coyote," I said, pausing to gauge his reaction. Silence. His face revealed nothing. "I, uh, have one in my truck." John's eyebrows went up.

"You mean, you wanna learn how?" he asked, unmoved by the insanity of my nocturnal request.

"Yeah. Can you teach me?"

John smirked, his eyes twinkling. "Let's go down to the barn."

"Right now?!" I said incredulously.

"Why not?" he said.

"Cool! Lemme run home and pick up my son. He needs to learn too. Be back in three minutes," I said, dashing to my truck.

Soon after, John, Ezra, and I encircled a coyote, which now hung vertically from a wide beam in his immaculate barn. Warm lantern light flickered across the coyote's white mesoderm while droplets of ruby-colored blood dripped delicately to the floor. Our breath condensed in the chilly barn air, surrounding each of us with small, ephemeral clouds.

"You try," John said, handing me his knife. I sliced away as he had, my strokes eager but clumsy. With John's assistance, I soon had a beautifully fleshed coyote pelt in my hands. Far more meaningfully, Ezra and I had received a patient lesson and indelible memory, rich in generous humanity. A lesson to live by.

• • • •

"The Amish no doubt have their problems," Wendell Berry once wrote.

"I do not wish to imply that they are perfect. But it cannot be denied that they have mastered one of the fundamental paradoxes of our condition: we can make ourselves whole only by accepting our partiality, by living within our limits, by being human—not by trying to be gods. By restraint they make themselves whole."

That's how I came to collect a coyote pelt. Perhaps I've learned that one's enough, accounting for why I didn't pull the trigger while staring one down this past fall. I want to live out Berry's—and the Amish community's—practice of restraint. A clue as to how to do so may be gained from the coyote. Staring down my gun barrel, I gazed upon a clever animal that has leveraged a fraught process for long-term success. Not merely a coyote—it was a coywolfdog. An animal that has accepted its partiality to make itself whole. If only I can do the same.

8
THEN I DO
SO DECLARE IT
Successional Loss of Habitat

*"There are some who can live without
wild things and some who cannot."*
—Aldo Leopold

wonder how many of my greatest joys can be traced to the severed head of a harbor seal. It's a convoluted thought process that goes like this: Some of the best places to watch birds, which I've long adored, are national wildlife refuges, which I've often visited. National wildlife refuges are public land, places to tromp around without garish No Trespassing signs leering from every tree trunk. Also great are America's national parks, national forests, national monuments—all places I've hiked, camped, climbed, and paddled. From Wrangell–St. Elias's thirteen million acres to Pelican Island's three and a half, each place has quickened my pulse, filled me with wonder, and was started—or at least heavily bolstered—by Teddy Roosevelt. Some historians have tediously long explanations for why Teddy protected so many places. I think his reason was simple: he loved nature. At first his love was bumpy and exploitative. Slowly, it matured. And at its root? The severed head of a harbor seal.

While you'd be forgiven for assuming the decapitated head was a prank, it was actually a gift, given to Teddy lovingly from a longtime family friend. Teddy adored it. He was an asthmatic and sickly child, making physical exertion difficult. The seal head provided a formative object of study without stressing his sensitive lungs. Teddy patiently fleshed it and prepared it with spirits, then placed it upon his shelf as a scientific specimen. "That seal filled me with every possible feeling of romance and adventure," he later recalled. Nature study took center stage; there was lots to learn and even more to collect. As he grew up, bird eggs and skulls turned to full skin rugs and body mounts, symbolizing travel, derring-do, and manhood. There was always another to hunt, a larger, more impressive animal. Teddy was hooked.

But nature yielded a paradox, too. Trophies had to be extracted, yet too much extraction eliminated the possibility. Natural trophies—real live species—were tied to particular places, some rugged and sublime, others barren and windswept. By the time Teddy abruptly assumed the presidency at the beginning of the twentieth century, places continent-wide faced all manner of exploitation, the species that inhabited them even more so.

The battle between exploitation and protection waged in Teddy's soul. Even the most one-sided hagiographies remind us of the sharp duality coursing within him. He loved animals. He also loved killing them. He didn't visit East Africa after his presidency to watch animals; he went there to shoot them. And his party succeeded mightily, dispatching over ten thousand animals. By the end of his life, he had snuffed out 296 different species of large mammal, if you're the accounting type.

Justifiably, these statistics sour many. Why such a glaring double standard, killing the very thing you love? It's a tempting rabbit trail I'll let run cold for now. Suffice to say, most hunters see little, if any, paradox in their craft. While Teddy likely shared today's hunting ethos, he did add one wrinkle: Teddy shot for the posterity of science. Many of his specimens went directly to the Smithsonian, or a host of other museums. He was aware that the killing spree was causing an extinction crisis. That's precisely why he grabbed his gun to go pigeon hunting. Passenger pigeons, in fact.

• • • •

You're likely familiar with the dispiriting tale of the passenger pigeon. How ten billion of the birds darkened America's skies when they passed overhead. Their abundance was apocalyptic, as one gobsmacked Ohioan bystander recounted: "Children screamed and ran for home. Women gathered their long skirts and hurried for the shelter of stores. Horses bolted. A few people mumbled frightened words about the approach of the millennium, and several dropped to their knees and prayed."

Holy Hitchcock! It wasn't just the darkening skies. Entire trees toppled under the birds' collective weight. The movement of their wings was described as a "mighty throbbing." No wonder the birds seemed inexhaustible, so perfect a resource for dedicated exploitation. That's just what happened. Right before Teddy's youthful eyes, the birds plummeted from billions to mere thousands. The freefall continued as trainloads of pigeons went east, feeding the growing cities.

Sensing extinction, Teddy saw a few stragglers and downed them. It was for science, he said, not gourmandizing. Future generations needed a record of this once-abundant bird. Caught in a positive feedback loop of decline, passenger pigeons dwindled until 1914, when lonely, geriatric Martha unceremoniously fell off her perch in the Cincinnati Zoo.

Had Teddy not been narrowly escaping his own death down in South America following his second term, I'm certain Martha's demise would have pained him. He wanted to protect species in life. But if he couldn't, then preserving them in death would have to do—tracing yet again to the severed head of a harbor seal.

Preservers feel compelled to preserve. So, while I question his decisions, I sympathize too. I relate all too readily, especially to the litany of flaws his fatter biographies describe, including an obsessive need for action, a visceral longing for violent combat, naïve charm, snap decisions, and adolescent bellicosity. His maturity was as stunted as a bonsai tree. "You must always remember," the British diplomat Cecil Spring-Rice once told a colleague, "that the president is about six."

• • • •

The concept of arrested development isn't limited to our twenty-sixth president. It's a focal point of ecology, too. Nature, you've often heard, abhors a vacuum. Landscapes are like gutters. They fill up over time, leaves and needles giving way to soil and—if your gutters are like mine—seedlings. Over time, one community of plants gives way to another, then another, resulting in a stable climax community. Stable, that is, until the next disturbance, be it a forest fire, a windstorm, or a disease outbreak. Continual and sequential change like this is the idea of succession. An abandoned farm field fills in with weeds, then shrubs, then saplings, and eventually a mature forest. Tilling, haying, or spreading pesticides and herbicides halts succession; it keeps the field a field, maintaining it in a perpetual state of immaturity, or arrested development. Your lawn mower does the same.

Ecologists talk about succession in three phases: primary, secondary, and climax. Surtsey Island, that little Icelandic nub that researchers watched progress from bare lava rock to a teeming throng of plants, insects, and gulls, is a case of primary succession, occurring whenever a barren habitat gets colonized. Secondary succession is everything else, all the habitats already colonized but giving way—succeeding—to other communities. The climax phase is marked by stability, but this is relative. Nothing lasts forever. Old-growth forests may harbor colossal, ancient trees, but they're susceptible to fire, wind, and insect infestations, too.

Of the three phases, Soulé was most concerned with secondary succession, which appeared in his list as "successional loss of habitat." To me, it is the Teddy Roosevelt factor of extinction, large, unwieldy, and hard to pin down. Perhaps the best way to do so is to follow my quest to find one bird—the northern bobwhite. Unsuccessful up north, I headed south, to Florida, ending up at the very place where Teddy's spree of protectionism and preservation sprang from.

• • • •

It was ironic to be searching for the northern bobwhite in our southernmost state. Bobwhite populations boomed in the Northeast during the same era that other species—like wolves and elk—disappeared. Family farms hit their apogee as forests were razed for timber and pulp. A cleared overstory allowed a healthy understory layer, a thick matrix of weedy undergrowth, small fields, and extensive hedgerows and fallow areas—perfect habitat for the bobwhite to forage and raise chicks. Bobwhite were prevalent, quickly becoming an important gamebird in the United States.

The era didn't last. Economies-of-scale thinking led small family farms to be replaced by industrial agriculture and mega farms. Field sizes grew. In Mississippi, for example, the average farm was 55 acres in 1942. Forty years later, farms had consolidated and the average ballooned to 290 acres. Pesticides and herbicides destroyed the weedy cover and bugs that newly hatched bobwhite need. Other land conversion happened, too, including urbanization and suburban sprawl.

For bobwhite, all those factors were bad. For Soulé, there was another factor to consider too: successional loss of habitat. Farm abandonment and a new cultural ethos had side effects: Denuded forests had a chance to regenerate. Canopies closed. Plus, another bear, not named Teddy, steered a historically novel approach to wildfires. In an incredibly successful and sustained US Forest Service campaign, Smokey convinced Americans to put fires out. Each and every one. Only you, Smokey said, can prevent forest fires.

The new policies were good for the safety of people living in fire-prone areas. But for game birds like northern bobwhite, Smokey may as well have been one of the four horsemen of the apocalypse. Bobwhite plummeted, becoming what the Cornell Lab of Ornithology describes as "a common bird in steep decline." So steep was the decline that despite birding my entire life I'd never so much as glimpsed one.

Reports on eBird took me to Florida's Kissimmee Prairie Preserve State Park. Unfortunately, the reports didn't declare the utter foolishness of a midday visit to a shadeless prairie in the early summer of the Sunshine State. With the exception of three park employees huddled around the gift shop's air conditioner and a heavy-bearded maintenance man who roared past me on a gravel-spitting ATV, I was utterly alone. From people, that is. Blistering heat did little to dissuade the prairie's inhabitants. Love was in the air. Meadowlarks sang, hawks soared, and butterflies bounced around my every step. A hundred yards up the trail, a wild boar rooted through the sand, surrounded by six chihuahua-sized piglets. What I didn't see was bobwhite.

Kissimmee Prairie is itself an endangered species. Natural, ungrazed prairies in Florida are few and far between. They're critical habitats for threatened or endangered species like burrowing owls, crested caracara, and grasshopper sparrows. With what we know about succession, natural prairies necessitate some explanation. Logic dictates the weedy communities should give way to longleaf pine or oak communities. Their arrested development lies in the grassland community's resistance to the historical, central Florida fire regime. With taproots protected underground, the grasses generate easily after fire. Fires are welcomed, as they eliminate shrubs and trees that would eventually shade them out.

Herein lies a conundrum of latter-day ecology. The necessity of fire in the maintenance of biodiversity has singed itself onto the collective conscience of conservationists and landscape managers alike. Smokey has been forced into overdue hibernation. It's widely known today how biological communities depend on fire's unpredictable regularity. Fires should happen. But can they? Today, subdivisions and sprawl shoulder up against so many natural communities. Can fires be safely prescribed without risk to nearby communities?

I left Kissimmee without a burning revelation. I left without bobwhite, too.

• • • •

Teddy had a revelation, however. His occurred in the Mississippi bayou, a year into his presidency, when he broke away from his duties to go on a six-day bear hunt. Teddy desperately wanted to shoot a bear, a trophy his walls glaringly lacked. Since time was limited, he needed to hunt with the best. The best happened to be a fifty-six-year-old ex-slave named Holt Collier.

As obscure historical figures go, Holt is as likable as he is perplexing. Born into slavery and unable to sign his own name, he ran away from his plantation at age fourteen and signed on with the Confederate Army. He saw combat in several states, eventually finding his way to Texas, where he worked as a cowboy driving cattle during Reconstruction.

Some of Holt's decisions were more head-scratching than Teddy's. Upon hearing of his former master's death, Collier returned to Mississippi determined to avenge it. Along the way, he spit tobacco, raced horses, and survived a few gunfights. Holt was unrivaled as a marksman. When he entered towns, he distributed venison to white and African American people alike. There was no box he fit into and no bear he couldn't kill. Courage and prowess took root early. When attacked as a young boy, Holt wrestled the bear, finally stabbing it to death. Far from a Roman gladiator, he was merely a boy with a pocketknife. His lifetime bear tally? Over three thousand. Here was a man with the bear necessities.

Unsurprisingly, Teddy was drawn to Holt's prowess and perplexities. If anybody could quickly get him onto a black bear, it was Holt. On a Friday morning, after his pack of terriers picked up the scent of bruin, Holt did just that. For hours he slogged through swamps, steadily gaining on the bear. When the exhausted bear plunged into a mucky slough, Holt bugled for Teddy, who was straggling well behind. Holt's dogs surrounded the bear, barking and lunging in a frenzy. One ventured too close. The bear grabbed it by the neck, crushing it to death.

The killing shot was supposed to be saved for Teddy. But the death of one of his favorite dogs incensed Holt. Patience gone, Holt jumped off his horse, flipped his gun around, and swung it like an oversized club. The gun rammed the bear's head with such force, it bent the barrel, mangling it beyond repair. The bear fell over, concussed. Holt tied the woozy bear to a tree just as Teddy rode up.

Teddy surveyed the carnage. In addition to the dead dog, two more were badly injured. Holt frowned as the bear groaned and gasped for air.

"Let the president shoot the bear!" shouted John Parker, a by-stander who had ridden up with Teddy and organized the hunt.

Teddy never raised his Winchester. He shook his head. "Put it out of its misery," he commanded Parker, tossing him a knife. Hesitantly, Parker approached the bear and plunged the knife into its ribs. Another onlooker, Ferris Buchanan, reported that Parker's knife failed to deliver a killing blow. Holt grabbed the knife and finished the job, slinging the bear's 235-pound carcass over the back of a horse.

According to biographer Douglas Brinkley, the moment held profound implications, reaching far deeper than just the surficial teddy bear craze it set off. Teddy's refusal was a statement. It further solidified an emerging sportsmen's code revealing how his—and the nation's—views had evolved toward wildlife.

This was a rare trophy that Teddy refused. Granted, the bear died regardless. That wasn't the point. The point is that Teddy wouldn't collect it, defining the role of the virtuous sportsman from the nebulous ether. From now on, neither young nor captured animals should be shot. There was a larger implication, too: if sportsmen were to harvest wildlife, they should also protect it. "For once," Brinkley wrote, "compassion overcame single-mindedness in one of Roosevelt's hunts." He had stood firm in the treacly Mississippi slough, youthful trigger itch replaced by mature reservation. Teddy had changed. He'd undergone succession himself.

• • • •

Having struck out on bobwhite in the Kissimmee Prairie, and craving the cooling breezes of open water, I turned my attention upon a scrubby, three-and-half-acre island in Florida's languid Indian River. Out in my mother's kayak on the river, no bird whatsoever seemed in steep decline. The airshow was nonpareil. Gulls and terns littered the skies, snowy egrets with bright yellow toes perched atop heavily stained mangrove limbs, and brown pelicans skimmed the water's surface with wide-splayed wingtips. I placed my paddle across the cockpit and trailed my fingers in the refreshing water.

"Paradise, eh?"

Startled, I glanced up to see a fisherman standing heron-like in a tiny alcove among the mangroves. He reeled his line in slowly, reflecting the tranquil atmosphere.

"Sure is."

"You from around here?" he asked.

"No, just visiting my folks. I'm from New York."

"Sorry to hear it," he said, assuming I spent my days fighting Manhattan gridlock.

"How about you?"

"Yup. Get out here quite a bit actually. Too peaceful not to."

I smiled. I had expected birds. I hadn't expected a kindred spirit. "You don't happen to know which of these islands is Pelican Island?" I asked, gesturing with my paddle tip.

"Just off to your right. Weave around this patch of mangroves and you'll see it. Surrounded by buoys, I believe."

I thanked him and paddled on, soon finding Pelican Island exactly as he'd described. The island, an emerald gem set in an aqua, coruscating crown, teemed with birds. They sparred and jostled each other endlessly, desiring the prize roosts. Coal-black cormorants stood out amid the great and snowy egrets, waterlogged wings spread out to the sky like a parish of Pentecostals.

My evening paddle was larger than birds, however. I had come to pay my respects to the place that set the course of American conservation. Here was a place where Teddy's vision fully matured, where his vision was keen and stable. "Is there any law that will prevent me from declaring Pelican Island a federal bird reservation?" Teddy famously asked in 1903. His question was sincere, not rhetorical. Silence. "Very well," he went on, "then I do so declare it."

Then I do so declare it. Six little words that played over and over, resulting in 540 national wildlife refuges, 150 national forests, 51 bird reserves, 18 national monuments, and 5 national parks. Pelican Island, all of three and a half acres, became the very first cog of a continent-wide system. With the stroke of a pen, Teddy stalled the steep decline of some of America's most iconic birds.

Yet just declaring things off-limits may not be sufficient anymore. When Teddy declared Pelican Island a refuge in 1903, it was five and a half acres. Forty years later, it had shrunk the same way Surtsey is, eroding away by wave action. Rather than oceanic waves, regular boat travel on the Indian River was to blame. While Floridians weren't using the island per se, their disuse was leaving a mark.

By the year 2000, iconic Pelican Island, America's original wildlife reserve, was down to a smidge over two acres. A few more years of fast-moving party boats and oversized yachts, and the little bird roost would sink like the *Titanic*. Titanic indeed, symbolizing egregious neglect and ineptitude.

But in the century following Pelican Island's inception, America learned. Three Mile Island, a hole in the ozone, acid rain, DDT, oil spills, and watching the Cuyahoga River catch fire proved embarrassing enough. From these ashes rose a phoenix in the form of the environmental movement. Aldo Leopold, Rachel Carson, and the inexorable return of bald eagles, helped along by the banning of harmful pesticides. The wave swept through the seventies, cresting in a whirling froth of effective grassroots initiatives and the Endangered Species Act. Sustainability appeared as a concept. And despite a mushrooming human population and avaricious economy, a sprig of collective humility popped up.

Pelican Island had to remain. Alarmed, in 2001 the US Fish and Wildlife Service jumpstarted a massive shoreline project with the help of the Army Corps of Engineers. Three other private organizations pitched in, some offering to match funds dollar for dollar.

While the late 1800s saw people blasting away at the island's birds for hat decorations, the early 2000s saw helicopters lowering in break walls on Pelican Island to avoid disturbing them. By the end of the project, a 165-foot-long oyster shell wave break had been created. To help the birds further, smooth cord grass and mangroves were planted along the island's perimeter for roosting and nesting.

America had gone from shooting birds to watching them, just as

Teddy had done during his time in the White House. Unsurprisingly, he was meticulous. Meticulous enough to help us see that though Pelican Island is secure, other habitat islands—like those on land—most definitely are not.

• • • •

It's obvious by now that Teddy's clear-eyed decision to protect Pelican Island didn't occur ex nihilo. As his life progressed, his outward actions evermore mirrored his maturing inner landscape. "By the time he was in the White House," writes biographer Candice Millard, "Roosevelt was not merely the most powerful elected official in the country, but one of its most knowledgeable and experienced naturalists." The birds of his life, you might say, had flown in to roost.

Despite the passenger pigeon lapse of his youth, Teddy kept an eye ever skyward. Documenting birds became an easy form of collecting. During his presidency, his duties greatly limited his travel to see new species. No matter. He focused his gaze outside the White House windows, keeping an ongoing list of all the birds to appear on the hallowed grounds. Though he never saw bobwhite, his list, ninety-one strong, included many of America's most-loved species: song sparrow, gray catbird, wood thrush, American redstart, red-eyed vireo, and black-and-white warbler.

His list provides a fascinating look at alarming trends many birds have faced. The White House's local landscape of large trees and well-tended shrubs hasn't changed much since Teddy left office. Even so, only the first two—song sparrow and gray catbird—still remain regular White House residents. The others no longer appear. What explains the disappearing act?

Unlike the disappearance of the northern bobwhite, the explanation doesn't involve the focus of this chapter—Soulé's successional loss of habitat. It's a slightly different, more straightforward reason—habitat loss—that we'll explore more fully in time. In short, instead of one rich habitat succeeding to another rich habitat, habitats around the White House have all succeeded to the sterile concrete jungles of economic development. The answer isn't found in the local landscape; it's in the larger landscape, namely DC's Rock Creek Park. For birds attempting to nest within the White House grounds, Rock Creek is critical. It's a staging ground, a jumping-off point. The park's vegetation and large trees provide needed habitat to disperse from. The White House provided a place to land.

Just like some of us who live out our entire lives in one county, natal instincts imbue birds born into the park to want to nest in the same place where they were raised. But sometimes, when all the suitable habitat is already taken, they're forced into adjacent areas. Like your children settling in the next town over.

Trouble is, the larger landscape has endured widespread and steady forest clearing. In its stead stands DC's metro area, swollen like a carbuncle. When Teddy left office, the White House was already an island. What changed was that nearby Rock Creek Park became one, too. Dispersal from the park became impossible. The resident birds in Rock Creek withstood the metropolitan siege as long as they could. But without supplies and reinforcements, they finally dropped off, giving way to the regular, hyper-competitive city slickers: house sparrows and rock doves. The Breeding Bird Census confirms this depressing fact, starkly revealing how forest nesters dramatically declined in Rock Creek Park. Some, like Kentucky and hooded warblers, have disappeared entirely. The park has become Surtsey, eroding into an unyielding metropolitan sea.

• • • ○

On our last day in Florida I felt closer to Teddy but still far from bobwhite. I couldn't bear to return to New York without laying eyes on the cute little quail with the same name as an old college custodian. My final hope lay in another little postage-stamp-size preserve called Helen and Allan Cruickshank Sanctuary, just a few minutes from my parents' retirement community on Florida's eastern side.

The 140-acre sanctuary of Florida scrub can be walked in an hour. Two if you bumble into an amiable gopher tortoise crossing a sandy path, as I had during a previous visit. The sanctuary is completely surrounded, hemmed in by subdivisions, strip malls, and a Starbucks. A former turpentine mine, the parcel was acquired in the nick of time as part of the Brevard County Environmentally Endangered Lands program.

It's too small a patch for bear or deer, but just big enough for tolerant bobcats who don't mind a steady stream of overflying aircraft and muffled traffic noise. The size was right for Ezra, too, whom I lured away from my mom's bison-sized TV with the promise of M&M's and Florida scrub jays. If we were lucky, we could lure the clever corvids to perch upon our outstretched hands.

Habituated to daily pedestrian traffic, the scrub jays didn't take long to find. They trailed us like stray dogs, hoping for a handout. Happily, we obliged, extending our hands with trail mix. Within seconds the jaunty birds landed, grabbed a few morsels, and flew off to stash their booty. A bird in the hand was great but birds on the head were even better. Soon multiple jays were picking through our hair. The seeds and nuts blended well with the landscape. The M&M's, however, particularly the orange ones, stood out in the tree crevices, as obvious as traffic cones on interstates.

Charmed by the jays, I almost missed two chicken-shaped birds tottering up the trail like stiff-legged friars. I knew them instantly, living examples of the birds I'd long stared at in my childhood field guides. Crisply painted with a gleaming white throat enclosed by a bold letter c. Despite the small habitat, the scrubby brush and saw palmetto offered the right mix of food and cover, the same habitat of early successional fields. For now, at least, it was adequate.

The question is, how much longer would it be? Change would come. Secondary succession would see to it; the biological community would reassemble and transform. Prescribed burns wouldn't work in this little patch, the threats too great for the hundreds of surrounding homes and businesses. What could maintain these conditions for the chunky little chickens in steep decline? Could anything arrest the development? Would the scrub inevitably concede to mature forest?

Like all birds, bobwhite have an ace up their sleeve. If the habitat worsens too much, they can utilize their short and stubby wings and alight for greener—scrubbier—pastures. The trouble is that the Cruickshank sanctuary situation is akin to DC's Rock Creek Park—there's nowhere left to depart to. North to citrus orchards, south to the subdivisions of Melbourne, west to Disney World, or east into the Atlantic. Places to colonize or disperse to are sparse. Successional loss of habitat may squeeze them out. But they'll have to grin and bear it; they're effectively tied to a tree in a Mississippi bayou, unable to go anywhere.

• • • •

But every shred and scrap matters, no matter how small. Pelican Island proved that. It also proves that while habitat can be taken, it can also be given back. And managed to benefit as many species as possible. Rarely, it takes but a simple statement: I do so declare it. More often, it takes vision, dedication, and public support—growing from the ground up. Grassroots stuff. Over time, movements can mature, succeeding into a more stable overstory of managed protection.

Protected places restore habitats. And us, too. Mornings with jays, afternoon strolls in a prairie, and quiet evening paddles around a little island that luckily wasn't overlooked. Protected places also show us, of course, that some of life's greatest joys can be traced to the severed head of a harbor seal.

9
WHAT DOES THE FOX SAY?
Environmental Variation

*"Oceans rise, empires fall
We have seen each other through it all."*
—Lin-Manuel Miranda, *Hamilton*

"What did the snail say when he went for a ride on the turtle?" Doug asked, glancing around at our half-frozen faces. We were all too wet and tired to care. A moss-covered board, which the rest of us had failed to notice, mercifully interrupted his joke.

"How do you all think this board got here?" Doug asked, staring down at my feet.

"What board?" I asked.

"The board you're standing on," Doug answered. We all looked down. Sure enough, a yard-long slab of wood, a two-by-six, was resting on the forest floor, partially covered in decaying, late-September leaves. Its perpendicular edges testified it had been milled.

We were well off-trail. The trees around us were several stories high; they'd clearly stood here awhile. The forest was in what ecologists would call "late succession," one the northern bobwhite would avoid. Why would an old board have been dropped here? We were stumped.

"Perhaps broken off from an old deer stand?" Steve guessed, scanning up in the surrounding trees. Steve was a pleasant, middle-aged engineer whose red mesh baseball cap hid little of his salt-and-pepper hair.

"No permanent stands are allowed in the park," Doug answered.

"And besides, wouldn't there be other boards nearby?" Doug was Letchworth State Park's longest-tenured naturalist. He had an unlimited knowledge of local history offset by a very limited arsenal of jokes. I'd been a grateful benefactor, loving cerebral challenges like this more than anything. A gifted teacher, Doug wasn't averse to exposing our ineptitude, too. Unwilling to be bested yet again, I stared at the board, willing it to give up its mysterious origin.

"How about from a paper mill?" I asked. Like much of the Northeast, Letchworth had been stripped bare by the turn of the nineteenth century. The sinewy Genesee River, which cut through the park, had a long history of boom-to-bust paper mills dotting its banks.

"Would've rotted away by now," Doug answered, clearly savoring his advantage.

"Was it for trail maintenance?" Sue queried, swallowing a handful of soggy trail mix.

"Do you see any trails around?" Doug replied sardonically.

"How about a remnant from the old Genesee canal?" I asked hopefully. A canal had briefly paralleled the river for transporting goods up to Lake Ontario. It was quickly replaced by a more efficient railroad.

"Again, wouldn't there be more than one board?" Doug challenged.

Silence. Drizzly rain pattered down on the leaf litter. Here we were, an engineer, a vet, and a college professor, all perplexed by a lone, mossy board at our feet. Didn't advanced degrees correlate with problem-solving?

Doug sensed our exasperation. "It's raining," he said, stating the obvious. None of us shared his unctuous smirk.

More silence. "What happens when it rains a lot?" he asked.

"The Genesee comes up," I said.

"And when it rains a whole lot?"

"It floods," Steve muttered.

"And?"

"Hurricane Agnes!" I shouted.

"Bingo," Doug said, giving me a golf clap.

"See those oaks down there?" he asked, pointing to the hundred-foot-high trees standing below the ridge we were on. "Agnes covered those. The river typically flows about 1,300 cubic feet per second in the summer. During some dry summer spells, you can hop across the river in shoes without getting your socks wet. But when Agnes hit in June 1972, it raged at over 90,000 cubic feet per second. Even standing way up here, much higher than the river's surrounding trees, we'd be ankle-deep in the Genesee. That's how this board got here. Water levels change."

• • • •

Despite living along the Genesee's fickle banks for nearly two decades, I've never comprehended change very well. Sure, I've watched it rise and fall every year after large rains and seen it overflow its banks often. But Hurricane Agnes was altogether different. Happening six years before I greeted the planet, it was what longtime residents referred to as a hundred-year flood. For a centenarian seeing just one large flood in a lifetime, it's an apt appellation. But a brief dig into the Genesee's history reveals that a hurricane of Agnes's magnitude wreaks fluvial havoc more on the order of once every three hundred years.

Past victims of the Genesee's fury, inhabitants of Rochester, knew well the river's threat. The Flower City had suffered severe damage in both 1865 and 1913. Fearing another hit, they successfully lobbied Congress for assistance. Congress sent in the Army Corps of Engineers, who completed a monstrous 245-foot-high dam in 1952, the largest flood-control dam east of the Mississippi, with a cost of $25 million.

The dam quickly proved a prescient investment. Just twenty years after its completion, Agnes stormed through the East, stagnating at the Genesee's headwaters. The swollen river came within a few feet of spilling over the dam's top and obliterating everything in its debris-laden path. Despite an exceeded storage capacity, the well-built structure held fast, sparing downstream communities some $200 million in damages. The corps obviously understood the river's variation far better than I did.

Upstream of the dam, Agnes sowed untold destruction. But as hurricanes go, it wasn't that strong. Agnes's catastrophic effects were due to the fact that when it moved northwest across Pennsylvania and New York's southern tier, it joined a low-pressure system and stagnated for five days, dropping over a foot of water. Granted, hurricanes have a certain regularity to them. But the other factors, like sitting in one spot and joining forces with another system, are what make the perfect storm. Extinction acts on species similarly.

• • • •

According to psychologist Paul Slovic, we live with subconscious Pollyannaism. We're prisoners of our experience, he explains, the knee-jerk part of our brains only considering past events we've experienced. "We don't go around calculating things in a scientific way; we just kind of are guided by our feelings, which are very much influenced by our experiences," he adds in *Thinking, Fast and Slow*. One 1962 study of people on a floodplain, much like that of the Genesee, found they were unable to conceive of floods bigger than the largest flood they ever witnessed.

In other words, if we don't live through something, we have a hard time believing it's possible. Plus, none of us can grasp time.

Ten years? Maybe.

One hundred? Probably not.

One thousand? Nope.

One million? No chance.

Added to our list of shortcomings is an inability to account for environmental variation. If it doesn't happen in front of us, or overnight, we miss it. Unless we freeze moments like yearly school portraits, we fail to perceive them. Hence the mind-blowing revelation of time-lapse photography. It also explains why warnings about climate change fail to quicken our pulse.

But one guy did understand environmental change. A long-dead Frenchman whose full name I promise to write only once: Jean-Baptiste Pierre Antoine de Monet, Chevalier de Lamarck. We'll just call him Lamarck. At the mention of his name, perhaps some lightbulbs are flickering. Yes, the giraffe-neck guy. The same guy who claimed that the long neck of the giraffe resulted from it being repeatedly stretched while reaching for food. This trait, he concluded, was acquired and passed on.

And you're right, his use and disuse theory—Lamarckism—is lamalarkey. But if any long-dead Frenchman with a pompously long name needed a little redemption, it's poor Jean-Baptiste.

Literally poor. Lamarck struggled with poverty his whole life. Despite publishing prodigiously, his books never generated revenue. Nor did his specialty—insects and worms—generate public interest. To satisfy his esoteric interests, Lamarck became a professor and turned to research. But whenever he tried advancing his scientific theories, he was either ignored or attacked by his acerbic colleagues. Ill-fated Lamarck couldn't even manage to make matrimony work, cycling through four different marriages. Toward the end of his life, he lost his sight and lived at the mercy of his daughters until an unceremonious death.

Poor, wrong, blind, and discredited—Lamarck had a rough go of it. We can't even pay our respects at his grave. Such a small courtesy is impossible, because the ground into which he was interred was merely a rental. Five years after his death, his remains were unearthed and relocated to a location nobody bothered to remember or jot down. Perhaps a mercy, as fitting his name on a headstone was bound to be difficult.

The sad reality of Lamarck's life is that one really sour idea—the giraffe-neck debacle—spoiled the whole jug of milk. He had brilliant ideas, too. So brilliant, perhaps, that his contemporaries weren't ready for them. His thoughts on environmental variation, which our man Michael Soulé listed among his vaunted eighteen, were way ahead of his time. They were ignored in his time, but they're relevant to us as we consider extinction.

"On our planet," Lamarck wrote back in 1802, "all objects are subject to continual and inevitable changes, which arise from the essential order of things. These changes take place at a variable rate according to their nature, condition, or situation of the objects involved, but are nevertheless accomplished within a certain period of time."

Okay, add wordiness to Lamarck's list of aforementioned faults. Regardless, truer words had not been spoken and his meaning was clear: nature is dynamic. At the time, prescient insight about nature's dynamism was nonexistent. Lamarck understood cycles. He understood the importance of large-scale, deep-time phenomena that well-exceeded human lifespans. Had Lamarck stumbled across a clearly milled board lying alone on the forest floor, he would have guessed its mode of conveyance faster than it took him to sign his name. "But a flood, of course!" I can hear him saying. "What else could have brought it here?"

Fossil gumshoe that he was, Lamarck knew how environmental variation affected extinction. He concluded, well before Darwin did, that ceaseless environmental flux caused species to either adapt or go extinct. He correctly reasoned that environmental change over long periods of time drove adaptations in the natural world. What he didn't know was how the adaptations evolved. Close but no cigar.

But since nobody else did either, I'd like to toss him a posthumous cigar. Mendelian genetics was still a long way off. "Genes" hadn't been discovered. Punnett squares, heterozygosity, and hybridization didn't exist either. Darwin's grandfather, Erasmus, wholly subscribed to Lamarckism. Darwin himself danced around it as he struggled to explain blind, cave-dwelling animals and the vestigial eyes of subterranean moles. He fed upon Lamarck's inchoate ideas concerning environmental variation and adaptation. Sure, Darwin deserved the scientific knighthood he received. But not at the expense of Lamarck becoming court jester.

On the matter of adaptation, after all, Lamarck was half right. The environment does cause changes in behavior, which do lead to a greater or lesser use of a limb or an organ. This is why marathon runners and Olympic athletes train at high elevations, to more effectively condition their heart and lungs. It also explains atrophy. No, these traits aren't inherited. But Lamarck didn't have all the data we have today.

• • • •

Some of the data we have today on the subject of environmental variation's effect on extinction is foreboding indeed. The recent form of environmental variation we're most familiar with is climate change. Since you've doubtless heard about the poor polar bears clinging to melting ice blocks, here's another example not so well known: fluffy, round-eared critters called pika. They look like oversized hamsters and live on rocky outcroppings and talus slopes of mountains across the West, ranging from New Mexico to British Columbia. All summer long they collect plants like fervent botanists and stash them under rocks and in subterranean burrows to munch upon come winter. Each pika is irrevocably tied to its larder.

The pika is also tied to snow and ice. These restrictions make them an indicator species, alerting scientists to the biological conditions of their ecosystem. One of those scientists, Erik Beever, is a USGS research ecologist who made the unsettling discovery that the little fluffballs have declined significantly across southern Utah, the Great Basin, and northeastern California. Writing in the *Journal of Mammalogy*, he concluded that the effects of the larger regional climate outweighed the habitat's local conditions. In other words, climate change was decreasing the quality of the pika's habitat. In 2016, he documented the pikas' disappearance from Utah's Zion National Park. Their toehold in Cedar Breaks National Monument, he added, was tenuous at best.

How does this pernicious form of environmental variation—climate change—affect pika? Beever hypothesizes that warmer temperatures can eliminate the pika's food supply or force pika underground for longer periods to escape intense solar radiation. Most studies reveal snow to be important for pika survival. Yet in many areas of the West, snowpack is declining. One study has documented a 20 percent decline since 1915. There's possible irony too. Snow has insulating properties. Without a thick enough snowpack, climate change may be causing pika to freeze to death.

That's but one example showing why Soulé listed environmental variation as a factor in extinction. Up in the pikas' mountain redoubts, a warming climate can pose the most serious of threats. Unlike other animals that can move up to higher altitudes to escape summer's heat, pika, quite simply, have nowhere else to go.

• • • •

Regardless of how dire a threat it poses, it is hard to get people riled up about climate change. It's a relatively slow process, and we're hopelessly desensitized to most visuals. That's why I took a different route during one of my conservation biology classes. In an effort to get the students outside and excited about nature, I devised a simple extra-credit scheme. If they photographed a fox, coyote, mink, bear, bobcat, or eagle and submitted it to me with a short write-up, I would award them extra points. As an afterthought, with a devilish grin, I added skunk to the list of possible animals. Nobody could ever be that desperate, I wagered.

Oh but they can, I soon discovered. The semester marched along as usual, assignments and test scores slipping as work piled up. With GPAs on the line, students went after the extra credit with alacrity. After all, it offered the feel of a treasure hunt—not another boring paper to write. Photographs poured in, my students locating the various species like seasoned bloodhounds. A mink arrived, followed by half a dozen eagles. Then, surprisingly, a blurry bear, taken at speed from a car window. Outnumbering all the others were fox and—you guessed it—skunks. All the fox photos showed just one mangy individual that had an extremely peculiar habit—according to many eyewitnesses—of eating pears not long after the clock struck midnight.

The skunk photos were more fascinating. It soon became obvious that many different individuals nocturnally patrolled the campus. I tacked them up to a bulletin board opposite my office door. Many a bemused colleague raised an eyebrow, but none protested the odd decor. Mark, the most curious of the lot, popped his head into my office one afternoon. "Remarkable how different they all are. Were these taken on campus?"

"All of them," I replied, relieved I wasn't the only human on planet

Earth intrigued by varying skunk pelage.

"This one here," Mark said, pointing, "is virtually all white. But that one is basically jet black."

"And check out those three in the middle," I said, all too happy to abandon my cluttered inbox. "The variation is nuts." Regardless of how grainy each photo was, no two skunks were the same.

"One might say," Mark said with a wink, "maybe not everything's so black-and-white." Mark was right. As Lamarck had deduced two hundred years earlier, variation reigned supreme. What united the skunks was their morphological diversity.

While novel to me, such an elementary observation wouldn't quicken the pulse of a seasoned zoologist. To such folk, our resident skunks were simply polymorphic, a trait common to many species. Like many aspects of nature, I wouldn't have noticed it had I not sent my students after skunks and tacked them to my wall. But the more I've considered polymorphism, the more obvious—and logical—it now appears.

Polymorphism is the result of discontinuous genetic variation. Males often look different from females, for example, a prime example of polymorphism called sexual dimorphism. Less obvious are blood types. Polymorphism includes any difference that can be categorized and that doesn't, at least proximately, result from mutation (like leucistic versus albino deer). Height and weight are not polymorphic, for example, because they're considered to be continuous.

Striped skunks are like zebras, each one boasting a unique stripe pattern. The stripes begin as a triangle at the head, then diverge down the back like an interstate with two off-ramps. The purpose of the stripes is to catch our eye like traffic cones, directing attention to the skunk's not-so-secret weapon—its paired anal glands. The glands can swivel independently and aim precisely at a distant target, or, if the situation calls for it, spray a fine, blinding mist. The chemical behind the mist is butyl mercaptan, gag-worthy even days after discharge. Other warning coloration, that we see on monarch butterflies and poison dart frogs, for example, wouldn't work on skunks. At night, when the skunk's predators are about, no colors stand out like white-on-black contrast. "You've seen me. I'm noxious," writes Natalie Angier. "Now buzz off."

A valid question arises here. If such an eye-catching, white-on-black pattern is so effective, why aren't all skunks patterned more similarly? In other words, why are some mostly white while others mostly black? The answer is that none of the patterns—mostly white, mostly black, or the others in between—have proven clearly advantageous. One morph may better dissuade predators while the other proves less hospitable to parasites. Or one may retain heat more effectively during winter while the other may attract mates more readily. With no clear advantage, natural selection has kept them all in play, a rich palette of polymorphism.

This isn't a rabbit trail. We've followed in the plodding, mephitic footsteps of the skunk because it reveals nature's most ingenious means of extinction prevention: adaptation. Polymorphism isn't a whimsical natural history sideshow, regardless of how it may entertain a colleague or two. It is an organism's built-in genetic response to ceaseless environmental variation; animal lives depend on it. It's also proof that environmental variation poses a real and present danger to all species. Lamarck knew that a dynamic world necessitates dynamic species. So, too, did Darwin. "It is not the strongest of the species that survives nor the most intelligent that survives," Darwin wrote. "It is the one that is most adaptable to change."

The question for us today, as we remember the pika, is this: Are the changes we're causing—like climate change—too fast for some species to adapt to?

• • • •

At face value, Soulé's environmental variation factor doesn't seem to jive with another time-honored ecological idea—the balance of nature. Who can forget, after all, when Mufasa told Simba, "Everything you see exists together in a delicate balance."

The line is memorable but grievously flawed. Balance implies that nature is static. If it changes position, it may spill, like crossing a room with a full cup of coffee. Because we're so inept at perceiving change, the idea of a delicate balance of nature seems apt. We look out our windows each morning to the same landscape we saw yesterday, and last year, and the year before that. Nothing seems to have changed—same trees, same shrubs, same birds.

What we miss is more profound. I, for one, fail to see the shallow Devonian sea that covered my yard and much of western New York. Every sedimentary stone my creek offers up, however, affirms the vast sea's presence, each riddled with fossil impressions of saltwater crinoids and brachiopods. Two hundred million years later, hadrosaurs thundered by, their tracks all over New York's southern tier. The dinosaurs were followed long after by a series of continent-wide ice sheets, the most recent—the Wisconsinan—stretching into the sky a mile higher than my roofline. All of this and then mastodons, hirsute with gracefully arching tusks, plodded across the ice-sculpted land. One such Snuffleupagus was exhumed from a peat bog not more than twenty miles from my front porch.

If judging by the longevity of reign, lions most certainly aren't the king of beasts; coelacanths are. Lions have ruled earth for thirty million years, coelacanths for over two hundred million. Long thought to be extinct, coelacanths shocked the world when a live one was caught off South Africa's coast in 1938. The creepy-looking lungfish, along with crocodiles, tuataras, and a handful of other living fossils, stand out for their relative stasis. While millions of creatures have died out around them, unable to adapt to an ever-changing planet, the coelacanth has hung on. The secret likely lies in their habitat. More than one hundred meters under the sea is one of the few places on earth where the environment doesn't vary.

"Everything you see holds together," Mufasa *should* have told Simba, "in perpetual flux." From a paleontological perspective, it's a better way to view zoological history. Ninety-nine percent of the world's creatures have gone extinct. And those creatures didn't go extinct slowly over time. Most went out in five major, profoundly indelicate moments, rare and unpredictable punctuation marks in the run-on sentence of life. A circle of life, maybe. A delicate balance, definitely not.

At this point, the idea of the balance of nature seems too deeply embedded in Western culture to remove. Bristling ecologists are no match for Disney. One such ecologist, Steward Pickett, repeatedly pushed "the flux of nature" in the 1980s. Unsurprisingly, the expression never cleared the walls of a few nerdy ivory towers.

Swimming away with the balance-of-nature hook makes me anxious. It subtly implies there's nothing left for us to do or change. As if all that's required is to board up the dilapidated house and keep people from trespassing. While there's nothing wrong with a preservationist, hands-off approach, I can't help but wonder if it's too late in the game for such a tactic. What about the whooping cranes and the Hawaiian geese that required reintroduction? And the heroic efforts to save Old Blue and her last remaining New Zealand robins? And the dedication needed to keep Pelican Island from eroding away? Not to mention the present-day dilemmas facing eastern timber rattlesnakes, alpine wildflowers, buckwheat, box turtles, bobwhite, and pika. Instead of clinging to the balance of nature idea, perhaps it'd be more fruitful to pursue, as environmental writer Bill McKibben has suggested, *our* balance *with* nature.

• • • •

So, what did the snail say when he went for a ride on the turtle? Later, I asked Doug. His answer: "Wheeeeee!" Like I said, Doug the naturalist was renowned for his knowledge, not his humor.

And what about the mangy fox a bunch of my students photographed munching under the pear tree? Fortunately, that ending's actually worth it. When news of the reliable fox spread, two students, Mitch and Katherine, independently decided to go for it, eager for extra credit.

If you're romantically inclined, you might guess how this played out. One particular starry night, both Mitch and Katherine happened upon the pear tree. They settled onto the grass near one another, hopeful, cameras in hand. They found more than just the fox. While their vulpine vigil concluded that night, their happy matrimony continues.

And what does the fox say? That two students seeking a glimpse of wildlife for extra credit make a great pair.

10

A QUADRUPED OF THE CLAWED KIND
Long-Term Environmental Trends

*"The hardest thing of all
to see is what is really there."*
—J. A. Baker, *The Peregrine*

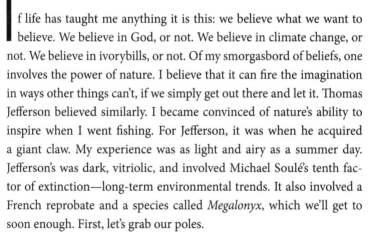

I f life has taught me anything it is this: we believe what we want to believe. We believe in God, or not. We believe in climate change, or not. We believe in ivorybills, or not. Of my smorgasbord of beliefs, one involves the power of nature. I believe that it can fire the imagination in ways other things can't, if we simply get out there and let it. Thomas Jefferson believed similarly. I became convinced of nature's ability to inspire when I went fishing. For Jefferson, it was when he acquired a giant claw. My experience was as light and airy as a summer day. Jefferson's was dark, vitriolic, and involved Michael Soulé's tenth factor of extinction—long-term environmental trends. It also involved a French reprobate and a species called *Megalonyx*, which we'll get to soon enough. First, let's grab our poles.

I've never relished putting worms on hooks. Judging by how much they squirm, they don't appear to relish it either. My fingers get gooey, worm guts ooze out, and well, it just seems mean. But the worst part of the whole worm-on-a-hook thing, hands down, is when you pull a wormless hook out of the water. Or you reel in a greedy little sunfish, worm now lost down its greedy gullet. Both results force you to find another worm and repeat the yucky process.

I'd been down on the dock of our summer cottage not ten minutes and was already reduced to my fourth and final worm. My hands were gooey, my thoughts were sour, and I'd caught nothing larger than a small, ugly perch. I cast out, felt a tug, and reeled in my line. This had to be a big one. Nope. On my line was another small sunfish, the worm nowhere to be seen.

Frustrated, I leaned back and recast, hoping the fish would fly off the hook and save me the time of releasing it. But with an added fish, my line was heavier than before. Instead of going out, it went up, circling an overhanging tree branch before dropping back down. It came to rest a foot above the water's surface where the surprised little fish wriggled in frustration. Before I could react, a large, dull black water snake struck the fish from a point of concealment on shore. With teeth lodged in the fish's side, the snake struggled to pull it back to shore.

My jaw dropped. I had unexpectedly become the antagonist of a dramatic scene in a rarely witnessed play. Unsure what to do, I began reeling in the line. Draped over the branch above, the line—complete with sunfish and now snake—went straight up into the air. With the four-foot snake now suspended vertically above the water, I paused, mesmerized. Due to the invisible fishing line, the gently swaying snake appeared to be hovering. I had become a twelve-year-old snake charmer, able to conjure snakes and lift them skyward.

• • • •

Nature would amaze us more if we weren't so used to it. Each spring, flowers bloom, trees leaf out, and birds suddenly drop onto our doorsteps. These regular events, involving mind-boggling complexity, are driven by nature's calendar, known as phenology. For some of us, cursed with the need to document, recording phenological events is second nature. The first hummingbird shows up on May 4, the first cardinal babies hatch on June 13, and the eastern phoebes begin their second brood on July 2. I'm not the only one in my house who notices phenology. Ezra sounded a lot like Paul Revere last spring when he tore through the house announcing the rose-breasted grosbeaks were coming.

But phenology has revealed a disquieting trend of late. Scientists with far more extensive records than mine have noticed that many biological events in the spring are happening earlier and events in the fall occurring later. While phenological shifts are not always bad (they can extend breeding seasons, for example), conservationists are worried. For untold millennia, ecological interdependence has put species in synchrony with one another. A bird's eggs hatch at the same time that insects become available, for example. The trouble is, phenological shifts do not appear to be occurring at the same rate or direction. Several studies have found that species higher in food chains—like birds—are not shifting as quickly as species lower down—like insects. This creates a mismatch.

Phenological desynchronization is a prime example of a current long-term environmental trend affecting biodiversity. While it may sound esoteric, Soulé considered it a critical piece of extinction's puzzle, affecting the abundance and distribution of organisms, ecosystem services, food webs, and even global carbon and hydrological cycles. Phenological shifts are driven by changes in temperature and precipitation. Yet another domino knocked over by that too-familiar villain, climate change.

Climate change skeptics like to point out the fact that the climate has always changed. True enough. But an inconvenient truth remains: the climate has changed—is changing—far faster today than it has in the past. Like the snake on the sunfish, hang on to that thought. We'll return to it. To understand the effects of long-term climate change and Soulé's extinction factor, you have to meet megalonyx.

• • • •

Megalonyx is the scientific name of the giant ground sloth. It means "giant claw" in Latin. Sadly neither a trip to the zoo nor a YouTube clip will provide any visuals. There aren't even any blurry, suggestive, Bigfoot-like photos to keep our imaginations alive. Giant ground sloths are kaput.

But contrary to Bigfoot and Nessie, megalonyx has yielded plenty of fossils. Almost as great as the beast itself, however, is Thomas

Jefferson's involvement with it. When he wasn't authoring the Declaration of Independence or doubling the size of the United States, Jefferson was down on all fours poring over fossils he had spread across the floor. His scrutiny led to faith. And his faith, you'll soon see, led to action. So intertwined was Jefferson with the giant ground sloth that the shaggy beast later assumed his name: *Megalonyx jeffersonii.*

Thomas Jefferson got his first whiff of the creature when he obtained a giant claw from miners toiling in a nearby saltpeter cave in western Virginia. Unlike me, Jefferson didn't box up his natural history treasures and stuff them under the bed. By day, he weighed and measured them, wondering what magnificent creatures they belonged to. By night, he dreamt about them, his fertile imagination running wild. Perhaps a little too wild.

In 1797, Jefferson committed one such fantasy to paper, which he decided to present to the American Philosophical Society. While Jefferson's wild speculation and cachet may have brought the house down, the paper's title sure didn't: "A Memoir on the Discovery of Certain Bones of a Quadruped of the Clawed Kind in the Western Parts of Virginia." In Jefferson's lively mind, "a quadruped of the clawed kind" implied only one beast: a vicious lion. And judging by the size of the claw, it was at least three times larger than any of Africa's lions. Best of all, he told his slack-jawed audience, the lion was alive. Striding about the West, ripping apart hapless herbivores as it patiently waited for Americans to discover it.

The giant lion's existence was as certain as Monticello's gleaming white pillars. Precious little was known about the western half of the continent. Or if the continent even had a western seaboard, for that matter. If the landscape stretched on ad infinitum, wouldn't it also be bursting with big and exciting creatures? Megalonyx was surely out there, as were great herds of bison, mammoths, mastodons, and who knows what else. Encouraged by the paper's response, Jefferson assumed the role of Disney's Gaston. They would find the beast. Some in the audience may have returned home to sharpen their pitchforks that very night.

• • • •

Contrary to what the more prosaic historical accounts suggest, Jefferson's foray into fossils can't be chalked up as a whimsical detour. It was much bigger than that; it involved nation building, patriotism, and savvy political maneuvering. Jefferson didn't just want an oversized, savage lion—he needed it. It would fabulously emblemize America's growing might. On a personal level, it would reinforce his unflagging faith in the fixity of species, namely that once created, a species's wick never burned up. Like many contemporaries, Jefferson firmly disavowed extinction. He simply didn't believe in it, a point we'll soon return to.

But the reason Jefferson needed a live megalonyx most was to silence a nerve-fraying, crud-throwing, ever-besmirching scoffer. A scoffer who roundly deserved to be silenced. Since I redeemed a long-dead Frenchman with a pompously long name in the last chapter, I won't refrain from sullying one here. The man's name was Georges-Louis Leclerc, Comte de Buffon. I'll mercifully call him Buffon—buffoon, if you please—and describe why he became such a thorn in Jefferson's side.

"America," Buffon sneered, "is an excessively cold and humid continent where big animals cannot survive, domestic animals become scrawny, and men become stupid and lose their sexual vigor." Sticks and stones, right? Who cares what a run-of-the-mill scientist said about the fledgling United States over two centuries ago? The problem was that Buffon wasn't just a run-of-the-mill scientist; he was a top-flight one, eminent even. A mathematical wizard, he wrote thirty-six encyclopedic and factual natural history volumes and jumpstarted the science of comparative anatomy. Although prodigiously productive, he made time for spewing invective and fatuous theories, largely intended for Jefferson's ears.

One of Buffon's theories addressed the worldwide distribution of animals. Species, Buffon suggested, sprang up in optimal centers. Places with a favorable climate and environment. Like France, of course. From there they gradually dispersed, ending up in less optimal, or, as Buffon relished saying, in "degenerate" locales like America. Upon arrival in America, species became degenerate themselves— small, weak, and ineffectual. And by association, plants, livestock, and people, too. Native Americans, he claimed with his chin out and nose up, "were feeble." All things in America, he continued, "shrink and diminish under a niggardly sky and unprolific land."

Jefferson grew incensed with such screed, stewing over Buffon's assertions throughout the American Revolution. Jefferson fought on two fronts. A public war for independence and a private war with Buffon. In the wee hours of the night, as ragtag militias and fortified battalions scurried to and fro around the incipient nation, Jefferson couldn't resist the urge to weigh his various bones yet again, placing femurs and vertebrae upon his scale, comparing the average weights of bears, bison, moose, and even mice, to counterparts in Europe. No detail was too small. Despite tumult all around, Jefferson assiduously documented everything, publishing it in his only book, *Notes on the State of Virginia*. A casual reader could mistake it for a fun checklist of the local fauna. It wasn't. Jefferson's forthright book was a pointed natural history manifesto. If it gained a wide readership, fine. But his book had a target audience of one. *Notes on the State of Virginia* would silence Buffon once and for all.

The squabble swelled to moose-sized proportions. Literally. So colossal was the American moose, Jefferson declared, that Europe's comparatively pint-sized reindeer could walk under one's belly without needing to duck. For proof—and at great personal expense—Jefferson exported a stuffed moose from Vermont to Paris. During its trans-Atlantic voyage, however, the moose began to rot. Its fur fell out. Not only that, the putrid specimen stank like the devil. With a wave of his uncalloused hand, Buffon blew it off.

But Jefferson was determined. If a half-decayed moose wouldn't suffice, he'd deliver the coup de grace with larger, more magnificent American beasts—mastodons and...megalonyx. First, he needed to find them. It was high time for a search party.

Jefferson's famous search party, of course, was Lewis and Clark.

Since many long and glorious books have been written about the two explorers, I merely wish to highlight one pertinent motivation for the journey: extinction. Jefferson didn't believe it happened.

A devout theist, Jefferson wasn't alone in his skepticism; extinction wasn't yet a widely accepted idea. Jefferson saw extinction as a violation of God's goodness. If God created animals and declared them good, why would he let them go extinct? Drawn to science, Jefferson lapped up the writings of classical natural historians. He saw nature's incredible interdependence and delicate synchrony. Like others, he faithfully recorded phenological events happening around him. Jefferson beheld a God-ordained balance. Extinction didn't cohere with that. Therefore, it couldn't exist.

All of this begged another question. If all the fossils around him belonged to real live creatures, well then, where were they? The West, the unexplored frontier, was the obvious place to look. "In the present interior of our continent there is surely space and range enough for elephants and lions," Jefferson wrote, "if in that climate they could subsist; and for the mammoth and megalonyxes who may subsist there. Our entire ignorance of the immense country to the West and North-West, and of its contents, does not authorise us to say what it does not contain."

Forgive Jefferson's choppy writing, questionable syntax, and British spellings. He had nations to found, wars to win, and illegitimate children to sire. Besides, his point was clear. Lewis and Clark weren't just after new routes of commerce; they were after Brobdingnagian mammals. America's preoccupation with size had officially begun.

Jefferson's hopes were soon dashed. Lewis and Clark didn't find mammoths, mastodons, or megalonyx. Worse, megalonyx didn't turn out to be a supersized lion. More careful anatomists revealed the bones and massive claw to belong to a large animal that was more likely prey than predator. It had short and stocky hind legs, an elongated, horse-like head, and a barrel-shaped body—a giant ground sloth.

• • • •

Though Lewis and Clark didn't find colossal creatures, they did find colossal herds of bison and a variety of species: bears, elk, wolves, deer, and pronghorn. "In every direction Buffalo, Elk, Antelopes & Mule deer innumerable," Clark wrote in his journal, "and so jintle that we Could approach near them with great ease." Bison were so abundant that the party found them everywhere. Breaking through ice, mired in mud, floating downriver, and rampaging their camp (crushing a gun in the process). So many and close were the bison that one calf even imprinted on the search party, faithfully following the amused explorers around.

High bison numbers are also confirmed by what Lewis described as their "faithful shepherd." At a place of a huge bison die-off, he wrote, "Wolves were there in such number, and were so stuffed with putrid meat, that Clark walked up to one and killed it with his espontoon."

Say what, Meriwether? Unless we live in a few remote corners of the United States, most of us today will live out our lives without glimpsing a wolf. And there was Clark, just over two hundred years ago, strolling up to a fat one and dispatching it with a casual jab to the ribs. The nonchalance of Lewis's entry suggests the feat could have been accomplished with a hot dog skewer.

At the time of America's founding, bison numbered between twenty and sixty-five million individuals. Let's assume a middle estimate—forty million. For comparison, Serengeti National Park, where I lived for a few years, boasts the world's highest concentration of any large mammal anywhere, wildebeest—at their peak about 1.3 million. Twice a year, as I hunkered over my laptop crunching numbers in my Serengeti research house, four million hooves thundered by. Their passing was seismic. The ground shook and walls rattled. Flies descended upon our house like a biblical plague. Incredible to behold yet unbearable to endure for more than just a couple of days. As I've heard some grandparents say about their grandchildren, we were glad to see the wildebeest come and glad to see them go.

That nonpareil experience was just 1.3 million. Forty million bison? More amazingly, how did European colonists manage to reduce that number to just 456 by 1889? Before I answer that, let's return to Lewis and Clark, megalonyx, and those missing hairy elephants. Where had America's biggest behemoths gone?

• • • •

I've heard it said that there are three sides to all debates: one side, the other side, and what really happened. With America's missing megafauna, one side is the "overkill" hypothesis. The other side is cutely referred to as the "overchill" hypothesis. The third side, what really happened, is probably a combination of both. Long-term environmental trends—climate change—may have stressed megalonyx to begin with. Shorter-term exploitation may have finished the job. Lest we stampede ahead too quickly, I'll explain them one by one.

The overkill hypothesis goes like this: About fifteen thousand years ago, *Homo sapiens* crossed the Bering land bridge and slowly spread out across the New World. These people, recognized as Clovis hunter-gatherers, systematically annihilated whatever mammals they could get their spearheads into. Slow-moving giant ground sloths were perfect prey, meaty and easy to dispatch. Bigger animals were better, offering more bang for the buck, or more sloth for the spear. Plus, the prey was naïve; they hadn't experienced meat-loving bipeds yet. Akin to Clark sliding an espontoon into an overweight wolf.

Proponents of the overkill hypothesis point no further than the trove of mastodon bones that show undeniable markings of human butchering. Other bones have spear points still embedded within them. Hypothesis one confirmed. Human predation definitely occurred. But, doubters ask, could small bands of early peoples really push an entire continent's worth of large mammals into extinction? It's a valid question, one that the bison's tale may shed light on.

But what about the theory linked to long-term environmental trends, the overchill hypothesis? To best explain this, let me complete your mental picture of megalonyx. Sit a hippo on his rump, give him a horse face, bartender-sized forearms, and oversized claws, and plant him next to a tree. Then visualize him rising up on two legs and yanking down tree limbs. These characteristics were well-adapted to life on the open savanna. Serengeti-type terrain featuring spaced-out trees, oceans of grass, and generally dry conditions—such was North America during the great ice age known as the Pleistocene, stretching from 2.6 million years back and ending just 11,000 years ago.

Right up until the arrival of those brainy bipeds over the land bridge, it was golden times for ground sloths. Outsized for most predators, zero chance for claustrophobia, and short shuffles between leafy buffets. Ground sloths took advantage, spreading everywhere. Twenty-some genera—various kinds—ambled about the New World, extending from Havana and the Caribbean to Alaska and Canada's Northwest Territories.

One such South American specimen, described by Cuvier and later collected by Darwin, was christened *Megatherium americanum*, meaning "the large beast from America." The successful sloth ranged throughout much of South America. Megalonyx got around too, its fossils found in 150 different sites spanning from Mexico to Alaska.

For ground sloths, the good times couldn't last forever. The climate changed. Whether it was advancing glaciers or a warming interlude, the dry savanna the ground sloths depended on was supplanted. Megalonyx was among the first to go. Other sloths, like those smoking Cubans in Havana, held out longer, some until 4,200 years ago.

Overkill proponents don't overlook this critical detail. The fact that sloths evaded extinction longer on islands suggests that spear-wielding people were the primary agent of death. Had the sloths been more accessible, people surely would have killed them with as much alacrity as they did those on the mainland. The Clovis bands, say overkillers, simply hadn't bothered rowing yet.

● ● ● ●

Climate change as a long-term environmental trend is one of Soulé's slipperiest factors of extinction for one principle reason: it hasn't always changed evenly. Within the last 2.6 million years of the Pleistocene, scientists estimate some fifty interglacial periods, warm periods that interrupted the overarching global chill. These oscillating warm and cold periods—interstadials and stadials—interrupt the cooldown unpredictably. Two recent colder stadials, the Last Glacial Maximum (23,000 to 19,000 years ago) and the Younger Dryas (12,900 to 11,600 years ago), were separated by a warmer interstadial. Did the large animals go extinct during the colder stadials, scientists wonder, or during the warmer interstadials? Both would have profoundly affected vegetation and the food web. Even now, scientists suspect we're in an interglacial period.

Lying behind these climatic ebbs and flows are three polysyllabic terms that drive most long-term environmental trends: eccentricity, obliquity, and precession. They're a mouthful, but hopefully more memorable if I relate them to a wedding reception I attended this past summer. While downing hors d'oeuvres, I asked a former student how he'd landed his sweet job as a graphics analyst.

"My socks," he responded matter-of-factly. My eyebrows went up.

"Yeah, during my interview I crossed my legs. This exposed my lucky Star Wars socks, which I'd forgotten I'd put on. Nerdy himself, my future boss knew I'd fit in right away."

Eccentricity, deviating from a norm, helped my student land a job. It helps ice ages, too, as the earth's orbit deviates from an exacting path around the sun. As does obliquity—tilting on the axis—and precession, best described as a periodic wobbling. These latter two are best left out of a job interview.

The sun is earth's ultimate energy source. Anything that affects it, affects life. Eccentricity, obliquity, and precession drive long-term environmental processes by altering the amount of sunlight that reaches earth. These are ultimately the forces that brought the mammoths, the mastodons, and megalonyx to their knees.

But wait. Don't long-term environmental trends move gradually, sloth-like? Aren't creatures adaptable to change? Why didn't they just adapt to the warming or cooling trends? These are fair questions, ones that overkill proponents like to raise. There are no definitive answers, though data is suggestive. Losses of animals weighing over one hundred pounds spanned the globe. Australia lost 90 percent in this weight class, South America 80 percent, North America 70 percent, and 40 percent for Eurasia. Africa, where large mammals likely coexisted with humanity the longest, suffered the smallest losses.

Losses mirrored humanity's expansion. Plus, smaller animals, those less targeted by roving bands of people, survived the calamity. Yes, the changing climate was certainly stressing the world's creatures. But exploitation, as humans spread out across the globe like an amoeba across a petri dish, likely hastened their demise.

• • • •

Yikes.

Millennia later, these two forces—climate change and exploitation—continue to doggedly trail us, like an imprinted bison calf. A convenient segue, as bison readily attest to humanity's avarice and exploitation. Though not Soulé's long-term environmental variation, a refresher on the bison's demise will come in handy later. Despite weighing a ton, the brawny beasts somehow survived the Pleistocene's megafaunal collapse. Then, as you know from accounts of Lewis and Clark and others, they swelled to some forty million.

You know the story after that. I'm an American with an overwrought conscience, so I'll spare you the gory details. European colonists found them and slaughtered them. Trainload upon trainload. By 1889, the "jintle creatures" had dropped like a piano pushed off an overpass, reduced to just 456 individuals. Forty million to 456. It was a passenger pigeon kind of bloodletting. Climate change is innocent. As are its three associates: eccentricity, obliquity, and precession.

• • • •

Today, climate change may not be innocent. Here in the Holocene interglacial, our exploitation is of a different sort, exploitation of long-dead plants rather than living animals. But the trend our greed is driving is equally disconcerting. Despite exciting green technologies, fossil fuel consumption continues, spewing carbon dioxide and other greenhouse gases into the atmosphere. In the preindustrial age, 280 parts per million of carbon dioxide circulated about the atmosphere. Today, the number has risen to over 415 parts per million. The gases are trapping warm air and increasing global temperatures unnaturally. In other words, this time climate change isn't the result of eccentricity, obliquity, and precession. While the climate used to change on the order of thousands or hundreds of thousands of years, now it's changing every year.

Signs are everywhere. Pika are dying, ice caps are melting, and glaciers are retreating. Since many alarming trends are out of sight and out of mind, skeptics remain. All of us, after all, believe what we want to believe.

I suggest an easier alternative to document the change: phenology. Just leave a pen and paper by the windowsill. When the birds appear in the spring and leave in the fall, jot it down with a date. Keep your notes. Refer back to them every few years. For climate change at least, base your beliefs upon that.

You might receive an added bonus. In the process of watching the natural world, your imagination might catch fire. And if newfound interest leads you down to a dock with a fishing pole in your hands, who knows what you may catch. The snake, by the way, eventually decided the fish wasn't worth it. With one last furious twist, it opened its mouth and dropped into the lake.

Jefferson managed to dislodge the fish he'd swallowed too. An added wrinkle—a virtue—in his complicated character allowed it. Regarding the existence of large mammals at least, Jefferson's mind was clearly open. For a long time, he believed in the continued existence of megalonyx, a clawed and fearsome American lion, roaming throughout the American West. His fossils were just too suggestive to think otherwise. Also, he badly wanted them to exist.

But two decades later, Jefferson did something profound, especially for a proud, accomplished, middle-aged American. He changed his mind. In a letter to John Adams in 1823, he finally acknowledged that megalonyx was likely gone. Extinction, he conceded for the first time, was a real possibility. He'd have to amend his theology.

You and I have far more data and fossils than Jefferson ever did. We also have the luxury of understanding what long-term environmental trends are and the damage they can cause, especially when coupled with short-term human exploitation. What we do with our enlightened understanding will dictate the fate of our fellow creatures.

History is rarely simple. It doesn't always reveal the best way forward. Acknowledging our blind spots will help. As will keeping an open mind. But for many of us who've had our heads in the sand, the first step toward curbing further extinction is simply to believe it's really happening. And that we're causing it. The same applies to climate change. Because for all of our innumerable differences, one thing we share: we believe what we want to believe.

11
Hog Wild
Catastrophe

"Whoever thinks the destruction of natural resources ended with the buffalo slaughter and the ravishment of our Eastern forests is neither informed nor observant."
—Ned Smith, *Gone for the Day*

Invasive species could be complicit in all of Michael Soulé's extinction factors. They compete with, prey upon, hybridize with, and spread disease to native species. They tend to disperse better, colonize better, and wreak havoc upon habitats. Perhaps Soulé should have made them a standalone extinction factor. Since he didn't, I've chosen to plop them here with catastrophe. I doubt he'd disapprove. Plus, I'd rather boar you sooner than later.

• • • •

The fading evening light was just enough to locate the directions for setting up my tent, but not enough to read them. No matter. How hard could it be? Certainly not too hard for a freshly minted, twenty-two-year-old, B-average college graduate. I brought the tent's long rectangular box up close to my face for a visual of what I was assembling. The photo showed a cute little red tent with two kids peeking out from the zipped-away door flap. Underneath were the words "Junior Dome Tent." Under that in small, ominous lettering: "Ages 8-14."

Crap.

I'd bought the tent hastily, grabbing it off a Walmart shelf just hours earlier, eager to hit the trails of Los Padres National Forest, a gem of chaparral, oak forests, and breezy panoramas of the Pacific. Just off of an intense week teaching fourth-graders about banana slugs and redwoods, I had raced impending darkness. I'd lost. Compounding my kiddie tent purchase, I hadn't come close to the campground I'd planned to sleep in.

California's crimson sun had long ago slid beneath the horizon, and it was too dark to keep going. I'd gone ten yards off-trail and now sat in my junior dome tent with a dilemma. Neither half of my body deserved the amenity of a roof. My upper half had made the terrible decision to buy the tent. But my lower half had motored me to it. I opted for an uncomfortable fetal position, symbolizing feckless stupidity. Pop-Tart crumbs pattered to my pillow—the balled-up, sweaty pants I'd hiked in with. A few Twizzlers and I was out cold.

Sometime later, the sound of rustling woke me. I lifted my head slightly, straining to hear more. It stopped. Then started. Then stopped again. Rather than the measured pace of footfalls, this was staccato, more like rooting or snuffling. I pried an arm from my mummy bag and checked my watch—five a.m. Eyes now wide open, everything was a blurry, navy-ship gray. The rustling was interrupted by a snort and what sounded like a gargled wheeze. Slowly, it drew nearer.

Bear. It had to be. My outdoor-ed curriculum had taught me that despite flying on California's state flag, grizzlies had been extirpated by 1924. This had to be a black bear. Could it smell my Pop-Tarts and Twizzlers? What other junk food had I stuffed in my bag?

Ever so slowly I unzipped the tent. Twisted live oak limbs encased my tiny tent in shadowy miasma. I eased to my feet, unwilling to wiggle free of my sleeping bag.

The rustling instantly ceased. Other than a lone frog peeping off to the right, silence blanketed the forest. Straight ahead, I saw it. Saw them, actually. Two burly, pork-barrel-sized shapes, each the color of anthracite. Disconcertingly, neither appeared to have a head. Other than overweight bear, decapitated megalonyx, or orcs crawling toward Mount Doom, no animal fit.

At thirty yards, I finally detected heads. Long and low to the ground, each snout was buried in the soil. I remained rooted to the door of my tent with fear and curiosity as the creatures approached. One evasive tactic remained, although it'd surely work better for a smoke-filled house: stop, drop, and roll. And pray.

I didn't need to. The lead creature hesitated, then halted. Before I could reach three Mississippi, both spun on their heels and bolted, dry leaves flying in their wake. Okay, definitely not ground sloths.

A long hour later, dawn finally broke. Curiosity replaced apprehension. Despite a free day lying ahead, I had to know the identity of my early morning visitors. Two instant oatmeal packets later, I slung my pack back on, hit the trail, and was soon back at the trailhead. Serendipitously, I found a ranger sitting in the cab of a muddied light-green truck. He clearly wasn't ready to begin his duties; a steaming Styrofoam cup was cradled in his hands. "Mark" glistened on a pin above his shirt pocket. He frowned slightly as I approached. "Mornin'," I said, awkwardly sliding off my pack and dumping it on the ground. He nodded but said nothing.

"Can I ask you something you might not believe?" I asked.

"Ask or tell?" Mark questioned.

"Uh, tell," I said. I liked him already—he was precise.

"I'm all ears."

"Okay. I, uh, saw something strange before sunrise."

Mark took a hesitant sip. He was obviously more concerned with not burning his tongue than anything I had to say. I continued regardless.

"I guess I saw two bears. But then again, I don't think they were."

Mark said nothing.

"To be honest, they looked sort of like South American tapirs. But I've never seen tapirs so I wouldn't really know." I couldn't help feeling like an imbecilic camper.

"I've never seen a tapir either," Mark said, looking through his windshield. He took another sip, apparently in thought. "What time did you see them?"

"Just after five a.m."

"What campground were you in?"

"I, uh, didn't quite make it to a campground. Ran out of daylight. But I was near Estrella," I added, hoping to avoid admonishment or maybe even a fine. Mark took the pen from his pocket and scrawled something in a logbook lying on the passenger seat. All I could see were columns and numbers.

Busted. How stupid could I be? Yesterday, the world's dumbest shopper. Today, the world's dumbest camper.

"You think I'm crazy, don't you?" I said, a last-ditch effort to strike rapport before my inevitable ticket. Perhaps I could yet get off with a warning.

"I don't," he said, tucking the pen in his pocket. He opened his truck door and stepped out. He started walking toward the kiosk.

"You don't what?" I asked, confused.

"I don't disbelieve you," he said. "I bet I know what you saw."

"You do?" I asked incredulously. "What do you think it was?"

"And," he said, ignoring me, "I'm really glad you told me. Do you have time for a quick story?" Just like that, Mark turned from tight-lipped to talkative. I nodded eagerly.

"Have you ever heard of a guy named William Randolph Hearst?" he began.

"I have!" I replied. The previous summer, my folks and I had gone for a tour of Hearst Castle in San Simeon. "You mean the mega-rich newspaper guy?"

Mark nodded, removing his full-brimmed, forest-green hat. "Hearst loved wildlife. And hunting. So he imported animals from all over the world. Zebra, giraffe, camels, bison, ostriches, lots of stuff. Over time, most of them died. But some, like the zebra, are still on Hearst's property. A few others broke out. Escapees went feral. And some have started breeding."

"These weren't zebra," I interrupted.

"I know," Mark said. "They were giant Russian boar."

My eyes widened.

"We've been trying to eradicate them for years. That's why I'm glad you reported them. Did you notice all the overturned soil as you hiked?"

I nodded, though I'd noticed nothing.

"Our oak forest has been ripped to shreds. Looks like it's been bombed. That's the boar. Nasty buggers. Hard to kill. We actually hired professional snipers to try to eliminate them at one point. So far, no luck."

• • • •

Story time with Mark convinced me that Hearst's Russian boar had become public enemy number one. Their elusiveness matched their destructiveness, a combo that has earned them a host of pejorative adjectives: exotic, alien, non-indigenous, non-native, unnaturalized, introduced, and the one we'll use—invasive. Before we get lost in the weeds (pun intended), let's start with a definition: an invasive species is any exotic species whose introduction into an ecosystem is likely to cause environmental or economic harm. Or, most sources agree, harm to human health. This, like many definitions concerning invasive species, reveals a common bias: a species's worth is relative to us; the concept is hopelessly anthropocentric.

The apple tree is a case in point. Apple trees arrived in America with Europeans. But instead of stealing land, exterminating species, and spreading disease, apple trees only spread good tidings. Sure, their leafy branches may have shaded out some natives. But mostly, they enhanced everything, providing sap, blossoms, buds, bark, twigs, shelter, and, of course, apples. Their introduction was an ecological, economic, and gustatory boon, not a bummer. By our definition, therefore, the apple tree isn't invasive.

A few seasoned naturalists I've hung out with have bristled when I've casually called a plant or animal invasive. When I pressed them why, their responses have been sincere, though vague. I think it's a reluctance to draw lines. At some point in history, all species took advantage of the Homestead Act. In other words, at some point every plant and animal invaded a preexisting habitat, a form of primary succession. Technically, everything's invasive. To call some invasive and others not, when limited to the narrow purview of brief human lifespans, feels arbitrary to naturalists with a long view. Pointing fingers is hypocritical, they say. We're invasive too.

It's an important point—humans as the ultimate invasive species. Soulé, who referred to the human race as a disease, agreed with it all too readily. I'll let you decide. But I will say this: humans, especially post-industrial Europe and the West, do share some alarming commonalties, mostly relating to restraint, or a lack thereof. Though apple trees can—and do—seed themselves through a process called naturalization, they exhibit restraint, old orchards tending to give way to mature forests. Apple trees are akin to George Washington stepping down from the presidency after two terms, refusing tyrannical rule.

Can humanity do the same?

Or at least not play the role of genie, offering magic carpet rides? While sea rocket and seagoing tortoises arrived by themselves, too many others haven't. Indian mongooses, Burmese pythons, Asian carp, zebra mussels, cane toads, Asian long-horned beetles, kudzu—all hitched a free ride with us. Wherever they've landed—Florida, Hawaii, Australia—what they've received has been the same: a whole new world. Little competition, few predators, and naïve prey. An all-you-can-eat buffet, a land of milk and honey, utterly devoid of checks and balances. To the victors have gone the spoils. To the vanquished—the reason for Soulé's fretting—extinction.

This is why Mark the ranger took me seriously. He had seen firsthand the effects invasive species can have without checks and balances. That unchecked, gluttonous Russian boar could eat every live oak acorn on the coast. After that, possibilities were as dour as they were numerous. Without acorns, native rodents, deer, and birds could diminish. Bereft of prey, bobcat, coyotes, and mountain lions could starve, emigrate, or turn to pets and livestock. Eventually, if trees toppled without replacement, nesting, roosting, and cover would disappear. Without shade, streams could heat up, stressing fish and aquatic insects. Critical dry-season water sources could dry up. Acorn woodpeckers, the clownish-looking birds that depend upon the oaks, could boom, bust, and never boom again. Dominos could topple in all directions, ramifying throughout the food web.

Why? Because one unhinged species unleashed another.

Ecology textbooks are littered with gloomy words to describe such scenarios, words like *unraveling, dismantling,* and *disintegration.* Euphemizers prefer *relaxation to equilibrium* while the realists use *floral and faunal collapse.* I prefer *trophic cascade,* which refers to how effects tumble through an ecosystem like a series of waterfalls. Whatever we call it, we can agree on this: it's a catastrophe.

But we can't have a concept without contention. To understand Soulé's idea of catastrophe best, let's rewind the clock and review an esoteric little debate between an Englishman and—you guessed it—a Frenchman (the last one, I promise).

• • • •

We'll start with the Frenchman, whose full name yet again proves irresistible: Jean Léopold Nicolas Frédéric, Baron Cuvier, whom we'll call Cuvier. Cuvier was clean-shaven, had a thin nose and hair thick enough to conceal a quill, perhaps even an entire inkwell. He adhered to catastrophism, or the belief that earth has been shaped by big, violent events. The Englishman was Charles Lyell. He had a strong chin, barely connected mutton chops, wispy hair, and he was an outspoken uniformitarian, thinking earth changed slowly, steadily, and predictably. In this case, history is too complex to label one right and the other wrong. Both were bright, iconoclastic polymaths with respective camps armed with brainy firepower.

Cuvier came to believe in catastrophism through the study of fossils. The more he examined them, the more he realized that whatever creatures they belonged to weren't around anymore. At least not around his forested French countryside. Were they living somewhere else, as Jefferson assumed? Just waiting for a search party to discover them?

Cuvier didn't think so. Unlike Jefferson, he believed extinction happened, that creatures existed for a while and then, for whatever reason, vanished. Although the issue of God's sovereignty rankled him, it was too teleological. Cuvier was a scientist, not a theologian. Politely he sidestepped. But while he didn't know why species went extinct, he did offer how: global catastrophes. In his mind, normal forces were small potatoes. "Our volcanic eruptions, our erosions, our currents, are pretty feeble agents for such grand effects," Cuvier declared. Species distributions, he argued, were dictated by global-scale catastrophes. The entire earth was affected by them, in fact. "Numberless living things were victims of such catastrophes," he wrote. "Inhabitants of the dry land were engulfed in deluges; others, living in the heart of the sea, were left stranded when the ocean floor was suddenly raised up again; and whole races were destroyed forever, leaving only a few relics which the naturalist can scarcely recognize." Noah's flood, he insisted, was a case in point. What else, Cuvier asked, could account for the wide variety of fossils he had of creatures no longer living?

Cuvier was talking about big stuff—serious terrestrial and oceanic upheaval, as if God periodically wrung out the planet like a sponge. Catastrophes, deluges, whole races destroyed forever. To him, a volcanic explosion was as minor as popping a pimple. Not nearly enough to annihilate a species. A worldwide series of volcanic explosions, on the other hand, like that set off by the meteorite sixty-five million years ago, was something else entirely. That's a legit catastrophe. So went the theory of catastrophism, an outlandish idea at the time.

Too outlandish for Charles Lyell, that is. Lyell had what most academics covet, an Oxford pedigree and cachet to match. He also had a well-regarded, multivolume book, *Principles of Geology*, toted around by many leading thinkers of the day. Jefferson and Darwin both had copies. In his book's three volumes, he pursued one singular idea and made it stick with a memorable catchphrase: "the present is the key to the past." The only catastrophe Lyell saw was Cuvier's bombastic ideas. To deflate them, he hurled obloquy.

Every geological phenomenon, Lyell argued, should be explained in terms of processes still acting today. Earthquakes, erosion, glacial movements, volcanic explosions, even the steady decomposition of plants and animals. Extinctions occurred gradually, by ordinary, often slow-acting forces. Catastrophes weren't needed to explain die-offs, simple observation was. Lyell's was a direct appeal to Occam's razor, parsimony grounded upon deductive logic.

Yet again, you can guess where this debate went. Both men were right. Lyell's routine, predictable die-off of species over time by natural processes is called background extinction. How routine is it? Paleontologists tell us that one species goes extinct every year for every million out there. If we just consider the ten thousand or so bird species, that amounts to one every four hundred years. Why earth hasn't run out of critters is because background extinction is generally offset by speciation. In a process called adaptive radiation, new species evolve to fill the void.

Against a backdrop of routine extinction, catastrophes occasionally occurred. Cuvier reasoned correctly: large numbers of plants and animals disappeared at unpredictable intervals. These are recorded in five extinction spasms, not including our current one. Each was truly catastrophic, like God conking earth with a cosmic frying pan.

History tends to see Lyell as the one with sober, coolheaded logic. But buried deep in his girthy book is an incongruous gem I can't resist exposing. Lyell believed that plants and animals were eternal. That they came and went in response to earth's physical conditions, ebbing and flowing, but never ebbing completely. "Then might those genera of animals return," Lyell wrote, "of which the memorials are preserved in the ancient rocks of our continents. The huge iguanodon might reappear in the woods, and the ichthyosaur in the sea, while the pterodactyl might flit again through the umbrageous groves of tree-ferns."

History is connected, of course. We'll never know how Lyell's words affected Jefferson an ocean away in Virginia. But Jefferson had the book and certainly read it. Nor was he averse to scientific flights of fancy. Perhaps Lyell's words tasted as sweet as one of Monticello's plums, fueling his spat with Buffon. We do know this: not long later, Lewis and Clark were sent out to find some eternal creatures.

• • • •

You have to admit it's a glorious visual—pterodactyls flitting through umbrageous groves of tree-ferns, reminiscent of Maurice Sendak's *Where the Wild Things Are*. If pterodactyls were flitting through umbrageous groves, one thing is certain: animal hoarder William Randolph Hearst would have acquired them. Sparing no expense, he would have had them shipped over and promptly released on his vast San Simeon estate. After clipping their wings, he surely would have hunted them.

Hearst lived large. One of the most critically acclaimed movies of all time, *Citizen Kane*, was based entirely on his outsized life. His parties were lavish, his megalomania great, and his philandering just as focused as his animal acquisition. Not long before the great stock market crash, Hearst imported two hundred Russian black boar, which he released onto his estate. As much as I'd like to cast aspersions, the boar I encountered at Los Padres hadn't descended from Hearst's herd. Contrary to what ranger Mark told me, the boar wreaking havoc across California—and the United States—had more likely belonged to a different California fat cat, George Gordon Moore.

Moore's boars definitely got out. Moore was one of Hearst's wealthy friends who shared a penchant for the peculiar hobby of importing exotic animals mainly to shoot. He lived nearby. To his credit, Moore openly admitted to letting boar loose not far from Hearst Castle. What happened next, however, is as dark as the inside of a pig snout.

Probably, Moore's pigs met up with domestic pigs. Not slop-eating, barnyard pigs. Other pigs brought over by Spanish colonizers way back in the 1700s. Long-emancipated porkers now as feral as they were hairy. Like wolves and coyotes, it's likely Moore's Russian boars and feral pigs hybridized. The result was an animal with a longer snout, coarser hair, straighter tail, longer legs, leaner hindquarters, and, on the males at least, tusks. Such hybrids were sleek and wily, perfectly honed for mangling ecosystems. Like coyotes in the East, here was another rare example of hybridization strengthening a species rather than weakening it. Unleashed on the south coast of California, these hybrids were as happy as pigs in … oak woodlands.

Hearst, Moore, whoever. The blame game is pointless. In the 1920s, our nation's eco-conscience hadn't fledged yet, and affluent folks were casting exotic wildlife about with handshakes and high fives. Ring-necked pheasants, chukar, Himalayan snowcock—everything went everywhere.

Everything still does. Each year, state agencies across the nation continue to hand rear and release exotic pheasants and fish for wildlife enthusiasts. And then there's me, armed with my advanced degree in ecology, plopping tulips in the ground last week. Granted, these species aren't invasive. They don't destroy ecosystems and economies. But tulips are from Turkey, for heaven's sake. Why can't we Americans just be content with what we have?

My rationale? A brief splash of color next spring. A smile as I walk about my yard. Ornamentals, we tell ourselves, are harmless. Except, of course, when they're not.

• • • •

Rumor has it that in the late eighties an expat living in Uganda wanted a splash of color, too. Instead of reaching for any of the thousands of local possibilities, whoever it was reached for water hyacinth, a purple plant native to South America. The plant went in the koi pond, where it innocently stayed until a hard rain. The pond overflowed and the hyacinth spilled into an adjacent river—the Kagera. It swirled its way downstream before coming to rest in Lake Victoria, East Africa's largest lake, upon which millions of people depend.

For water hyacinth, it was a dream come true. Warm, nutrient-rich water. Nobody to eat it, and endless sunshine. Fast-forward to the 1990s, a few years after hyacinth had found its way to the lake. The imperialistic plant choked the shoreline in thick, movement-stifling mats. Unable to navigate, the fishing industry died. Mosquitoes boomed in the stagnant water, malaria rising along with them. Local economies crumbled.

In the early 2000s, I visited the lake a few times. Other than one feeble attempt at windsurfing well offshore, I never swam. Nobody did. Despite daily temperatures routinely in the nineties, the lake's refreshing waters were off-limits. Water hyacinth had created the perfect stage for a three-part tragedy involving worms, snails, and people. The play goes like this: The worm lives in the snail. Eventually, it pops out and swims, searching for a larger, human host. If it finds one, like an African fisherman hauling in his nets, the worm attaches and burrows through the skin. It doesn't stop until deep into the body, often lodging in intestinal lining.

A few carefree, asymptomatic years later, the worm migrates to the blood vessels where it causes fevers, chills, and inflammation. If untreated, a nasty, long-lasting, and sometimes fatal disease called schistosomiasis, or bilharzia, results. Unfortunately, the nastiness doesn't end there. Fat and happy in its human host, the female worm lays eggs. To grow best, the eggs need to return to the original host—snails. It's an unglamorous mode of transit but stinking effective. Eggs get pooped out. More often than not, the free ride is courtesy of unwitting and impoverished Africans lacking sanitation and sewer systems. Back in the lake, the eggs reenter snails and the circle of death continues. A cycle as ingenious as it is worrisome.

Schistosomiasis owes water hyacinth a debt of gratitude. Snails fare better in still, stagnant water, exactly what a blanket of plants creates near shore. And since people have few economic livelihood options other than fishing, they're forced to risk the disease. Just think: you can paddle out into the world's largest lake—Superior—dip a cup into its cool, clear waters, and drink without filtration. In Victoria, the world's second-largest lake, you can't even get a boat past the hyacinth.

"I think it pisses God off if you walk by the color purple in a field somewhere and don't notice it," wrote Alice Walker, likely in regard to the late-fall bloom of asters. But I think her words apply more urgently to hyacinth. Failing to notice the ravages of this invasive and the harm it has caused to powerless people is even more indicting. The desire for a simple splash of color in a koi pond can make a splash all right, in this case a tsunami.

At the heart of Soulé's catastrophe is a web. Ecosystems are strung together by innumerable gossamer strands connected to one another invisibly, and sometimes counterintuitively. "When one tugs at a single thing in nature," John Muir wrote, "he finds it attached to the rest of the world." When water hyacinth, Norway rats, dandelions, or European starlings land somewhere new, they tug at many strands. Sometimes the world resists. But other times, like in the case of Russian hybrid boar, it simply can't.

• • • •

Invasive boar aren't eternal beings as Lyell guessed, but they're pretty darn close, rooting their way around the earth for millions of years. Though the average pig weighs in at 150 pounds, some behemoths tip the scales at 450. They put on weight as effortlessly as they raise piglets. Once a sow passes her first birthday, she can produce a five- or six-pig litter every year thereafter.

Erase your image of timorous pigs cowering inside from a big bad wolf. And unfortunately for ecosystems everywhere, this little piggy hasn't stayed home. With bottomless stomachs, the nose of a bloodhound, and above-average athleticism, wild boar genes acted like steroids for the feral pigs. Consider this: five-foot-high fences can be scaled or burrowed under. Able to go where they please, wild boar decimate crops, destroy historical sites, shred golf courses, spread disease, and pass on parasites. Everything they do competes with native species. There are only two words for any tree trying to regenerate in a land populated by feral pigs: good luck.

Boar-caused damage has been so severe that people are taking to extreme measures. A recent article, titled "Oinkers and Choppers," describes the advent of a new sport: chasing down pigs in helicopters. For a modest sum, partakers arm themselves with AR-15 semiautomatic rifles, hang out of the whirlybirds like paramilitary troops, and fire at will on all things porcine. Due to the pigs' destruction, or perhaps because it's Texas, few people have disapproved. I agree, blasting away at boar with semiautomatics from overflying helicopters doesn't seem humane. But what else can be done? In the United States, the federal government puts their annual damage at a cool $1.5 billion. In the words of one USDA researcher, wild boar are "the worst invasive species we'll ever see." From an ecosystem's perspective and all the native species within it, they're an unending flood, a chronic disease, or daily falling meteorite. A catastrophe.

• • • •

When a catastrophe occurs, we all have to do our part. My unique chance came when my mother called me late one night a few years back.

"Mom, are you and Dad okay? It's almost midnight."

"We're fine. You'll never guess the reason I'm calling."

"What's up?"

"I've got a gift just for you."

"A gift?"

"Trust me, none of your siblings will care." Oh no. While my mother scored on some gifts, she whiffed on others. This lead-up sounded like it'd be the latter.

"Go on," I said, curious.

"You know how I often enter raffles?"

"Yeah."

"Well, I entered one this summer at the Harford Fair." My mother is a compulsive raffle hound. Surely, a dozen turkey calls were headed my way. Or a lifetime supply of forest-scented candles. "I didn't win the grand prize, which was a paid vacation to Hawaii." Hawaii? Wow, these raffle prizes sure outclassed a basket of bath soaps.

"But I did win first prize."

"A free trip to Alaska?" I asked hopefully.

"Not exactly. But it is a free trip."

"To where?"

"Tioga."

"Where?"

"I think it's a little town in Pennsylvania."

"Oh." My heart sank.

"You have an all-expenses-paid trip to hunt wild boar in Tioga, Pennsylvania."

My mother paused as I processed this info.

Three seconds later I shouted into the phone: "I accept!"

Wild boar! Overdue razorback revenge! A decade later, here was a chance to get back at the Californian colossals who had sent shivers down my spine in my junior dome tent. Rather than self-indulgent, this foray was for the betterment of ecosystems and society. If I succeeded, there'd be one fewer invasive animal with a Hollywood ending. Plus, enough pork to sink a ship. What could be better?

Well, the hunt could have been better. Several months after my phone call, I was ten feet up in a tree stand in Tioga, Pennsylvania, sitting next to a bearded guy named Joel who knew a lot more about hunting than I did. His coat smelled distinctly of bacon grease. "Now listen," Joel said. "The pig here's gonna come rippin' up that fence line." Joel paused, pointing out the ramshackle chain-link fence twenty yards in front of us. "If she slows, even for a second, you gotta shoot her. Since all you got is this bloody open-sight, you're gonna need to make your shot count."

The "bloody open-sight" was Joel's name for the ridiculously old, short-barreled gun now trembling in my hands. Passed down from my grandfather, it lacked a way to mount a scope. The night before, when I'd removed it from the leather case, a Prohibition-era rodent nest had fallen out. Accuracy was out of the question. In my inexperienced hands, shooting was akin to throwing a frisbee in a blizzard.

I'd meant to practice. But lesson preps, labs, and parenthood hadn't afforded the time. I'd fired a grand total of three times, each practice shot punching me in the right shoulder and missing the target by a mile. One hundred years ago, the gun might've commanded a pinch of tobacco and three beaver pelts in a Saskatchewan backwater. Nowadays, it commanded retirement, to be hung above a mantle in a woebegone hunting shack. Right now, in this tree stand, the rusty relic was all I had.

Joel's walkie-talkie crackled. Where I heard only crackly static, he heard the boar's whereabouts. "Okay, our beater's on a nice black hog," Joel whispered. "Yup, she's following the fence line. Should be here any moment now. Get ready." I tensed, lightly teasing the trigger with my index finger.

The beater, whom I'd met briefly before the hunt, was a rosy-cheeked, pimply high schooler with black, greasy hair falling out of a loosely knit Steelers hat. He had patchy facial hair, an unfastened blaze-orange vest, and a can of Skoal outlined in his back jeans pocket. Too much of his neon green boxers were on display, gravity tugging inexorably on his trousers.

He was called a beater, I learned, because his job was to thrash through the underbrush, beating out the boars. Ideally, toward paying clients. Despite my nerves, I felt for the kid. No way people lined up for this job, running through the brush as hacks like me took aim. Aiding the beater was a ten-foot-high fence. I tried to ignore the tattered, boar-sized holes in several places.

The fence, I was told, completely surrounded our "wilderness" hunt. For the beater, it served as a giant funnel. Tree stands were positioned at corners and other strategic spots to speed up the average hunt. Classic canned shooting, the hunting equivalent of a fast food drive-thru. Perfect for trophy hunters, particularly the inept, the impatient, and posers like me.

"Here he comes!" Joel said. "And he's a biggie!" He touched my forearm lightly. "Remember, if he stops, shoot." At that moment a hideous, asphalt-colored creature with small beady eyes stepped out of some rhododendron. It looked like a creature in serious need of braces and a nose job. Not nearly as big as Californian boar but still sizeable, with scraggly hair covering its dense, compact body. The boar braked, detecting our scent. Its back arched as it sniffed the air. "Now!" Joel said.

BANG! I recoiled against the tree. The boar squealed and took off, a puff of black hair suspended in the air where the boar had been. "Did I get it?!" I asked excitedly. A quick glance at Joel extinguished my hope.

"Nicked it," he said, frowning.

Embarrassed, I stared down at my gun barrel. Nincompoop!

Unable to hit a potshot at twenty paces. Broadside, too! Dark, answerless questions flooded over me. Why hadn't I practiced more? Why was I using an antiquated weapon? Why hadn't my mother won the grand prize of the raffle? And why, for heaven's sake, was I shooting pigs in a petting zoo?

"Is my hunt over?" I asked sourly.

"Well, you only get one pig," Joel said. "This one's yours. Now he's ticked off. Getting another shot'll be tough to impossible. No use sitting up here anymore." Joel smiled as he started down the ladder. Obviously, I wasn't the first inaccurate fool he had coached.

As soon as our feet hit the ground, the beater jogged up with an imploring look.

"Nicked it," Joel told him. "Pig's pretty mad. Hug the fence, Jay. We'll cut the corner and wait. If we can't get him at the next bend, that pig'll hole up and we'll have to call it a day." Stoically, Jay nodded, packed another pinch of Skoal in his lip, and went off to hug the fence.

A few minutes later, we were crouched down by a large, freshly fallen oak. Joel's walkie-talkie crackled anew. Joel listened a second then turned it off, not taking his eyes off a thicket to our right. "You know the rule. If that sucker stops, shoot. Take better aim this time," he added, winking.

I knew the rule. But this time, the boar didn't stop. It careened out of the brush at a fast trot, hugging the fence line. The sucker wasn't stopping; it was now or never.

BANG! My ears rang, the recoil again punching me backward. But miraculously, the boar crumpled into a heap.

I'm not sure who was more amazed—me, Joel, or Jay, who suddenly appeared. The boar—my boar—was stone dead.

Another miracle soon followed. Knowing my father was out to breakfast, I slyly called my mother. Ten minutes later, I had procured funding for a wall mount of the boar's head.

And years later, yet another miracle. Innately ugly, the mounted boar had long been relegated to an out-of-the-way spot above the dryer. One day, Linda unexpectedly asked, "What if we try hanging it in the dining room?" I stared at her. She was serious. Maybe boar heads had recently appeared in *Martha Stewart Living*. Or maybe she'd hit her head on a tusk one too many times while unloading laundry. I certainly had. Either way, invasive species that it is, the boar took over the central room of our house.

I'll never know if boar mounts are avant-garde or retro. Trust me, it's no white stag; there's nothing majestic or magnificent about it. Just a wiry-haired, long-snouted, beady-eyed pig, homely and expressionless—the Abe Lincoln of the swine world. A mount of the boar's butt couldn't be much worse.

I rarely notice the boar anymore, even though it leers down at me while I eat my supper. None of my family does either; we're used to it. In that sense it's an apt symbol of our relationship to most invasive species. But we ignore them—wittingly or not—at our peril. They can start as innocently as planting a flower to spruce up a koi pond. Not long after they can take over a lake, destroy a fishing industry, and cause inestimable suffering. Others can root their way through forests and creep up on us in the dark. After that, no number of choppers, semiautomatics, or raffle prizes can take them down. It's bad for us but far worse for the native wildlife the invasive species compete with and prey upon.

Managing such a catastrophe won't be easy. But acknowledging the problem is. Easier, I've learned, than hitting the broadside of a boar.

12

HOW IN HALEAKALĀ?

Extinction or Reduction of Mutualist Populations

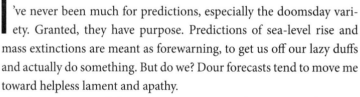

"When we see ourselves as part of nature, we understand that saving nature is really about saving ourselves."
—Ami Vitale, *National Geographic*

've never been much for predictions, especially the doomsday variety. Granted, they have purpose. Predictions of sea-level rise and mass extinctions are meant as forewarning, to get us off our lazy duffs and actually do something. But do we? Dour forecasts tend to move me toward helpless lament and apathy.

Case in point: While prepping a Human Ecology course a few years back, I slogged through a prosaic book titled *Sparing Nature*. On the bottom of page 156, I ran across the following: "In New Orleans, Louisiana, there is little protection left from hurricanes because artificial structures have altered the natural buffering effects of the Mississippi Delta. Even without a major storm, the Louisiana coast loses one acre of land to the encroaching sea every twenty-four minutes. The loss of the marshes may have huge economic costs and lead to substantial loss of human life should New Orleans get a direct hit from a hurricane."

The book came out a full two years before Hurricane Katrina. While not a prediction per se, the author, also an ecologist, foresaw the disaster. We know what happened next: the Category Five hurricane claimed over 1,800 lives and incurred $125 billion in damages, making it the costliest natural disaster in US history.

If this clear-eyed warning existed in print a full two years before

Katrina, why didn't anybody try to prevent it? I have a few guesses. First, probably only environmentally minded bibliophiles like me read the soporific text. And second, predictions are just that—predictions. There's a chance they won't happen, too. Why bother preparing for something that may not come to pass? For lazy folks like me, predictions provide a rationale to sit tight and lament. Apathy is easier. Sandbags are heavy.

But there *are* two environmental predictions I love. Both of them actually spurred action. One prediction was thankfully wrong and the other was gloriously right. The wrong one sent me immediately to Hawaii. The right one sent videographers to Madagascar, a full 130 years after it was made. The wrong one involved youthful irresponsibility and Hawaiian honeycreepers. The right one involved youthful irresponsibility, a moth, an orchid, a famous bearded guy, and an encyclopedic monograph titled *Fertilization of Orchids*. Like a hummingbird in a flower garden, I'll flit about the two predictions interchangeably.

• • • •

My heart sank when I read my ATM statement: $649. Half of that would go to the red-eye flight to Maui. Gas and airport parking would knock out more. At best, I'd have $200 for ten days. Forget island-hopping. There was little margin for error, and hitchhiking would be my only means of transport. But with thriftiness, luck, and my junior dome tent, perhaps it was doable. It had to be. I had birds to see.

When I called home, I kept my details vague.

"Going to Hawaii for about two weeks, Mom."

"Hawaii?! Why?"

"Some birds there are predicted to go extinct soon."

"Birds?"

"Honeycreepers," I clarified. "Gorgeous little things with long, curvy bills. Everything I've read has predicted the extinction of the honeycreepers to happen within the next ten years. I desperately want to see them before they vanish. They're endemic," I added, wanting to come across smarter and less impulsive.

"Endemic?" my mom asked.

"It means they're native to the Hawaiian Islands. They're only found there."

"Oh. So, you're going to *all* the islands?"

"No. Just Maui. Can't afford the rest."

A pause. It was obvious my mother was processing my latest wild idea. I plowed ahead. "May never get this chance again. I have a two-week break here from teaching. Can't think of any better way to spend it. Sitting around the cabin would get boring." Silence. I knew what my mother was thinking. I headed it off. "And believe it or not, a ticket home to see you costs more than this Maui flight I found. An opportunity like this doesn't come around every day."

"How's your truck running?" Dad asked, cutting in. It wasn't unusual for him to eavesdrop on my conversations with Mom.

"Oh, hi Dad."

His question about my truck was a good sign. Dad had bought me a little slate-gray Toyota pickup and taught me to drive the puny stick shift in California's busy central coast where I was teaching outdoor education. The truck had a carpeted back with a camper shell, perfect for camping, which I'd done plenty. Though I couldn't be sure, his question foreshadowed consent, perhaps because my seat-of-the-pants plans reminded him of one of his own questionable phases when he'd cruised around the country in a Volkswagen camper van.

"Superb. Only stalled a few times last trip."

"Glad to hear it. Isn't stick shift great?"

"Sure is," I said, feeling optimistic I'd receive his blessing.

"How are you funding this trip?" he asked, without a segue.

Shoot. My mother surely wondered as well. But her maternal love let me keep the details of my penniless life to myself. Not Dad. Pragmatism had replaced the dubious decision-making days of his youth.

"I should have enough," I said airily. "I'll camp the whole time. Maui's easy to get around in." Granted, I had no idea what I was talking about.

Silence. I cringed, drawing circles on my cabin floor with my big toe.

"You know," Dad finally said, "someday your epitaph will read: 'An opportunity like this doesn't come around every day.'"

I winced. I had student loans to repay. My dad would have been happier if I was saving money instead of blowing it on birds. But to me, this was money's purpose. Plus, the lure of tomato-red 'i'iwis and 'apapanes was too strong. I knew my carefree college years were behind me and budgets and 401(k)s loomed ahead. But before the guillotine of responsibility lopped off my head, I had to spy out a few endemic honeycreepers.

"It's just ten days, Dad," I said. "It's not *that* irresponsible. Remember, there are far worse twenty-two-year-olds out there!"

● ● ● ●

At one point, there most certainly was a worse twenty-two-year-old. In his youth, Charles Darwin had a similar exchange with his own father, Robert. Robert, too, had been pragmatic. He wanted Charles to live responsibly, become a well-regarded clergyman, and honor the family name. But like me, Charles was obsessed with frivolous outdoor pursuits, which rankled his father. When Charles asked his dad to fund his five-year trip around the world on board *The Beagle*, Robert flatly refused. To him, it was a "wild scheme" and a "useless undertaking." "You care nothing but shooting, dogs, and rat-catching, and you will be a disgrace to yourself and all your family," Robert had warned him. The fact that *The Beagle* was named for a dog probably didn't help.

If not for his uncle, Josiah Wedgwood, Charles never would have set foot on a seaworthy vessel. Wedgwood mercifully interceded, arguing not that the trip needed Charles, but that Charles needed the trip. His nephew was restless, Josiah reminded Robert, a restlessness quelled only by a protracted journey and limit-pushing adventure. I hope Wedgwood added that opportunities like this didn't come around every day. Whatever he said worked. With an exasperated sigh, Robert finally conceded to underwrite his son's expenses.

• • • •

The Beagle, we know, ferried Charles around South America all the way to the Galápagos. I was headed to Maui. Although I wasn't intentionally emulating Darwin, the fact that the two archipelagos were quite similar wasn't lost on me. Both were formed from magma as a continental plate drifted over one of earth's mysterious hot spots.

Since both the Galápagos and the Hawaiian Islands emerged straight out of the sea like Surtsey, they each boasted unique flora and fauna that arrived via their own power and then evolved. Castaways arrived by wings, flippers, or clinging to debris. You know about Nene and giant tortoises. Fearless finches arrived too. In the Galápagos, one species radiated into fourteen. In Hawaii, one—the European rosefinch—exploded into fifty-four, today called honeycreepers.

Who didn't arrive to these archipelagos is equally noteworthy. Until people dropped the gangplank for goats, cows, rats, dogs, cats, Indian mongooses, sugar cane, and dozens of others, Hawaii lacked mosquitoes. Zero.

Before the mozzies arrived, the millennia were halcyon for honeycreepers. But their absence also meant they lacked immunity to another more sinister, soon-to-arrive stowaway, one that hitched a clandestine ride within a bevy of imported birds: malaria. Avian malaria invisibly stormed the Hawaiian beachheads, joining forces with habitat loss, mongooses, and cats to push many honeycreepers toward extinction. Their days, I had been warned, were numbered.

"All animals are equal," Orwell's pig Napoleon said, "but some animals are more equal than others." That's the honeycreepers. As I'd told my mother, honeycreepers are endemic, meaning they're restricted to where they evolved. Such singularity makes losing them that much more grievous, the biological equivalent of Stonehenge being cleared for a parking lot. The lobelia flowers the honeycreepers feed on are botanically singular, too. Like the birds, they've evolved in isolated conditions without competition. Evolving together, the lobelias and the honeycreepers grew interdependent. The honeycreepers depend on the lobelias for food while the lobelias depend on the honeycreepers for pollination. As one goes, so goes the other. *If* one goes, conservationists worry, so goes the other. This is what Soulé meant by his twelfth factor—the extinction or reduction of mutualist populations.

• • • •

My first few days in Maui went swimmingly. Literally, in fact. Without bilharzia to fear, I swam in translucent pools that shimmered under the spray of diaphanous waterfalls. Platter-sized sea turtles surfaced in front of me along the rocky, emerald coastline. Wild oranges and mangos picked along the roadside supplemented my steady oatmeal diet. Campgrounds were plentiful, people were friendly, and my wallet wasn't completely skeletal yet. But I'd stuck to the rich lowlands long enough. With my pack full and tattered Rand McNally in hand, I knew the time had come to ascend Maui's dormant volcano, Haleakalā.

I'd successfully hitchhiked to the volcano's main road up. The trouble was, nightfall was coming and traffic was sparse. Most cars were zipping past, pretending not to see me. Worse, there wasn't anywhere to camp, each side of the road flanked by large, opulent homes, half-hidden by decorative gates and fences. Haleakalā's rounded peak loomed navy blue in the distance, the night's first stars twinkling just behind it. If I didn't get picked up soon, I'd be forced to sleep on the roadside.

Twenty minutes later, my situation hadn't improved. Perhaps, I wondered, a gracious person would let me pitch my tent in their yard. To my left was a friendly-looking, apricot-colored house with a terracotta roof. The open driveway gate must be an omen, I thought. Stooping from the weight of my pack, I forced my feet up the driveway, marveling at how the paving stones snugly interlocked. The doorbell glowed orange, eyeing me ominously. I swallowed and pressed it. Seconds later, an auburn-haired lady with perfectly even bangs cracked the door open, not a soupçon of warmth in her wary eyes. Apprehension dripped off the small part of her face I could see.

"Hi," I said, conjuring the friendliest tone I could. "I'm, um, heading up the mountain but don't think I have enough daylight left to make it up. Would it be okay if I pitched my tent in your yard? The next campground is far up the mountain."

The lady's furrowed brow and unblinking stare conveyed the obvious: there was no way in Haleakalā that human flotsam like me was going to sleep in her yard. Her silence suggested she was thinking how best to tell me to buzz off.

"It's okay," I said, "I'll keep going." I turned to head back down the driveway. The door shut abruptly behind me.

Back on the road, the sky seemed darker. I envied people in their warm and comfortable houses, sitting down for a nice dinner. Forlorn, I kept walking, forcing myself to turn and face the intermittent cars. When one neared, I raised my thumb and smiled, hoping to move the passing motorist to compassion. But instead of slowing, it sped up, eager to leave the scruffy-looking axe murderer behind. My heart sank into my heavy, worn sneakers. Why had I come to Maui? Why hadn't I gone home to see my folks? Why did I care so much about a handful of honeycreepers?

• • • •

One hundred seventy years earlier, Darwin felt similarly as he journeyed on *The Beagle*. Seasickness plagued him mightily and he hadn't even been able to leave his bed for days at a time. All he had was a rocking boat, a churning stomach, and Charles Lyell's ponderous book about uniformitarianism and eternal pterodactyls. "Excepting when in the midst of tropical scenery," Darwin scrawled in his diary one homesick night in 1832, "my greatest share of pleasure is in anticipating a future time when I shall be able to look back on past events; & the consciousness that this prospect is so distant never fails to be painful."

Preach it, Charles. I understood that great adventures often involved suffering and loneliness. But the thought offered little solace. Having resigned myself to a miserable, all-night hike, I didn't bother turning around to face the headlights of a car zooming up behind me. Out of habit, I put my thumb out. Like all the others, it whizzed passed me.

But wait. Brake lights! Without hesitation, the driver performed a dangerous U-turn, blew past me again, did another U-turn, then pulled up alongside. It was an open-top, muddy Jeep Wrangler. A wild-haired kid about my age smiled. "Goin' up the mountain?" he asked, an unlit cigarette dangling from his mouth.

"Yes!" I practically shouted, ignoring the fact that this kid would have failed a driver's test twice in the span of ten seconds. I didn't care. Careening off a cliff seemed better than walking all night with bricks on my back.

"Jump in, man," he said, motioning to the seat next to him. "I work up there. Are you staying at Hosmer's Grove?"

"I'd love to," I said, disbelieving my good luck.

"Sweet. I'll drop you there. I'm Andy, by the way," he said, extending his knuckles for a fist bump.

Andy delivered me directly to Hosmer's Grove. Though I politely declined cigarettes and a few other controlled substances, I readily accepted three chewy granola bars, a half-empty bottle of water, and explicit directions on where to find honeycreepers.

The next morning, the Good Samaritan's directions proved unnecessary. Not more than a minute after stumbling bleary-eyed out of my tent, I saw my first 'i'iwi. The gorgeous bird bounced about the limbs of a lobelia, probing its pale, sickle-shaped bill deep into filigree red blossoms. Starstruck, I sat down on a rock and stared, drinking in this holy grail of honeycreepers.

Morning chill sent a shiver down my spine. It was cold up here. Which also explained why Haleakalā Volcano had proven a final redoubt for the honeycreepers. Malaria-carrying mosquitos were sparse this high up, safeguarding the birds. The 'i'iwi flitted nonchalantly about, oblivious to its imminent, forecasted doom. The bird's decurved bill, I noticed, was ideal. Perfectly sculpted for deep plunges into each flower's corolla, the cant of the bill mirroring each blossom's unique angle. Until that point in my life, it was the niftiest bill I'd ever seen.

• • • •

Nifty bills are a marvelous way to illustrate what Soulé meant by extinction or reduction of mutualist populations. Instead of using the ʻiʻiwi, however, I want to detour to the Andes Mountains of Ecuador, where, with a dozen college students in tow, I recently spied an even niftier bill. The bill didn't belong to an outsized raptor or a multicolored toucan; its owner, rather, was a hummingbird. While other hummers sport more iridescence and feathery frippery, none match the swordbill's bill. Not even close. At eleven centimeters, with an eleven-centimeter tongue to match, it's longer than the length of the bird's entire body. Far too long to preen with. While most birds scratch and primp with the bills, the swordbill is relegated to using its measly, nearly invisible feet. When perched, the swordbill holds its head at a forty-five-degree angle out of necessity, not haughtiness. It is the longest bill, relative to body size, of any bird alive.

While the swordbill's bill length seems as unnecessary as a monster truck in suburbia, evolution is never extravagant just for the heck of it. There's a method to the madness. Just like Hawaii's lobelias that are best accessed with the decurved bill of the honeycreeper, the Andes harbor a plant with nectar best slurped through a serious straw: passionflowers.

Passionflowers have trombone-shaped corollas, an inner whorl of floral leaves that vary from six to fourteen centimeters long. These act like an annoying measuring stick at a theme park. If you're not this tall—or this long, in the hummingbird's case—forget it. Go try the kiddie section. In the case of the passionflower, the world's 344 other hummingbirds all drew the short straw; its nectar is tantalizingly out of reach. As a result, swordbills enjoy quiet, uninterrupted dining, the most obvious advantage of this arrangement. No time is wasted chasing other species away, or being chased.

And for the flower? Dependable pollen delivery. A sip of nectar is ecologically tantamount to tipping the pizza delivery guy. Extending the analogy, not all pizza is delivered quickly and hot. Some drivers are irresponsible or can't find your house. Late, misdelivered, or nonexistent delivery happens all too often in the promiscuous world of plant sex. This forces flowers to produce more pollen and nectar than necessary just to ensure a smidgeon actually arrives to another plant for fertilization. The passionflower's elongated corolla safeguards against this. Of many willing suiters, it chose the swordbill. The two wed, coevolved, and are locked in a codependent marriage 2.4 million years strong.

'I'iwis and lobelias, swordbills and passionflowers—cross-species, coevolutionary pairings abound in nature. They dance in synchronous beauty, each species benefiting from the other's devotion. Such relationships are symbiotic, or what Soulé would call a mutualism. There is a key difference, however. In symbiosis, each organism's life wholly depends upon the other. Mutualisms lack such urgency; they're just friends with benefits. Termites and microscopic animals called protozoa are symbiotic. Termites can't digest wood without protozoa (they lack the necessary enzymes). Protozoa need a place to live. So the two have worked out an arrangement where the termites let the microscopic critters hang out in their guts in exchange for free digestion. Termites would die without protozoa and protozoa would die without termites. Which came first? I'm too chicken to guess. Hit up some other egghead.

In a mutualism, an animal may suffer without its partner, but it won't necessarily die. Examples are legion: cattle egret and Cape buffalo, two-toed sloths and moths, greater honeyguides and honey badgers, warthogs and mongoose. All these pairings benefit one from the other. It's not hakuna matata, but it's close.

Soulé wasn't interested in the perks of mutualisms. He was worried about how they affect extinction. The relationship is a gamble. Each species has bet on the faithfulness—and longevity—of the other. But if a catastrophe happens, like the chance arrival of a malaria-carrying mosquito, it's not just one species whose survival is at risk—they both are. When Hawaiian lobelias bet on honeycreepers, they didn't factor in a bunch of beached canoes on Hawaii's shoreline, filled with invasive species and mosquito-infested bilge water.

But as you may have learned via high school dating, too much codependence can spell disaster. Sure enough, a smattering of other plants similar to the swordbill's passionflower went extinct when their sole pollinators, for lots of the reasons we've already hashed out, disappeared. Fortunately, species can sometimes wiggle out of codependent relationships. Susanne Renner, of Ludwig Maximilian University, led a study that sequenced DNA from forty-three different passionflower species. When swordbill numbers dropped between two and four million years ago, some passionflower species abandoned their long corollas. More precisely, natural selection favored shorter corollas in several species. No longer were the eggs all in one basket; they'd been divvied up. Renner's work brilliantly showed adaptation, how coevolution isn't always a one-way ticket.

• • • •

Darwin's trip aboard *The Beagle* wasn't a one-way ticket either. His eventual return to English sod allowed him to make many predictions, some altering the course of biology. A lesser-known one he made in 1862 is my favorite in the long history of science. Probably because it reminds me of the ʻiʻiwi and the wondrously improbable sword-billed hummingbird. Also, because he made it during a turbulent time in his life that involved a simple, yet revelatory, gift of flowers.

Long after Darwin returned from his five-year odyssey, he hit a rough patch. *On the Origin of Species* was drawing a backlash, his health was poor, and he was mourning the loss of his favorite daughter, Anne. Amid this, his friend James Bateman stopped by. Since Bateman came from Kew Gardens, perhaps it wasn't surprising he brought flowers. But the flowers themselves *were* surprising: Malagasy orchids. The orchids, *Angraecum sesquipedale*, were well named. *Sesquipedale* means "one-foot-and-a-half," appropriate for the pale-petaled orchid's tremendously long spur, which held nectar at the bottom.

Flowers in hand, Darwin immediately put his myriad barnacle, worm, and pigeon experiments aside. Lightweights like me might have admired them on a windowsill. Not Darwin. For him, the orchids were exciting lab subjects, much more than mere condolence. He poked, prodded, and sketched the plants, scratching his temples. Three years later he pumped out *On the Various Contrivances by Which British and Foreign Orchids Are Fertilized by Insects.* Regardless of Darwin's scientific chops, this title didn't leap off the shelves. Other than a few unruly-haired, pocket-protector types, nobody noticed. Those that did referred to it by a shorter, more manageable name: *Fertilization of Orchids.*

Notwithstanding the book's lukewarm reception, it was an important contribution to biology. It took *The Origin of Species* further, as Darwin plunged into the real power of natural selection. The ideas blazed a new trail, leading to a brave new world of coevolution, whereupon natural selection acts upon two separate species relative to one another. Plus, it lent sorely needed scaffolding for a bunch of fuzzy ideas, sorely needed by botanically minded boffins. Coevolution, the scientific world realized, was like Oz, hidden behind a curtain, orchestrating symbioses, mutualisms, and all manner of interspecies affairs. Other terms—commensalism, parasitism, and hyperparasitism—soon arrived in the furrow that *Fertilization of Orchids* plowed.

While the scientific community was slow, the importance of Bateman's orchids was immediately obvious to Darwin. Excitedly, he dashed off a letter to his friend Joseph Hooker. "I have just received such a Box full from Mr. Bateman with the astounding *Angraecum sesquipedale* with a nectary a foot long," he wrote, before continuing, "Good Heavens what insect can suck it?" The nectary Darwin referred to was the flower's long corolla.

That's the context—now the cool part. You already know about the swordbill and passionflower song and dance. Well, the longest corolla recorded to date was fourteen centimeters. The Malagasy orchids Darwin received from Bateman were more than twice that long—thirty centimeters. That simple measurement was all Darwin needed. His mind, full of coevolutionary ideas, filled in the rest.

Darwin never went to Madagascar. Nor had he ever seen an insect capable of reaching thirty centimeters into a pollen tube. Yet he knew such an insect must exist, for no other reason than natural selection required it. "In Madagascar there must be moths with probosces capable of extension to a length of between ten and eleven inches," he boldly predicted in *Fertilisation of Orchids*.

It was gutsy. And not only because Darwin flouted the metric system. Wolves were circling his house in Downe. Critics and naysayers were salivating for a chance to undermine his reputation. A prediction like this offered the perfect opportunity to dismantle evolution's scaffolding. All they had to do was prove no such insect existed.

Darwin knew he'd gambled big. Just like he'd predicted the eventual discovery of transitional species—intermediates—in *The Origin of Species*, now he predicted the existence of a Malagasy moth with a mega-long proboscis. His gambles were contingent, bets hedged against the prospect of discovery. For his critics to disprove him, they had to search. If their search turned up nothing, Darwin could always argue they hadn't searched hard enough.

So maybe not so gutsy. Darwin's gambles lacked an expiration date. Turns out they didn't need one.

Exactly twenty-one years after his death, the moth Darwin predicted was found, precisely where he said it would be, deep in the Malagasy forest. *Xanthopan morganii* was a sphinx moth, a subspecies of one discovered much earlier in Congo, one it's unclear Darwin had been aware of. The Malagasy moth was milky white, darting about with a supersized proboscis, a straw-like appendage rolled up on its snout like a party kazoo.

Despite the smoking gun, corks remained on the champagne. Science is rigorous. It demands behavioral evidence, not existential plausibility. Nobody had actually witnessed the moth feed.

Regardless, the moth became known as Darwin's sphinx moth, its Latin epithet, *Xanthopan morganii praedicta*, meaning "the predicted one." The name finally justified itself, nearly 130 years later. In 1992, determined videographers ventured into Madagascar's remnant forest scraps and set up their equipment alongside *Angraecum sesquipedale* orchids. They sat back and waited. Sure enough, the moth eventually appeared, unfurled a ridiculously long pixie stick, and sank it deep within the long corolla. Darwin's prediction, at long last, had been documented.

I rewatched the dramatic footage, available on YouTube, just the other day. Neither intense nor sublime, the condensed version I saw showed a single, unassuming, star-shaped plant. The ghostly moth soon materialized out of the forest's gloom and hesitantly approached. It hovered, sipped, then fluttered off. That's it, a simple fast-food drive-thru. Simultaneously ethereal and pedestrian. Just another mutualistic encounter among the billions endlessly ongoing around us.

• • • •

Soulé's extinction or reduction of mutualistic populations isn't as esoteric as it sounds. People have long understood it in starkly different contexts. The most obvious example is bison and the people who depended on them.

Bison provided Plains Indians everything: Skin for tipis, clothing, bedding, moccasins, quivers, and knife sheaths. Bones for knives, needles, awls, and hoes. Horns for cups and rattles. Sinews for bowstrings. Bladders for containers. Fat for soap. Tails for fly swats. Dung for fires. And nearly everything else—meat, marrow, liver, brain, intestines, even nose gristle—for eating. "We told them the country of the buffalo was the country of the Lakota," Red Cloud said in his last address to the Oglala people, in 1903. "We told them that the buffalo must have their country and the Lakota must have the buffalo." Many decades later, John Lame Deer concurred: "It's hard to say where the animals ended and the human began."

The continent-wide bison slaughter in the late 1800s wasn't just for meat and hides. Nor was it merely to clear the land for cattle. Native American settlements inconveniently blocked the path of western expansion. "I would not seriously regret the total disappearance of the buffalo from our western prairies," said our eleventh secretary of the interior, Columbus Delano, adding, "in its effect upon the Indians, regarding it as a means of hastening their sense of dependence upon the products of the soil." Even though Delano had fought for African

American civil rights and helped establish Yellowstone National Park, a desire for genocide remained. "The civilization of the Indian is impossible," Delano concluded, "while the buffalo remains on the plains."

Sadly, his sentiment was by no means unique. General Philip S. Sheridan heartily agreed. "If I could learn that every buffalo in the northern herd were killed I would be glad," Sheridan said. "The destruction of the herd would do more to keep the Indians quiet than anything else that could happen."

Since we're discussing extinction rather than ethnocentrism, we'll leave the upsetting ethos of the nineteenth century alone. The point is that people have long understood the importance of the creatures they—and others—depend on. Remove the bison and the Native American goes with it. The result is a socioecological trophic cascade. Or, in plainer language, a sad domino effect.

But there's a bright side, too. For one thing, not all predictions bear out. Hawaii's honeycreepers, I'm happy to report, continue to sip from lobelias. Plus, as Darwin showed, clear understanding allows prediction. Will our greater understanding and growing concern for the world's creatures help us prevent their extinction? My ten-day trip to find the honeycreepers for $649 proved that anything's possible. As did the discovery of Darwin's sphinx moth. So even though I dislike predictions, I predict it will.

13
THE CARDINAL RULE
Competition

"Victory breeds hatred, for the conquered is unhappy. He who has given up both victory and defeat, he, the contented, is happy."
—The Dhammapada

A womb of sorts. A foldable chair nestled against the wide base of an old, gnarled red oak. Warm air trapped between four layers of flannels and fleece warding off the late October chill. A rabbit-fur hat pulled low. Compound bow across my lap, chin melting into my chest. Early dawn darkness. Stillness. Far off, an evaporating tremolo of a screech owl. Cozy, quiet, perfect … for falling asleep.

Minutes? An hour? Whenever I did awaken, a large-antlered buck stood before me, a school-bus length away. His heavily muscled fore-quarters glistened, anchoring a stout neck, alert face, and gracefully curving antlers touched off with gleaming white tines. His large, liquid, inky-black eyes studied me, awaiting the merest flinch. Was I a harmless growth affixed to the oak? Or a sinister ambush? He stomped, confirming his growing suspicion. I was helpless, incarcerated by the buck's keen perception. Standing, or drawing a bow, was impossible.

I'd blown it again. Each fall presented one big buck opportunity. Three years previous, I'd shot at an oblivious six-pointer. But the poorly nocked arrow fell off my bow, landing just beyond my boot tips. With a smirk, that buck dashed off. The next year, another buck. That time, a sapling branch spoiled my arrow's trajectory, sending it skittering into the leaf litter. Last season, I finally hit one. The buck ran off and I waited for it to drop. It didn't. After a thirty-minute wait, I recovered my arrow and examined it. Blood revealed a nonfatal shot, two inches behind the vitals. Two days of steadfast, earnest searching with an expert-tracker friend turned up empty.

And now this. Asleep at the switch. Inexcusable.

A doe emerged at the opposite field edge, one hundred yards away. The buck swung his massive head and stared at her, his radar-dish ears remaining locked on me. I knew this trick. Even the faintest rustling of my jacket would send him bounding. I held fast.

Luck! A second doe emerged, following the first. Hormonal urges overrode caution. The buck's ears swiveled toward them. Any second, he'd pursue, the urge to procreate dictating his steps.

Now or never.

Heart pounding, I eased off my chair, raised my bow, and drew. Adrenaline coursed through me, making my arms shake. For stability, I eased one foot forward.

My boot snapped a twig.

The buck jerked back to face me, muscles tensing.

Focus. Focus. I squinted through the mist, lining my peep sight up just behind his glistening shoulder. One ... two ... *SNORT!*

The deer's explosive alarm sent a shockwave through my tense body. My arm flew upward and my arrow released, launching skyward, into the stratosphere. The magnificent buck remained rooted, bewildered. He stared at me, still unsure what I was.

But I knew. I was an arrowless, witless, deerless idiot.

"Trying," Homer Simpson wisely told Bart, "is the first step toward failure." Why hadn't *my* father offered me the same sage advice when I'd started hunting? Somehow, all my neighbors harvested big bucks as easily as they downed six-packs. Even the pimply high schoolers who'd barely gotten their driver's licenses managed to. Was this just a profound string of bad luck? Was I innately terrible? Or, was my ancestral line the problem?

My dad liked nature. But he liked books more. He spent his career teaching English. Mornings before school, we constructed five- and six-letter words out of "Raisin Bran" and "Grape Nuts." Rather than teaching me how to read buck scrapes, he taught me "sit on a potato pan, Otis" and other palindromes. To cement my fecklessness, he passed along his father's ancient gun, an artifact better suited for a museum than my unsteady hands. Without hunting coming through my DNA, I've had to learn through trial and error. My mentor, YouTube, hasn't helped much. Lots of trials and lots of errors.

"If a thing is worth doing," G. K. Chesterton once wrote, "then it's worth doing poorly." Right or wrong, I've run with Chesterton's sentiment. Hunting is worth doing, even poorly, I've realized, for everything *else* it offers. It's quiet out there. No infernal copier machines, honking cars, or sitcom blather. The tranquility is accentuated by babbling brooks, wind whistling through the treetops, and the occasional soul-stirring staccato honking of a passing skein of geese.

It's beautiful, too. Snow-covered forests stop the heart at dawn: Sunbeams stab through the boughs, turning aspen leaves lambent and making dewdrops sparkle like sapphires. Diffident grouse descend from hidden roosts like fat little friars. Squirrels start their querulous games of freeze tag. Crisply marked chickadees perch upon hats and peer into gun barrels. Even the forsaken gully behind my house, strewn with radiators and bed springs, becomes Rivendell at daybreak. Back against a tree, my thoughts wander and cross back upon themselves. When they've traveled enough, they sit contentedly, like a fox in the snow. I hunt, I've found, for peace and beauty.

• • • •

I also hunt for deer. I love to match my wits with theirs. They smell, hear, and see better than me, but perhaps I can outsmart and outwait them. I'm competitive. "They're men," quips a top birder's wife in *The Big Year*. "If they stop competing, they die." While there's truth in this, competitiveness isn't contingent upon the presence of a Y chromosome. Females compete too. Nor is it unique to people. The rest of the world's biota compete just as intensely as we do. Competition rules them, in fact. While people often relegate competition to games, in nature, it results in death. But it creates beauty, too. Mind-blowing, forest-at-dawn beauty.

How does competition manage this seeming paradox? For one thing, competitiveness and aggression aren't synonyms. They're related but extricable. To understand how competition—Soulé's thirteenth factor—can drive extinction, it's helpful to tease them apart. Let's start with how competition creates beauty first, before we get to its nasty side.

• • • •

A moment ago, a male and female cardinal clung to opposite sides of my feeder. Their beautiful, yin-yang symmetry demanded my attention. The male, Tim McGraw of the bird world, set off his ketchup-colored body with a Zorro eye mask and a jaunty crest of head plumes. The female was more muted, like hummus. We'll call her "Faith," because we're talking about relationships here.

For the past two weeks—early April—Tim has sung his little syrinx out, a song that birders mnemonically remember as *purty, purty, purty,* preceded by a few down-slurred whistles. More jarringly, Tim has also repeatedly rammed his head into our front window pane. Although he appears dumbstruck, he's really lovestruck, convinced his reflection is an amorous interloper. Hormones in overdrive, he's bound and determined to claim our yard, and Faith, as his own. For now, he's fine with the robins on the lawn and voracious wrens scuttling about. To a limited degree, he competes with them, what biologists call interspecific competition. But right now, with flirtatious femmes fatales flitting about, other male cardinals are literally driving him witless.

Within-species contests—intraspecific competition—lead to unparalleled spectacles in the natural world. It's the stuff of nature documentaries: sparring lions, head-butting bighorns, grappling polar bears, and the large-antlered deer I always miss. It drives the other-worldly beauty around us, too. Rainbow-colored lorikeets, splendid fairywrens, and my favorite, the King of Saxony bird-of-paradise, a snowy-white bird with psychedelic plumes that trail behind it like handlebar streamers when it flies.

Competition accomplishes this through a force called sexual selection, which consumed Darwin once he finally pushed his Malagasy orchids aside. "The sight of a feather in a peacock's tail, whenever I gaze at it, makes me sick!" he wrote to a friend. Not sick like awesome. Sick like, get me a bucket, fast! Growing public vitriol from *The Origin of Species* was surely a source of Darwin's nausea. How the peacock's tail had become so fantastical was another.

If we ever stop to study them, peacock tails should make all of us sick (peacocks are peafowl. Peahens, the females, are too). The male's tail is an eyeful, blue-green iridescence set off by over a hundred eyespots, called ocelli. What sets a peahen's heart aflutter is the angle of the dangle, the way the ocelli reflect light. Peafowl plumage color is structurally based, not pigment-based. Optical interference Bragg reflections relating to the nanostructures of the barbules to reflect light.

Catch that? Me neither. The point is, peacocks win peahens by the way they wield their tail, or train. If the male rattles his tail seductively, and the season and sun are right, females swoon. Sultry vocalizations, desirable turf, and Andrea Bocelli singing in the background help. This suite of behaviors, known as redundant signaling, increases the odds the male will outcompete others and pass his genes on. Poor performers don't mate.

But as usual, there's a catch. Extravagant plumage and long, heavy trains weigh down peacocks like X-ray blankets, making them more vulnerable to predation. If too heavy, they're unable to skirt a leopard or an Indian civet's claws, and succumb, their DNA slipping down a predator's digestive tract. The weaker die off, the best live, the pulsing heart of natural selection; Darwin swiped Herbert Spencer's handy phrase "survival of the fittest" to explain it. Survival of the fittest explained predator avoidance but lacked a handy term for the peacock's crazy tail—for why male cardinals captivate and why countless species shimmer, shine, sashay, and sing.

To explain the puzzle, Darwin bent over his desk and cranked out an 898-page corker entitled *The Descent of Man and Selection in Relation to Sex*. The reason birds were beautiful, he argued, is because females made them that way. High-strung males, desperate to impress, competed in any way they knew how. Over millennia, via sexual selection, they were physically and behaviorally shaped by it.

As with Darwin's orchid book, reaction was tepid. Blatant references to sex were taboo, especially his assertion that sex drove the world. Moreover, females did the choosing? For Victorian tastes, this was too much female agency. By the dawn of the twenty-first century, however, Darwin's wild idea had been confirmed. Like it or not, sexual selection was a world-shaping force.

For better or worse, Darwin knew the biological world was sexually charged and that intraspecific competition lay at its heart. Other competitors we know too well, of a capitalistic bent, have long known it, too. The multibillion-dollar-a-year makeup industry is a case in point. As are the endless diet plans, hair loss products, cosmetic surgery labs, tanning salons, fitness gyms, and fashion companies. If you need a refresher, tune in to *The Bachelor*. But the success of *The Bachelorette* reminds us that in human societies, the waters are muddied—it's less clear who's choosing whom.

• • • •

Who's choosing whom is clear with the cardinal pair clinging to my feeder and—for now at least—to each other. Faith holds the cards. Tim will do anything for her attention. He has devoted his life to it, in fact. Instead of a long, heavy train with a hundred ocelli, Tim sports the red of a firetruck, which is great in breeding season but makes him stick out like a sore thumb on a monotone, midwinter afternoon. His crimson not only catches Faith's eye, but also the sharp eyes of the neighborhood raptors. Somehow, Tim must evade these well-honed, songbird-killing machines. His plumage mustn't betray him.

All winter long, Tim stands out like a British redcoat but behaves like a wary militiaman. Instinct instructs him to hold still in dense raspberry tangles and lie low. Grab a seed here, a withered berry there. A week turns into months. Rumors of his death are greatly exaggerated. With resourcefulness, luck, and my birdfeeder, he survives the bleak midwinter. Come spring—right now—his time-tested genes make Faith's heart palpitate. His sheer existence means he's a survivor, DNA worthy of her investment. In this seasonal evolutionary dance, a positive feedback loop has triggered Tim's brilliant color and outlandish behavior. But she will only mate with him if his territory, where the green grass grows, is rich, too. Knowing this, Tim sings incessantly—*purty, purty, purty*—loosely translating: Keep off! Get lost! Scram!

• • • •

Which brings us to the nasty side of competition. And though I hunt for peace and beauty, I've found nastiness, too. It comes via a concept called the competitive exclusion principle, which I'll illustrate with—what else—a hunting story.

With just three acres of my own, I hunted for years on a friend's land a few miles down the road. It was a great arrangement. I watched over the property in exchange for the privilege to hunt. Last year, while getting out of my truck early one morning, a truck I didn't recognize pulled up alongside me. The driver's window went down to reveal a heavyset man with bushy eyebrows. "Better enjoy it," he said smarmily. "I've leased this property out for next year."

"Really?" I asked, confused.

"Yeah, the owner said he wasn't using it so he leased it to me." Ugh. It was true. While I'd gotten permission years earlier, my friend probably assumed I'd quit. My heart sank.

"Good for you," I replied, giving him an exaggerated thumbs-up. My sarcasm was noted. Bushy-Eyebrows Man rolled up his window and roared off, a victor's smile surely stretched across his face.

I'd just been excluded, a victim of ecology's fundamental competitive exclusion principle. It's an ironclad rule stating that two species with similar niches cannot exist sympatrically, meaning, in the same environment. One will always outcompete the other. If the outcompeted species can't emigrate, it goes extinct. I had been outcompeted. Since I hoped to avoid extinction myself, emigration was my only option. I would have to hunt someplace else.

• • • •

But wait. Doesn't the rule state that species will always be outcompeted by other species? Cardinals aren't the only birds at the feeder. There are lots of different species. Chickadees, nuthatches, sparrows, titmice, blue jays. All of them are eating seeds in the same environment. Doesn't the competitive exclusion principle contradict this? Shouldn't there only be one species eating seeds? Shouldn't the others have been driven to extinction? Why, pray tell, are there so many birds eating the same stuff?

Pat yourself on the back if you remember the math whiz Robert MacArthur, one of the two founders of island biogeography theory. MacArthur pondered this very question, hence his reemergence here. Not content to sit back and pontificate, data-hungry MacArthur took his question to the north woods of Maine. While his discovery was great, his method was commonplace: he birdwatched. He just sat under some spruce trees with a notebook and watched who did what. Five warblers showed up. Right away he noted that they all fed on the same thing—insects. The magic, he found, was that they all did it differently.

MacArthur's analysis revealed a fascinating insight: the warblers formed a guild, a "loose agreement" to divvy up the resource pie. Tree crowns and the outside edges were claimed by the Cape May warbler. The Blackburnian warbler also remained high but foraged slightly lower than the Cape May. Black-throated green warblers overlapped with Blackburnians but stayed nearer the trunk. Bay-breasted warblers foraged lower still, sticking to the canopy interior. Yellow-rumped warblers claimed everything else, extending all the way down to the forest floor. If your eyes glazed over, the point is: guilds promote coexistence. It's called resource partitioning and explains how species coexist without emigrating or going extinct. Also, it's always more complex than we think.

Lest competition ruffle our feathers too much, let's switch to fur. Natural selection can drive size changes to help species divvy up the pie, too. In nature, it's not always go big or go home. Going small can help just as much. In the North American canine lineage, sympatry forbade two large, similar canids from coexisting. Wolves went big. Only large animals—moose, elk, deer—could satiate their larger caloric demands. That left smaller prey, like rodents and rabbits, for another canid, coyotes. Coyotes took note and adapted with aplomb, their smaller size allowing a scrappy life along the edges of wolf packs. They were better suited for living alongside a two-legged predator, too—us. Smallness meant they didn't have to eat as much, and they could melt away more quickly. Better for raiding dumpsters, nabbing roadkill, and grabbing the occasional sweater-wearing lap dog.

Species have gotten smaller or bigger, and sliced the pie for millions of years. All well and good. Zoomed out, competition has actually allowed species to proliferate and ramify following the five major mass extinctions. It has allowed adaptive radiation, accounting for Darwin's Galápagos finches, Andean hummingbirds, and the Hawaiian honeycreepers. So, if competition creates biodiversity, why would our North Star, Soulé, include it among his extinction factors?

Mostly because of the human-caused catastrophes that have made competition even nastier than usual. Rampant development and resource extraction have made a side salad of ecosystems, tossing species about like croutons. We've mentioned many: water hyacinth, Russian boar, Indian mongooses, European starlings, goats, cats, rats and malaria-carrying mosquitos. While the natives are used to competing, they're not always ready for new foes, like a featherweight boxer forced into a heavier weight class overnight.

· · · ·

At the root of the competitive exclusion principle, resource partitioning, and sympatry is the niche. It's one of my favorite ecological words, partly because nobody knows how to pronounce it. Since I'm no exception, I lean into the awkwardness in my college classrooms, jutting out my chin like a French aristocrat. "Neesh," I proclaim, rarely having to wait long for eye rolling. I also like how easy it is to understand, referring to a plant or animal's position and role within an ecosystem. Wolves, for example, are top-level predators. By preying on the old and the sick in an elk herd, their presence weeds out inferior genes. By killing, they create food for a host of other species, such as bear, fox, eagles, wolverines, crows, and magpies. I can't resist applying the concept to my students, too. "What is *your* niche?" I ask them as they hoist their backpacks on and file out. Some are trying to figure out that very question. Others are only thinking about lunch.

The idea of the niche is important because if a species goes extinct, its ecological niche becomes vacant. Vacancies can cause domino effects—trophic cascades—that ripple through the ecosystem, tantamount to a factory closing in a small town. Without jobs, people leave. The school soon closes, then the bank, followed by the bingo hall, diner, and lastly, the gas station. Each closing causes another and another. Like a game of Jenga, it's hard to predict which pulled out piece will bring the whole system crashing down.

This is the dark side of competition, begging a larger, more philosophical question: What is humanity's niche on the earth? Few have recognized the downside of competition as cogently as writer-farmer-philosopher Wendell Berry. "There is no denying that competitiveness is a part of the life both of an individual and of a community," Berry writes, "or that, within limits, it is a useful and necessary part." That little clause, *within limits*, is his central concern. In essay after essay, Berry rails against our inability to limit ourselves, spurred on by the unregulated competition of capitalism. "The danger of the ideal of competition," he writes in *Home Economics*, "is that it neither proposes nor implies any limits. A community cannot survive under the rule of competition."

It's not a digression. Berry's social commentary addresses extinction, too. Endangered species and capitalism are as interwoven as an oriole nest. I'll let our latter-day prophet speak for himself: "It [the ideal of competition] proposes simply to lower costs at any cost, and to raise profits at any cost. It does not hesitate at the destruction of a family or the life of a community. It pits neighbor against neighbor as readily as it pits buyer against seller. Every transaction is meant to involve a winner and a loser. And for this reason the human economy is pitted without limit against nature. For in the unlimited competition of neighbor and neighbor, buyer and seller, all available means must be used; none may be spared."

This is big picture, Voldemortian competition, humanity's ongoing duel with all the world's creatures. Since it's the ultimate cause of the sixth extinction, we have to address it. Unlimited competition, now governing most of the world's nooks and crannies, is ruthless to the least adaptable. They won't make it. Since we're born into the system, our entanglement isn't surprising. But our complicity is. Paying lip service to the endangerment capitalism causes is rearranging deck chairs on the *Titanic*.

• • • •

It's a monstrous problem. I don't know how to answer it either. If there *are* answers to be found, outside seems like the best place to look. It's partly why I grab my bow and keep heading out on dark, chilly, October mornings. Returning home emptyhanded isn't a bad thing. Nor is it bad to be pushed off the choicest places. Good places are limited. Everything's limited. Not everybody can win. Perhaps it's even okay to get outsmarted by deer and sail arrows over a big buck's back. Hunting is humbling. A temporary sting of losing assuaged by a long-term gift of humility. Every trip reminds me to savor what I have. To appreciate—peace, quiet, tranquility—all those things that are free. Most importantly, hunting has taught me that for every winner that competition fosters, there's a smarting loser, too.

"Insanity," as the saying goes, "is doing the same thing over and over again and expecting different results." So this past November I tried something new. Instead of cramming myself in with others on public land, I called a generous farmer friend to ask if I could hunt on his vast acreage. "Absolutely," he said benevolently, "as long as I get to hear about the nice deer you get!"

A week later, midway through deer season, I pulled into my farmer friend's unmarked road. Giddiness warded off the early morning chill. Maybe today was my lucky day. A free morning and over a hundred acres stretched out before me. Finally, I was lord of the manor. Full permission and zero competition. I put on my gloves and rummaged through the trunk for my folding chair. I'd place it at the base of an old gnarled oak and watch the world awaken. And when a big buck strolled by, I'd be ready.

Headlights. A car pulled off the main road and eased over the potholes just behind mine. Not a souped-up, testosterone truck that threatened to squish me, but rather a rusty, low-slung sedan, sporting a partially dented roof with rust around the fender. A car with nowhere to tie a deer carcass, unless bungeed to the top. Certainly not the emblematic vehicle of the typical hunting fraternity.

Let me guess—this land was leased, too, and the farmer had forgotten to tell me. Here we go again. Nothing like an altercation to start an otherwise perfect day. Today, however, I wouldn't surrender with sarcasm. If this hunter wanted a fight, I'd give him one. My hands balled into fists. I spoke before the window finished rolling down.

"I've got permission to hunt here!" I blurted. "The owner is a friend of mine."

Silence. This guy wasn't expecting a verbal fusillade. At least not before six a.m.

A hand shot out the window. Not a middle finger. Nor a fist. A peace offering—a handshake. "Good morning!" a voice said warmly. Several other voices offered greetings, too.

I took off a glove and shook the hand. The shake was solid, sincere. I crouched, peering into the car's unlit interior. Even in the darkness, it was clear that every seat was occupied. Smiles were ear to ear across four faces, all looking like human marshmallows in puffy camo coats.

Now I understood why the sedan was scraping bottom. "You teach at Houghton?" the driver asked.

"Uh, yeah," I said, my feistiness deflating.

"We've met once out here," he said. "A couple years back."

I studied him. Sure enough, while I couldn't pull out a name, his face rang a bell.

"Bob," he said, reading my mind. "And you are?"

"Eli," I said. "And I'm really sorry. I didn't know…"

He waved it off. "Wanna hunt with us?" he interrupted. "We're gonna try to drive 'em on foot and we'd love to have another good hunter!"

I was speechless. Bob's neighborliness disarmed me, turning the competitive exclusion principle I'd grown so accustomed to upside down. My words stumbled out. "Thanks, but I, uh, have a place already picked out on the far side of the hill."

Bob looked at me earnestly. It was obvious that his hunting life had evolved completely differently, built upon cooperation, inclusion, and community. A vital community, one Wendell Berry would say "draws its life, so far as possible, from local sources" and solves its problems "by nonmonetary exchanges for help, not by buying things." Trust undergirded Bob's hunting community, a community I wasn't ready for.

"You sure?" Bob asked.

"Yes," I said, nodding. I was sure. I wasn't ready because, well, I wasn't a good hunter. I missed deer more than I hit them. I fell asleep too often. I wasn't ready to put my incompetence on display.

"Yeah. Thanks, though. I'll take you guys up on it sometime!"

"Sure hope so," Bob said. "It'd be great fun."

From one brief interaction, it is clear Bob won't ever strongarm me to hunt with him and his friends. He's not that type; I'm the one who has to be willing. The buck, as they say, stops with me. And perhaps if I say yes next time, it won't bound away.

14
THE LUNATIC EXPRESS
Predation

"I find solace, inspiration, and exhilaration in nature. Issues there are boiled down to the simplest imperative: survive."
—J. Drew Lanham

Bear spray has always intrigued me. Probably because it comes in a cylindrical canister, has serious warning labels, and you use it when you go hiking. In other words, it's just like bug spray, or "insect repellent," for haughtier types. Although one can rip your leg off while the other can bite unnoticed, both enemies are theoretically warded off by a simple spray. When you're hiking in wild country in the summer months, you need both sprays. Forget either one, I've been told, and you're hosed. But you can remember both, I'd like to add, and also be hosed. Hence my intrigue.

Not long after hitchhiking through Hawaii and pitching my junior dome in a convenient dumpster, I loaded up my pickup with a new tent, sleeping bag, backpack, water filter, Pop-Tarts, and three cylindrical canisters: bear spray, bug spray, and Quaker Oats. These items had helped me fearlessly savor many iconic western landscapes.

Glacier National Park was the latest icon in my sights. Little green tents in my trusty Rand McNally guided me like navigational beacons. They marked cost-effective campgrounds with coin-operated showers and kindly hosts who trundled around the loops in golf carts. Little did I know it, I had plunged into nomadism. A time rich in experience and short on income. While traveling down lonely highways and through even lonelier backcountry, existential questions consumed me. Should I get married? Go to grad school? Buy a chocolate lab and move to Alaska? All three?

Smaller questions squeezed between them. How were the trail conditions? What was the weather forecast? Did I need to pack a tent? Small questions, but consequential. Maybe not life or death, but close to it. Where could I get answers? Perhaps an equation?

• • • ○

Life and death equations, it turns out, do exist—Lotka–Volterra equations. They're nonlinear differential equations with a wisp of Italian flair. While the instantaneous growth rates and bevy of constants are simple for some, they're too obtuse for a mathematical dunce like me. But when they undergo linearization, even I can see the beauty of the graphs they produce: simple harmonic motion, or a series of gentle rolling hills, one imposed on the other. Predators and prey waltzing together under snow-laden boughs.

The equations are algorithmic models, showing how predator and prey populations follow a predictable rise and fall. The hunted fall first, causing a brief rise in the hunters. But soon after, buffet tables laid bare, the hunter population falls again. Fewer predators means a rebound in prey, and so on. Up and down, up and down, like a roller coaster in a theme park's kiddie section.

The curves are the result of a savvy guy named Charles Gordon Hewitt. In *The Conservation of the Wild Life of Canada*, presciently published in 1921, Hewitt graphed nearly a century's worth of fur-trapper data he finagled from the Hudson's Bay Company. Zeroing in

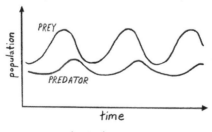

Lotka–Volterra curves

on the lynx and hare and plotting their interactive effects over time, a predictable pattern emerged from the boreal forest: cyclical, dynamic, and demonstrable. The relationship proved perfect for mathematical modeling.

While the equations are eye-crossing, the model isn't. It's surprisingly simple. Huge ecological phenomena are ignored. Take competition, last chapter's innards. Particularly the subtle, moment-by-moment, often indirect competitions within populations of species, or guilds. Like all the jockeying that MacArthur's warblers did in the North Maine Woods. Competition features too many such strands, too many trophic levels, too many variables to keep the puddle pellucid for long. Overwhelmed, some ecologists develop physics envy. Teasing out relationships is difficult when the real world of ecology is like trying to see stars from a rooftop in Beijing. It's even tougher to write reliable equations. Competition is simply too big and ghastly for Lotka–Volterra.

Disease is ignored too. Even without the lynx, disease can cause the hare population to cycle. As can fluctuations in the resource base caused by fires, flooding, or succession. Lotka–Volterra equations assume a prey's pantry is eternally stocked. Newsflash: it isn't. Lynx aren't the only one whose larder runs low. Unchecked, prey species have a bad habit of gluttony, eating themselves out of house and home. When they do, they crash like kamikaze pilots.

Here's the proof: On two far-flung, lynx-free locales—Yukon's Jacquet Island and Prince Edward Island—hare populations still ebb and flow every eight to eleven years like a lagomorphic tide. Disease and food scarcity team up to nullify a hare's chances of a hopping good time. Checks and balances on the islands are dynamic and hard to track. Disease, cover, burrow sites, food supply—the warren of population determinants pop up like a game of Whack-A-Mole, er, Hare.

Checks and balances are critical for the maintenance of biodiversity. They keep one population from becoming too numerous and wiping out others. For ecosystems, there is such a thing as too much growth. And as we've discussed, there can be too much growth in economies, too, though such slogans won't get any politicians elected. Over two hundred years ago, one clean-shaven Englishman knew all this. Not Darwin or Lyell, though both were influenced by him. The man of the moment is Thomas Malthus, who had big ideas of his own. Big ideas that are still well worth considering.

Malthus invested in dour prognostication rather than facial hair. In 1798, he published a far-reaching essay that went by the innocuous title *An Essay on the Principle of Population*. In it, he argued that while populations increase exponentially (1, 2, 4, 8, 16…), food sources only increase arithmetically (1, 2, 3, 4, 5…). "The power of population is so superior to the power of the earth to produce subsistence for man," he wrote, "that premature death must in some shape or other visit the human race."

For Malthus, an examination of the natural world revealed an obvious truth: if unchecked, animals outstrip their food supplies. Predators provide one of those necessary checks, which you're tiring of hearing about. Humans, he added, are perched atop the food chain and lack such checks. In Malthus's logical mind, a grim eventuality awaited such an apex species: war, disease, famine, or some ugly combination thereof. On one side of the threshold, fun and games. On the other, bloodshed and tears. Crossing the threshold, he opined, was inevitable. All of which posed a dilemma, a Malthusian dilemma.

● ● ● ●

My family has a dilemma now too. Just three days ago, we took a major familial step and took in a feline. Lynx-like, except for an absence of ear tufts, daintier paws, and scragglier, orange-and-white fur. Hopelessly cute and incorrigibly curious. While the kids are in love with the kitten, Linda and I already rue our pandemic-addled impulsivity. It was a flat-out terrible decision. Wrong on so many levels. Much more importantly, it was one David Lyall, back in 1895, made as well.

Don't confuse David Lyall with Charles Lyell, the English uniformitarian who padded Darwin's and Jefferson's personal libraries with both sound and fanciful ideas. Compared to Charles, David Lyall's life was simple; all he had to do was keep a candle burning. He was an assistant lighthouse keeper tasked with trimming paraffin through long and lonely nights. With a wife and young child to support, Lyall moved out to Stephens Island, a dinky island taller than it is wide, off the coast of New Zealand. New Zealand's treacherous channels had caused many shipwrecks and cost hundreds of lives already. By night he watched the candle. By day he watched the birds. Tibbles did too. Tibbles was Lyall's cat, whom he'd brought out for companionship with his family away on the larger island. Unbeknownst to Lyall, Tibbles was pregnant. A seemingly minor detail, but in the greater landscape of extinction, wildly important.

Tibbles didn't just watch birds. She killed them, dropping each victim one by one at Lyall's feet. Lyall couldn't identify them. A citizen scientist ahead of his time, Lyall skinned the corpses Tibbles brought in, dried them, and sent them off to more accomplished naturalists for help with identification. Meanwhile, Tibbles kept up her efficient extermination program and birthed a litter of kittens, increasing her appetite for destruction. For Tibbles and her wide-eyed kittens, this was a paradise city where the grass was green and the birds were pretty.

Actually, the birds were brown, dumpy, and looked like they'd had their tails hacked off with a meat cleaver. Mouse-like, they ran among the rocks. Their wings were useless. Millions of years of isolation had reduced the little bird's keel, the bone to which flight muscles attach, to a rudimentary nub. Gone, too, were the barbs and barbules, the neat Velcro-like hooks that keep flight feathers robust.

Happy on the ground, the bird didn't care a whit. Flight made little sense when food, shelter, and love were all to be had on terra firma. Nor were there any mammalian predators to flee. Until Tibbles and her litter of cute, curious, and avicidal kittens, that is.

Just one year after arriving, Lyall wrote a letter to the mainland. "The cats have become wild and are making sad havoc among the birds," he penned. Like a news correspondent at a warzone, Lyall documented the carnage. But for whatever reason, he didn't intervene.

Perhaps he thought the birds were inexhaustible. Or that they had separate, intact populations on other isolated islands.

Nah. Amateur though he was, Lyall was too scientifically-minded for that excuse. I think, rather, Lyall was just like my kids and cat lovers everywhere. He overlooked her misdeeds because he'd grown attached. Now, that love extended to her cuddly kittens. Around him, the unidentified bird's trajectory was mirroring that of a skydiver. His own letters attest to it, now confirmed by visitors to Stephens Island. One month after his letter, an editorial appeared in *The Press*, a newspaper distributed in Christchurch. "There is very good reason to believe that the bird is no longer to be found on the island, and, as it is not known to exist anywhere else, it has apparently become quite extinct. This is probably a record performance in the way of extermination," the editorial added bleakly.

Yes, I believe that Lyall's hesitation can be boiled down to one simple reason: he didn't have the heart to annihilate his villainous feline horde. He had created his own Malthusian dilemma, his cat population's exponential growth quickly outstripping the food supply. Decapitated birds, dainty piles of desiccated feathers, littered the island. But other than writing a few somber letters, Lyall didn't act.

Clearly, the cats had made it wonky. They were ubiquitous. Sustained by handouts from come-and-go, hospitable lighthouse workers, the cats lacked checks and balances. But the birds had checked out. Every single one. Ironically, once exterminated, the birds were officially named—Stephens Island wren.

In such a small, bounded system, the sad beauty of the Lotka–Volterra equations were on full display. Tibbles and her exponential offspring were the lynx. They had overshot the sinusoidal curve, causing the wren—the hare—to flatline. But Stephens Island tragically veered off. Beneficent handouts prevented a wren rebound with temporal cycling. Systematic annihilation complete, the island faced its own Malthusian dilemma.

Regarding predators, the Stephens Island wren hadn't been totally naïve; it had long offered up its body to New Zealand's native laughing owls. With the owls, however, the wren had occasionally had the last laugh, slipping into the island's tangled vegetation and leaving them hungry. Like the lynx and hare, the owl and wren had forged an uneasy truce, predicated on population booms and busts and survival of the fittest. While the owls couldn't penetrate the thicker vegetation, the cats could, picking their way out with a feathered corpse in their jowls.

Alas, the story of the Stephens Island wren nearly had a hero. In 1898, a few years after Lyall left, a different lighthouse keeper, Robert Cathcart, arrived and immediately noticed the bird carnage. He came out guns blazing. Whether motivated by vengeance or target practice, we'll never know. A self-made Billy the Kiwi, Cathcart stepped out of the lighthouse and fired at everything with four legs and a tail. At long last, checks and balances had arrived. In his first nine months, he mowed down well over one hundred cats in his felicidal spree. Deadeye though he was, even Cathcart couldn't kill them all. Like Russian boar in the United States, some were too wily and eluded him.

Twenty-six years later, even the cleverest cats were finally destroyed. At long last, Stephens Island was cat-free. For the wren, it was too little too late. The island's namesake bird was gone, its detached, faded feathers flying further over the Pacific than the bird ever did.

Resilience and fragility, nature knows both. The Stephens Island wren grimly represents the latter. Sixteen stuffed specimens scattered across the globe's natural history museums are all that remain. If you see one, like I did in London's Natural History Museum, you might notice the bird's Latin name, *Traversia lyalli*.

Typically, naturalists count it a high honor to have one's name attached to a species. Two naturalists who had received specimens from Lyall fought for the honor of Stephens Island wren, in fact. Neither succeeded. Sadly, the genus went to a money-minded curio detailer, Henry Travers. With apologies for the pun, Travers made a killing on the wren, netting what in today's currency would be about $3,000 USD per specimen. And the second part of the binomial? That's for David, of course. An indelible memorial for the myopic cat lover who reduced the world's tally of flightless songbirds by one-third. Dubious honor indeed.

David Lyall. Poster child for how small changes, however innocent, can have catastrophic consequences. The traits he displayed—awareness and inaction—linger with us today. I, unfortunately, am a case in point. I am fully aware of the cat-infested world we live in. I'm also aware of the effects of unchecked predation. Aware yet complicit. I can't blame my lonely, quarantined kids. It was I who sanctioned—championed even—my family's first kitten.

• • • •

How bad is *Felis catus*? According to *Cat Wars: The Devastating Consequences of a Cuddly Killer*, horrendously bad. Authors Santella and Marra list a cool thirty-three extinctions that cats have significantly contributed to around the world. Not to mention two diseases, toxoplasmosis and rabies, which they spread with flea-bitten aplomb.

At last count, there were eighty-six million American housecats. That's one per every three households. According to the Wildlife Society, nearly one-third of our slinky pals routinely slip outside and murder two animals in the average week. Bloodlust momentarily satiated, they return back inside to use the litterbox, lap up the dredges from a cereal bowl, and sleep off their murderous spree on the loveseat cushions.

Granted, some cats get neutered, declawed, and are forced to hydrate from the toilet. But most suburban cats have it made in the shade. Strays not so much. Deprived from steady Purina Nine Lives rations and flea collars, strays are the real psychopaths. Numbering at least forty million in the United States, strays take three times the amount of prey.

Regardless of the hostility I show the strays that show up at my place, they consider themselves part-owners, patrolling it with the vigilance of a Buckingham Palace guard. They slide under my shed, mark their territory in our porch plants, and eerily peer into my living room windows like literal peeping toms. You can see the bewilderment in their yellow-green eyes. Their DNA is scrambled, domestication and persecution creating a fierce and fearful mendicant.

The house we bought came with cats. The single woman we bought it from introduced herself: "I'm Tracy, the crazy lady at the end of the road with nine cats." Tracy's words, I quickly realized, lacked hyperbole. The house was a cat condominium, completely outfitted for furry quadrupeds. During our first walk-through, quasi-feral cats squirted out from behind washing machines and from under beds. One natty-haired cat peered haughtily down on us from atop the fridge. Clumps of fur blew across the wood floors like tumbleweed. All cats were welcome, even the most geriatric. They could come and go as they pleased, using the convenient cat doors and gentle-grade ramps.

Undeterred, we bought the place. And while Tracy moved on, her entourage of strays dug in their furry heels. Bird lover, I was eager to see them go. I sealed the cat doors and cut handouts out entirely. A few hard winters, rivaling those of Valley Forge weakened the troops. Facing starvation, most eventually uprooted, looking for Meow Mix from kinder country dwellers down the road.

With the coast clear, avian affirmative action went into full effect. I gave the place back to the birds. Before long, bird feeders hung on all sides of the house, loaded with grape jelly, suet, millet, and sunflower. Bird houses—thirteen at last count—sprouted on poles, posts, trees, and shed walls. Gardens were enhanced, old Christmas trees were turned into shelter belts, and strategic brush piles soon rivaled the Tenochtitlan pyramids.

It worked. The twitterpated birds spread their tweets to every corner of the county. They came like clockwork, pecking, preening, and posturing. Nature's fetching palette was on display: goldfinches, red-bellied woodpeckers, blue jays, indigo buntings, purple finches—an avian rainbow arced over my yard.

But like David Lyall, I was shortsighted. Reversing the biblical account, my Noachian bird blessing preceded the flood. Openhanded benevolence made my home awash in rodents. Unwittingly, I'd created a perfect storm: food, shelter, and most important of all, neither claw nor whisker of a tail-flicking cat. Rats, mice, voles, rabbits, wood-chucks, possums, chipmunks, gray and red squirrels advanced in waves. Despite my best defense, they laid siege. I employed every tactic I could. Cracks were sealed, traps laid, and shotguns fired.

Enemy setbacks were only momentary. For every chipmunk I interred, another took its place. On and on the mongrel beasts came. Nothing worked in the Sisyphean struggle. I was outmatched. One errant-shooting professor against dozens of rumbly-stomached opportunists. Nature abhors a vacuum. Conditions were too good, the offerings too delectable, for the critters to look elsewhere.

The garage and the basement fell to the rodents first, soon followed by the walls and crawlspaces. Mouse nests appeared in duffle bags, droppings blanketed dresser drawers, sounds of scratching reverberated in the walls, and then—*eek!*—a mouse brazenly scurried across the kitchen floor during dinner.

Amid the home invasion, the truth became clear: my actions were precisely the opposite of David Lyall. Despite an advanced degree in ecology, I'd turned my yard into an upside-down version of Stephens Island. While that system went sideways by the addition of a supreme predator, mine did so by subtracting the very same one. Without predators, the rodents' temerity vanished.

Unlike many, I'm not averse to cohabitating with a handful of mice, provided they act respectfully. But if they're gonna live the good life under my roof (or in it), I want them on their nimble little toes, trembling as they chew through the insulation.

No number of traps and shotgun blasts can instill the fear I want them to have. Only one creature will do—a lynx. Only a slant-eyed cat can cause fear and trembling among the rodent population. For the Lotka–Volterra equations to produce those marvelous graphs, the prey needs a predator. And so I sanctioned a kitten.

• • • •

Grizzlies also elicit fear and trembling, I learned many years ago in Glacier National Park. There, the towering peaks rimming the Going-to-the-Sun Road reduced my truck to matchbox proportions. I inched along the hairpin bends, easing off the accelerator as I passed bemused mountain goats with Darwin-sized beards. Awestruck, I pulled into the St. Mary Visitor Center for a backcountry permit and sorely needed advice.

The screen door slammed behind me as I entered. Two rangers stood behind a topo map pressed under plexiglass at the counter. One, with beady eyes under a black unibrow, motioned me forward. "I'm looking for a memorable, one-night trek into the backcountry," I said, placing both palms on the map. "Chasing beauty and solitude," I added. "And it'd be fun to see wildlife, too."

Like an inchworm, half the ranger's unibrow arced up. He leaned forward, assessing me. "Looks like you're in shape."

"Decent."

"Look no further than the Stony Indian Pass trail. It's twelve miles to the campground over some glorious country. What day you going?"

"Uh, today, actually."

"Oh." The ranger's skepticism was obvious. "You'll have to really move, then. Plus, radar shows there may be a front movin' in 'round dinner time."

"A front?"

"Yeah. Rain showers. Though could be snow higher up."

"Do I have enough time?"

"If you don't smell the flowers, which there'll be plenty of. Park here," the ranger said, pointing to the map. "Once you sign in at the trailhead, you'll follow this route. Yellow blazes all the way." His index finger glided along the plexiglass. "Here's your campground. Doubt you'll see a soul once you get a few miles in though."

"What about the nighttime temps?" I asked, trying to show him I wasn't totally flying by the seat of my pants.

"High forties, low fifties. But with the front, all bets are off."

"Thanks for your help," I said, grabbing a map from the stack.

"Oh, and one more thing," he said, smoothing his beard. I turned, one hand on the doorknob. "Lots of wildlife out there. Bears especially.

Hang your food, make plenty of noise as you hike, and leave nothing smelly in your tent."

"Does that mean *I* can't sleep in my tent?" I asked, grinning. The inchworm above his eyes remained flat. "Will do," I said, miffed he hadn't appreciated my humor.

Yes, I'd hang my food. But I sure as heck wasn't going to make noise. I wanted to see wildlife, not chase it away. I knew bears were out here. That's partly why I'd come, to feel the thrill of deferring my top spot on the food chain. While a dangerous encounter was always a possibility, the odds of survival were grossly in my favor. Relative to the number of backcountry hikers, precious few had scary run-ins. Statistically, I was far more likely to die just driving to the trailhead. Besides, my bear spray was holstered to my belt. As long as I grabbed the bear spray and not the bug spray, and didn't spray it in *my* face, I'd be fine. All the backcountry called for was coolheaded logic.

Coolheaded logic deserted me even before I reached the trailhead. There, in a moment of acute stupidity, I pulled my heavy Walrus tent out of my backpack and stuffed it back in the truck. I'd slept many nights without it on my meandering trip across America. For the next eight hours, I needed to move like Legolas, not Gimli. If it rained, I could always make a shelter.

The trail was just as epic as the humorless ranger predicted. Mac-Gillivray's warblers and western tanagers sang in the cool forests, which gave way to meadows affording expansive views. Good idea, I congratulated myself, to leave that lead-weighted tent behind. While certainly not springy, my legs were still serviceable ten miles in. Feeling good, I eyed an elephant-sized boulder and scrambled atop. Endless miles of coniferous forest stretched from horizon to horizon, interrupted only by a green meadows and a handful of castellated peaks. I took a long swig from my Nalgene, sprawled out on the warm boulder, and shut my eyes. Ah. The good life.

Raindrops. The oversized type that are widely spaced and splatter. Reluctantly I sat up. While I'd catnapped, a dark curtain of clouds had stolen the sky. Better not get wet, I thought, ruffling through my pack.

When I pulled out my balled-up rain jacket, a small paperback book fell out. It was *Sackett*, by the well-known author Louis L'Amour. "You *need* to read Louis L'Amour if you're traveling out west," my dad had said months earlier, thrusting the book into my hand. "It'll change your life."

Whoops. I hadn't used my rain jacket for so long, I'd forgotten I'd stuffed the book in it back in Wyoming. The raindrops slimmed and steadied their cadence. Doubts fell with them. Without a tent, could I really stay dry? Could I build a rain-resistant shelter?

Decision time. If the rain continued, I'd need to start construction now. While the ranger had told me a front was coming, he'd never told me about its intensity or duration. I could slide under the boulder I was on. It was lopsided, affording a tiny overhang. The recess at the boulder's base was just large enough to contort into. Good for wind and lightning protection but not much else.

Then, as if a switch flipped, rain changed to snow. Big, fluffy flakes. It wasn't wetness I had to be worried about, it was air temperature. Even if the boulder could keep me dry, there was no way I'd be warm enough. Left leg falling asleep, I stretched it out in front of me. A night here would be cold and cramped indeed. An involuntary chill ran down my spine. I looked at my watch: 5:23 p.m. A trickle of water ran down the boulder, puddling beside me. This wasn't a shelter, it was a gutter. My sleeping bag would be damp in no time. I'd be a saturated sponge by nightfall. No, this wouldn't do.

My only other option was retreat. Hiking out exactly as I'd come in. My truck was parked twelve miles away, a stone's throw from Lake McDonald Lodge. At best, four hours of daylight remained. I'd spent the last few months driving around the West doing lazy day hikes, not training for an Ironman. If I retreated, I'd have to move fast. At dusk. Precisely the wrong thing to do in grizzly country. Both options were bad. Staying risked hypothermia. Returning risked exhaustion and bear mauling. Indecision gripped me. Stay or desert?

• • • •

One hundred years earlier and a continent away, African and Indian laborers faced the exact same quandary at the beginning of the twentieth century when building a railroad from the coast to Lake Victoria on behalf of the British. About midway through the operation, near what is today Tsavo National Park, two lions developed a taste for the workers. They began to prey upon them. What started as a sprinkling turned into a downpour of attacks. Roughly one victim every two days—135 in all. With every man dragged off into the bushes, the workers' anxious fear increased.

With ghostlike evasiveness, the lions dodged everything the British threw at them. They avoided poison-laced goats and skirted by armed, all-night vigils set out to shoot them. The railway workers were stuck, damned if they ran away or stayed put. If they deserted, they faced waterless, inhospitable terrain, and maybe a mauling. Staying ran the risk of being dragged out of a tent and devoured. Only one solution remained: finish the job as quickly as possible and get out of the death zone. Fear proved a powerful motivator. Track was laid in record time and the project soon finished. Aptly, the railway became known as "The Lunatic Express."

• • • •

Unable to decide, I noticed *Sackett* in my hand. Why not read a little? Perhaps it would clear the dark thoughts enshrouding me. I managed nineteen pages before I reached the following passage:

> High up as I was, snow could be expected nine months out of the year. And when snow fell, that valley up above would fill up and the stream would freeze over. Anybody caught in this valley would be stuck for the winter.
>
> Yet a heavy rain could make that narrow chute impassable for days. Allowing for rain spells and snow, there were probably not over fifty or sixty days a year when a man could get in or out of the valley...Unless there was another way in.

It left me with a worried, uneasy feeling to think I was in a jug that might be stoppered at any time.

I paused and looked up. Falling snow now made it impossible to see across the valley. A droplet of chilly water ran off my nose and onto my open book. Page nineteen swelled upon contact, the ink smudging. I, too, was in a jug. At twenty-two, I wasn't ready to be stoppered. I stashed the book in my pack and eased out from the crevice. For the last two months, oatmeal and bug spray had proved their mettle. Time to put my faith in the third member of the holy trinity. Work your magic, bear spray.

I did the math. Twelve miles to cover in a little over three hours. An average of four miles per hour would bring me back to my truck just before nightfall. Since the average human walking speed is 3.1 mph, I would need to increase my speed by a fourth and eliminate all breaks. A miscue, like losing the trail or veering off on a wrong fork, would be inauspicious at best. As would bumbling into a grizzly fanny. Although doing something felt better than cowering in a crevice, it ushered in a whole new constellation of stress. Ursa major stress.

Fatigue quickly proved a moot point. Fear overwhelmed it. Just an hour ago, all I could think about was oatmeal and rest, so wholly did lactic acid and hunger govern my body. Now, adrenaline supplanted both.

Fear also overrode my insistence on hiking in silence. For the first time, I didn't want to see wildlife. I desperately hoped to avoid it. With a voice somewhere between Kermit the Frog and *The Little Mermaid*'s Scuttle, I've never been big on singing. That all changed. Hymns, Warren G, Disney, Alan Jackson—everything I knew came pouring out. To this day, I pity all the poor innocent creatures within earshot I passed that snowy Glacier evening.

But it worked. Glacier's bears—and my sudden acute paranoia—remained at bay.

• • • •

That's the way predation works. Predators attack the prey's mind far more than the body. As twilight fell, my imagination cooked up a grizzly around every bend. Misshapen stumps, boulders, and shadows twisted into ursine shapes, making me hesitant and hyperaware. It's the effect wolves have on elk. It makes elk edgy and avoid certain places, decreasing the time they spend feeding. All of which gives plants a chance to grow, mature, and allow for succession. Just by existing, top-level predators create healthier ecosystems.

Hold your hares! Don't lynx directly drive down prey with a predictable, Lotka–Volterra curve? Yes, but the hares suffer from stress as much as they do direct attack. A study in the *Journal of Animal Ecology*, for example, showed that a hare's reproductive output declined significantly when exposed to stress. The methodology called for the researchers to daily expose pregnant hares to a salivating, bloodthirsty dog—on a firm leash—for minutes at a time. Not only did the hares produce fewer and smaller young, they also produced much higher levels of the stress hormone cortisol.

Cases like Tibbles and the Stephens Island wren only really happen when humans are involved. In ecosystems that humans haven't mucked up, predators don't mess up ecosystems, they enhance them. With millennia-old checks and balances, predation rarely drives a population all the way to extinction. It can temporarily suppress prey populations that render them vulnerable to other factors, but predation's direct effects—killing—are disproportionately small. Normal, trophic-level exchanges necessitate small populations of top predators. In the contexts they've evolved in, they can't kill fast enough to hold prey populations down. Even if they occasionally manage to do so, like lynx, they'll soon cycle downward, too. So, if you're fearful when out in nature, you're in good company. Predators rule with fear and loathing, monstrous effects indeed.

The disproportionately large effect that predation has on prey populations is exactly why Michael Soulé feared losing top predators. And why it's his fourteenth factor. Take them out and herbivores explode. This causes the landscape to suffer and disease to spread easier. Plus, top predators are numerically few to begin with. Their susceptibility to extinction is higher from the get-go.

• • • •

Only a lynx can spike a hare's cortisol count. Only man-eating lions can cause track to be laid in record time. Only a housecat can make chipmunks think twice before breaking into my basement. And only stupidity can make me think I could hold off a surprised 1,300-pound bruin with a can of spray.

Thankfully, I never had to use it. I stumbled into Lake McDonald Lodge at 9:36 p.m., twenty-four miles behind me, and collapsed onto a deep leather couch in front of a roaring fire. I sank into it like a coffee stain, unable to move a muscle. If my emotions that night were graphed, they'd mirror the rolling hills of the lynx and hare. Highs and lows, joys and fears, and now, fatigue and immense relief. Profound contentment fell over me as the flames danced. Two hours later, logs reduced to orange embers, the desk clerk walked over, concern plainly evident on her face. She looked predatorial, a beaklike nose supporting half glasses and fast-blinking eyes. "Do you have a room, sir?" she asked, clearly suspecting I didn't. I glanced down at my full canister of bear spray. Temptation.

"Uh, no," I replied. "I'm headed out." The truth was, if I got a room here, my shoestring budget would be in smithereens. There'd be no cash for gas, or worse, oatmeal. The clerk didn't move. Slowly I heaved myself up and holstered my spray like a sidearm. Feeling one hundred years old, I slung my pack back over my aching shoulder and shuffled out into the snowy drizzle.

Sore, poor, and forced outside, I could have pitied myself. Everything I had—my shelter, truck, and food—was substandard. But my smile was irrepressible. The clerk was tethered to her desk. One she'd return to the rest of the summer. She was a lynx bound to a population of hares.

Me? I was free. With oatmeal, bug spray, and bear spray, I could go as far as my truck and my feet would take me. I'd never quit worrying about Malthusian limits. But now was the time for pushing my own. In a moment, I'd nestle down in my cozy sleeping bag and dream about bears I never saw. Tomorrow I'd strike out for someplace new. To enjoy another journey on the lunatic express.

15
THE KEYS OF ST. HUBERT
Disease

"The living of life, any life, involves great andprivate pain, much of which we share with no one. In such places as the Inner Gorge [of the Grand Canyon] the pain trails away from us."
—Barry Lopez

"Life is a disease," George Bernard Shaw wrote, "and the only difference between one another is the stage of the disease at which he lives." Though depressingly bleak, Shaw's words ring truer for me every year. Regrettably, humans are all-too-familiar with disease. We can't escape it. Unsurprisingly, the world's other creatures can't either. Humans spread disease to other animals. And animals spread it right back. The COVID-19 pandemic has heightened public awareness of disease in general. But lost in the discourse are the ways disease causes extinction, why Soulé mentioned it as a vital factor to consider. Since it's tricky to disentangle the human experience from disease, I won't bother. I'll level our gaze at the world's more reviled creatures—bats, ticks, rats, and a fungus blight—and show how disease has brought me down, too. But before we get to those buggers, let's start with a cute and charismatic one—the raccoon.

While driving my daughter to her clarinet lesson last fall, I spied a portly raccoon in the middle of the road. "Indigo, check out the raccoon! This isn't something you see every day." Oddly, the raccoon didn't run off as we drew up alongside it. "Do you see it?" I asked.

"No. Where?"

"Look down. It's right below your window."

"Oh, how cute!" Indi exclaimed.

Normally I would have agreed. But not this time. Something about the way it shuffled alongside us troubled me. As did the raccoon's marked disregard for our car, now just a few feet from his rotund body. The raccoon turned its bank-robber face up toward ours. Its soupy eyes lacked typical wariness. The fur running down its back was thin and wiry. Only my bighearted daughter could declare this haggard creature cute. Late for the lesson, I left the vacuous raccoon behind us. A mile later I second-guessed myself.

"I should have run it over," I said aloud, instantly regretting it.

Indi's eyebrows lowered accusingly in my rearview mirror. "You're joking, right?"

"Actually, no."

I had to explain myself.

"Well, typically raccoons are nocturnal. So that's a red flag."

"What's a red flag?"

"Uh, something that's sort of weird or alarming. Also, did you notice how the coon didn't seem afraid?"

"Maybe it was just a nice one," Indi said. You could count on her to give other creatures the benefit of the doubt.

"Plus, I don't like how close it was to our house. Hope it doesn't shack up underneath the back deck. And did you see its eyes?" I added.

Indi nodded. "They looked watery."

"Yeah, kind of sickly."

Indi fell silent. At eight years old, she still wasn't sure why these characteristics warranted running the raccoon over. I wasn't sure either. It was a bright and beautiful Saturday. I let it go.

Two hours later, clarinet lesson over, we were back home at the kitchen table.

"Dad, the raccoon's here!" Indi said, pointing at our back door. I walked over to the door, crouched, and looked through the glass panels. It was indeed the very same animal. Same watery eyes, wiry fur, and fearless, languid movement.

The raccoon teetered over to where I crouched, as if walking on Legos. Just a half inch of glass between us. Reacting to either me or its reflection, the animal placed its humanlike hands on the glass. For an animal known for fastidiousness, this one's paws were filthy. With a pry bar and revolver, the strung-out, masked bandit could've robbed us blind.

There were plenty of places for the raccoon to live in the surrounding forest. It didn't need our house. This turf was spoken for.

"Get lost!" I yelled, banging on the glass. The raccoon didn't flinch. "I said, get *LOST!*"

At this the raccoon's vacant eyes focused, blazing hatred. It bared its teeth and hurled itself at the door.

Shocked, I leapt backward. Indi covered her mouth, eyes wide. Wires crossed, intimidation was lost on this raccoon. It had forsaken a life of creeks and crayfish for one of violent home invasion. Only one possible explanation existed, what I had suspected on the road. "Disease," Hosea Ballou once stated, "is the retribution of outraged Nature." Witnessing this kamikaze attack on our back door, I heartily agreed.

• • • •

Rabies. Nothing else explained such atypical behavior. Thanks to Louis Pasteur's vaccine, rabies no longer instills fear in the masses. But back in medieval Europe, the disease had everybody looking over their shoulder. Mostly for wandering, salivating dogs.

The most paranoid made pilgrimages to Liège, Belgium, where they'd pray to St. Hubert, the patron saint of hunters, to spare them. Others stashed iron keys in their walls or wore them around their necks on lanyards. If bitten by an animal, they'd race to the nearest furnace and heat their key up. With the key glowing red, they'd sear the wound, hoping to sterilize it.

Medieval peasants, in a time before morphine and painkillers, were far tougher than me. I can't fathom such agony. But folks had ample reason to endure it. A severe burn was far better than the excruciating death that accompanied rabies.

The disease is well worth fearing. Some of its symptoms include anxiety, confusion, partial paralysis, agitation, hallucinations, and in its final phases—hydrophobia. Hydrophobia—the fear of water—is particularly heinous. Just think, you were bitten on the bum by a wild-eyed dog while out planting turnips. Now you're in the disease's latter stages. In the midst of your frothing and convulsing, the mere thought of water makes you recoil. The one substance that most dying people ask for is the very substance you'd die to avoid. Instead of drinking, you'd rather sink your teeth into the lady across the street putting clothes on the line.

Rabies accomplishes all this by assaulting the central nervous system. It's like an evil computer hacker, capable of reprograming a motherboard. After being bitten, a dog's twenty thousand genes are completely altered by the five-gene virus in mere weeks. During this period, the dog's nerve cell transport system is hijacked.

Growing up watching *The Little Mermaid*, I always assumed Ursula the Sea Witch had rabies. After all, she was unpredictable, discolored, and violent. Yet had Ursula had rabies, she would have sought Ariel's brain rather than her melodious larynx. That's what the virus covets most. The virus's journey takes time—weeks, or sometimes months. This interminable spell, while the virus is heading north, is called the incubation period, the lull before the storm. Without treatment during this vital window, the fat lady—Ursula—will sing. Once the virus reaches the brain, it's curtains. The brain inflates like a balloon and all hell breaks loose. The technical term is encephalitis.

Many nasty diseases actually give us a grace period. But the grim irony is that we don't react in time. Mostly because, as I'll soon illustrate with my own bout with Lyme disease, we don't recognize early symptoms or, in my case, shrug them off as something else. Regarding Lyme, a swollen tick on your leg is a pretty good clue. But if the tick that got you was tiny, or it got you in a place you can't see, the window of intervention drops like a guillotine.

The same reasoning holds true for rabies. If a wild-eyed coon leaps upon you and clamps down, odds are you'll promptly seek treatment upon prying it off. Or, as in *Old Yeller*, you'll shoot your dog to prevent an inevitable—and far worse—end. Those are the obvious cases. But what if a bat nips you with imperceptible teeth while you're asleep? In the morning, chances are you won't notice the nick on your arm, or you'll assume it was a mosquito or a spider. Hi ho, hi ho, off to work you'll go, utterly unaware of the chiropteran saliva marching through your nerve cells like the advance foot soldiers of a Roman siege.

Fortunately, I didn't learn about such a scenario as a child. The prospect of rabies-carrying bats nipping me as I slept would have upset many a peaceful night I spent sleeping under bats in our rickety old cottage. Maybe my mother knew, however. Because each time bats swooped over her, she went ballistic, shrieking and ordering my dad to do something. Momentary inaction was followed by a barrage of thinly veiled threats.

One evening before we'd gone to bed, my dad made the mistake of opening the fireplace door. Out flew a dozen bats. Everybody grabbed a tennis racket or broom and swung, ducked, and squealed. Such moments of pandemonium, with sanctioned use of sports equipment indoors, were the apogee of my childhood summers. We whacked light fixtures, furniture, each other, and only occasionally a bat.

Living with bats led me to take them for granted. At dusk every night, an army of bats took over the lake. Mosquitos and gnats didn't stand a chance with the aerial masters of echolocation. So plentiful were the bats at our summer cottage that my father even lassoed one while casting one evening from our dock. By morning, the bats had reentered our cottage and hung quiescently in the rafters above my head to sleep off the buffet. Other than occasional droppings that pattered onto my bedspread, they didn't affect me. So I didn't understand—and therefore derided—my mother's hysteria. But her reaction wasn't totally unfounded. Bats are the third leading vector of rabies in the United States, following raccoons and skunks. Sleeping with bats carries risk. Astronomically low, but as you now know, rabies is a poor choice for an exit.

But the disease is undeniably ingenious. Any virus that can turn a cute, nocturnal raccoon with a proclivity for washing food into a diurnal, teeth-baring menace stands atop the medal stand in my book. It's the virus behind werewolf legends, too. But as far as Soulé and extinctions are concerned, rabies is meekly ineffectual. It's too lethal for its own good, killing victims too efficiently. A crazed coon may spread rabies to a very surprised cow, but it'll never run down a deer or fox no matter how bloodthirsty the virus makes it. If rabies turned raccoons into cheetahs, or caused them to sprout wings, it'd be far more effective. But rabies does infect winged mammals—bats—a boon from the virus's perspective. Due to their penchant for roosting communally in warm, moist environments, it's not surprising that bats have played host to a slew of viruses. Marburg, histoplasmosis, Ebola, Nipah, and, in my neck of the woods, white-nose syndrome.

• • • •

White-nose syndrome was the reason why our annual summer matches of bat tennis and our mosquito-free skies abruptly ceased. The clouds of bats that darted about our heads on evening canoe trips dissipated like a mist.

Originating in Europe, white-nose syndrome insidiously slipped into little brown bat colonies, the same species that called our cottage home. It made wintering bats itchy, causing them to awaken more frequently than normal. Hibernation and insomnia don't mix. Like an old man making multiple trips to the bathroom, the bats left their hibernacula on little sorties, impairing their energy and water balances. Compared to the glory days, the lake in recent years has been batless. Without this marvelous predatory check, gnats and mosquitoes boomed. Chiroptophobes must pick their poison. Bats in the belfry or mosquito blood drives? I choose bats, rabies risk notwithstanding, hands down.

What I saw on my little lake in Pennsylvania was sadly indicative of a much larger trend. In 2008, the International Union for Conservation of Nature listed little brown bats as their lowest conservation priority, citing them as a species of "Least Concern." Ten years later, the bats' status was upgraded to endangered, counts of hibernacula—their winter refuges—having declined by an average of over 90 percent.

Regardless of Batman and Robin's efforts, people and bats have never mixed well. Today, however, challenges facing bats are greater. Houses are better sealed than they used to be. Caves and crevices are disappearing with every new development. Loss of habitat had already put bats on the rack. White-nose syndrome cranked the wheel to the breaking point.

• • • •

Extinction, of course, is multicausal, hence why Soulé cited eighteen factors that contribute to it. Though we're dealing with them one by one, they're a dense raspberry tangle, intertwining and sprouting from one another. Disease is but one. Others, like habitat fragmentation and invasive species, are strongly linked to it and can directly cause epizootic events, or zoonoses, jargon for disease outbreaks. Though it effectively suppresses populations, disease only rarely accounts for the final death rattle.

As a case in point, consider Christmas Island, a little chunk of rock sticking out of the Indian Ocean just south of Indonesia. There, ship-jumping black rats took out two native rats, the Christmas Island rat and the bulldog rat. The new rats didn't prey on the others, they simply passed their diseases on, like Europeans passing measles-laced blankets to Native Americans. So, while we're quick to blame rats for spreading disease, we should realize they've been victims, too. Generalizing is tough to do in conservation; there's always an exception. As Charlie Brown would say, "Rats!"

If disease-caused rat extinction doesn't quicken your pulse, remember Hawaii's honeycreepers. When the mosquito, *Culex quinquefasciatus*, arrived, sixteen honeycreepers living at low elevations promptly died, victims of disease—avian malaria and avian pox—to which they lacked resistance. The lucky survivors were those that lived higher up and out of reach of the invasive mosquitos.

But none of the losses to bats, rats, and birds is equivalent to what amphibians have endured. For every four animals critically endangered by disease, three of them are amphibians. With their thin skin, frogs are the fragile vase in the living room. These otherworldly creatures live in liminality, straddling terrestrial and aquatic realms, all the while sprouting limbs and breathing through their skin. This makes amphibians particularly susceptible to a tongue-twisting disease, chytridiomycosis, caused by a fungus: *Batrachochytrium dendrobatidis*. Say that five times fast. If you're not in the mood, call it chytrid fungus.

It's unclear whether chytrid fungus is new or if its virulence is increasing. After appearing in its present epizootic form in Australia in the early 1990s, it soon hopped to Africa, the Americas, Europe, New Zealand, and Oceania, perhaps mirroring movements in international trade. When chytrid attaches to a frog, it builds up on its outermost layers of skin. When the number of chytrid's zoospores exceeds a threshold of ten thousand, the frog begins to have trouble breathing, hydrating, osmoregulating, and thermoregulating. Not long after that, it croaks.

• • • •

To understand why conservationists are concerned about chytrid fungus, consider what the fungus has done to one of America's most iconic trees. Not far from my home is a quaint little eighty-two-acre sanctuary that the Nature Conservancy rescued from a peat-mining operation in 1957. Had the peat been dredged, the bog would have reverted to a less acidic, freshwater pond. Lots of cool carnivorous plants—sundews and pitcher plants—would have succumbed. Also, I'm pretty sure the lone American chestnut tree would have disappeared too.

Yes, a real, living American chestnut tree. Over fifty feet tall and capable of casting sweet shade in summer. In case the story's hazy, just over a century ago there were four billion chestnut trees growing in the eastern United States. A chestnut is the perfect tree. Large, straight-grained, rot-resistant, and a prolific food provider for wildlife. This was the tree that sustained America's most numerous bird—the passenger pigeon—so abundant that overflying flocks periodically blotted out the sun. For forty million years, American chestnuts survived all their floral, faunal, and saprobic adversaries.

Then, in just forty years, they died. A dendrological blink. In 1904, a fungus from Asia was discovered on chestnut trees in the Bronx Zoo. The fungus was another tongue-twister, *Cryphonectria parasitica*, and caused cankers to swell up on the trunk.

Like rabies and white-nose syndrome, chestnut blight doesn't kill its victims quickly. Rather, it leaves the root systems alive, often indefinitely. With intact roots, the American chestnut continually sends up stump sprouts. The sprouts reach head high, develop cankers, and die. The blight knocked chestnuts out at the knees, reducing the redwood of the East to an early successional-stage shrub. Walk around certain cutover forests and you'll see them, armies of adolescents loitering about, wishing with all their cambium to regain their rightful place among the canopy dwellers.

Several have. Like the lottery winner at Moss Lake. It stands off the trail, a few feet from the water's edge, easy to miss unless you're looking for it. Rest assured I didn't discover it. I was shown the tree by a confidant who was likewise shown. A scrap of local knowledge passed down, like favorite swimming holes, held in trust. Trivial to some, I value this survivor, and two others I've found since, immensely.

I take nearly all my classes to go see it. I wander off the path, weave around hemlocks and red maples, and stop. Casually, I lean back against the chestnut's trunk and hope that the most observant will notice it. Or the nut husks, resembling rolled-up hedgehogs, lying at their feet. Most don't. Rather, they glance at their watches or feel for their phones peeking over the top of their back pockets.

I can't blame them. Most haven't heard of the American chestnut. Nor do they know that its death represents what many call the greatest ecological disaster to strike the world's forests in all of history. I point out the tree, run my hands over the rough bark, and relay the chestnut's demise. For years, I've told my students about the inherent dangers that disease outbreaks and zoonotic spillovers pose on a globalized world. Now, after COVID-19, I no longer need to. To give them hope, I mention the American Chestnut Foundation's efforts to bring back the chestnut, and the dedicated few attempting a trial-and-error technique called hypovirulence, which tries to kill individual cankers by injecting them with viruses obtained from other chestnut survivors. Like a flu shot for trees.

Why, I ask them, has this lone chestnut beaten the odds? After a mumbled hypothesis by whatever student is most uncomfortable with silence, the class stares at me, awaiting judgment. I offer none. Truth is, I'm not sure why. This particular individual's existence, and a handful of others dotting the region, are a mystery. Perhaps Moss Lake's slight acidity safeguards the roots? Or maybe this tree has a mutation that confers resistance? I like to point out nature's unsolved mysteries. It reminds my students there's so much we still don't know, and lots for them to do. I fight the urge to fill the airspace. Instead, I encourage the class to touch the tree, get up close and personal with it. Some trees, I'm convinced, must be hugged to be understood.

• • • •

Sooner or later, nearly all of us will get up close and personal with disease. While some of Soulé's other extinction factors may have seemed esoteric and abstract, disease isn't one of them. We avoid learning about it at our peril, as it often visits us like a thief in the night, or, raccoon at our door. Disease can affect us singly or stop a whole world in its tracks. Unable to be contained, it spills over.

Since our concern is for how disease affects extinction, a concluding soliloquy about Lyme at first glance feels irrelevant. Trust me, it isn't. Granted, Lyme hasn't put other species directly at risk. Rather, it affects us. And while the physical toll isn't pleasant, the psychological toll may eventually be far worse. Because the vector of Lyme—deer ticks—infect us with more than just spirochetes. They infect us with fear. Fear that, in the long run, may cause more species extinctions than all other diseases combined.

• • • •

Like many who get infected, I never saw the tick that bit me. So, as the disease quietly incubated, I loaded the wagons and headed west, eager to spend a sabbatical in Oregon with my family. For the next four months, I'd balance part-time teaching with writing, research, and recuperation, before we'd head back east. While we sang songs and played the license plate game, spirochetes were using my body like a petri dish, multiplying and spreading ill will. Symptoms started with backache. By Idaho, I developed headaches, body tingling, and general malaise. Symptoms like these send sensible people to the doctor. Me? I dropped my family off in Oregon and immediately flew off to help a colleague start a semester course in Alaska. Surely it was just temporary fatigue or a passing flu. Besides, it was nothing the Land of the Midnight Sun couldn't cure.

Alaska's beauty distracted me from my pain but didn't cure it. Somewhere in Denali National Park, while photographing pika near the Savage River, the bottom fell out. My chest burned, my back seized up, and my head felt like a moose was sitting on it. I needed help. Three days later, I was back in Oregon and in the ER. A few days after that, too sick to get out of bed, I got a call. "You've tested positive for Lyme disease," the doctor said matter-of-factly.

Everybody's battle with Lyme is different. The short story is, through my family's love and nurture, Oregon's sublime beauty, and God's grace, I gradually recovered. While the details of my year of belabored convalescence aren't important, how Lyme changed me is. My story is hardly unique. If Lyme changed me, it has—and will continue to—change others too.

Up until Lyme, nature had always been the rudder steering my ship. My woodlot adventures as a boy gave way to grander forays to East Africa's savannas and Ecuador's Amazonian headwaters as I grew. Nature gave everything, demanding only insect repellent, calamine lotion, and willingness to go out.

But lying on my bed in Oregon with Bell's palsy immobilizing half my face, my steadfast rudder had snapped off. Benevolent nature had withdrawn her hand. Suddenly, I saw nature differently. The view out my window changed, from one of glistening boughs and singing birds to a vast reservoir for disease. I became fearful. If I ever recovered, I vowed to never go out again. Anything that could make me feel this awful simply wasn't worth indulging in. I'd find new passions. No more hiking, hunting, or birding.

During my months of recovery, I stayed true to my word. Fear held me hostage, making me what Jim Gaffigan calls "indoorsy." Fear also made me miserable. Unsurprisingly, innocent, short forays began. Walks around the yard. One hundred yards down a trail. As my strength slowly returned, I ventured farther. And the farther I ventured, the happier I became. My interest in nature, I realized, was as indelible as a leopard's spots. Lyme-riddled or not, scrubbing it out was nigh impossible.

But is it impossible for others whose interests don't run so deep? A niggling doubt suggests otherwise.

How might the fear of catching Lyme keep people from going outside? Well, because we all know oodles of indoorsy folks. You may be one yourself, this book representing your main outdoor foray. The truth is, I understand the rationale of people who prefer to stay indoors. Staying inside is easier. Most homes, mine an exception, hold nature nicely at bay. Plus, homes turn our inner control freak loose. Dirt can be swept, spills mopped up, and temperatures adjusted. Need a breeze? Turn on the fan. Exercise? Hop on the elliptical. A taste of nature? The National Geographic Channel. Our hermetic chambers more than suffice.

Plus, nature is as fierce as it is fickle, providing plenty of other reasons to huddle inside. A typical calendar year in many parts of the United States brings: soul-sucking summer heat, sunburn, rainstorms, lightning, hail, mosquitos, gnats, deerflies, spiders, nettles, snakes, poison ivy, thorns, bees, bears, bats, and rabid raccoons. At one time or another, all of these have dampened, burned, frozen, scratched, surprised, dehydrated, stung, bitten, petrified, needled, and threatened me. And now another: ticks. Nasty, bloodsucking, black-legged ticks. Ticks that flatten an otherwise healthy man in mere weeks.

Before Lyme, I looked down on indoor types. Soft, timid, and boring, they knew not what they were missing. After Lyme, however, I envied them. Disease-free, they knew exactly what they were missing: general discomfort and most of all, Lyme. In recent years, due in large part to three hundred thousand new Lyme-bodies like me annually, New York's Department of Environmental Conservation has posted ominous signs at the entrance of every natural area. "Attention: Lyme in this Area," the signage reads. I ignored them for years. Disease happens to other people, I thought, not me. Now, I study the little yellow signs as if they were eye tests. I pause and contemplate heading back to my car. True, I can't stay out of nature. But those signs remind me of my mortality. Of the legion of ticks waiting to crawl up my pantlegs.

• • • •

My thesis is worrisomely simple: fear prevents attachment. Staying inside prevents Lyme, but it also prevents a relationship with nature. Without that, where will our interest, love, and motivation come from? Why will we care about extinction at all?

Risk aversion promises a safer life, but not necessarily a better one. A friend and colleague, who's hoping to climb Denali one of these years, has a framed quote by Teddy Roosevelt hanging on his office wall. Every so often, when the academic treadmill becomes too tedious and I feel like I might asphyxiate under a pile of ungraded papers, I barge in. We exchange pleasantries and recent bird sightings while I keep one eye on Teddy's words: "It is not the critic who counts; not the man who points out how the strong man stumbles, or where the doer of deeds could have done them better. The credit belongs to the man who is actually in the arena, whose face is marred by dust and sweat and blood."

Sometimes, Teddy's words are enough and I return to the stack of papers. More often, I peek down my fourth-floor corridor and make sure the coast is clear, grab my bag, and bolt. An hour later, I'm down on hands and knees, peering at moribund ants stuck in the purple-veined bottom of a pitcher plant. Without regular desertions, I reason, I'd be half-digested too.

Teddy understood suffering's merit. He knew that suffering and joy wrap around each other like a double helix. That some of life's deepest joys can't be attained any other way. This conundrum explains why people who are close to death can experience life most profoundly. And why people run marathons, punish themselves for the Olympics, and climb mountains. Where was Vice President Teddy when he heard the news of McKinley's turn for the worse? On top of a mountain, of course.

If Teddy could carve out the time to scale mountains as the vice president, then I could do so as a college professor. That's why a few weeks ago, I was back at it, my eyes on another high peak. Hoping to impart a lesson of joyful suffering, I brought Ezra along. We decided on Lower Wolfjaw, a lesser-known Adirondack forty-sixer. Hoping to catch the blessed little window of good weather before the blackflies, we opted for late May. Sure enough, no blackflies. Nor the faintest hum of any bug, for that matter. But that didn't mean we skirted suffering. What we lacked in bugs we made up for with ice. The latter half of the trail was half-frozen, perfect for wiping out and postholing up to our crotches. Conditions befitting Elsa, Olaf, and the odd snow leopard, not my son in worn-out sneakers.

With his shoe size going up every month, I couldn't justify buying him a pair of hiking boots. Poor kid. He may as well have strapped greased watermelons to his feet. He slipped, slogged, and struggled. "I think there's enough daylight to hit one more peak before heading down," I said, looking at Ezra. "Wanna do one more?"

"I'm good," he said, his mouth full of Cheez-Its. That night, we celebrated our feat the same way I had growing up, with Spam. "It's just so good!" Ezra exclaimed, reaching for another piece. Obviously, it was the experience—not the Spam—he was referring to.

• • • •

Some of our experiences in nature aren't so good. Lyme disease and the rabid raccoon clawing at my back door are examples of that. As are all wildlife-related diseases. Insidious and recalcitrant, the faster we eradicate them the better. The problem is, there's no fool-proof way to do it. Louis Pasteur rescued us from the jaws of rabies with a slick vaccine. But other measures, like the decision to coat the earth with DDT to curb malaria, caused an ecological meltdown. Until there's a cure, preventing Lyme will be tricky, too. The disease isn't just about ticks and deer, and avoiding it isn't as simple as tucking pant legs into socks, stylish though it is.

Like extinction, Lyme is multifactorial. Ticks are tiny, adaptable, and exist in three life stages, one of them virtually invisible. As larvae and nymphs, they prefer rodents, especially white-footed mice, of which 40–90 percent carry *Borrelia burgdorferi*, the spirochete bacterium that causes Lyme. In the adult phase, they like feeding on deer. But any old four-legged fur bag will do, like the sixty million stray cats roaming the United States. Drop an ungulate bomb on the country—annihilate every single antlered beast—and we'll still, sadly, have Lyme. Nuke the rodents and the ecosystem will collapse. Take out bats, as we've seen, and insects increase. While we loathe the diseases they carry, each critter helps assure a healthier ecosystem.

This makes wildlife disease a double-edged sword riddled with tradeoffs. If we safeguard humans entirely, other risks increase. Wiping out mosquitos is a poor choice for curbing malaria. Bats and pangolins shouldn't be killed because of coronavirus fears. Nor should raccoons because of rabies. While species must be safeguarded, some individuals, once infected, can't be.

The big bad raccoon huffing and puffing and threatening to blow my house down was a case in point. A wiser course of action would have been to call animal control. But as a rebellious Edward Abbey wannabe living well over an hour from the nearest dispatcher, I wasn't about to. Even if my call went through, it was unlikely they'd respond quickly. I grabbed my .22, opened my daughter Willow's bedroom window, and told everybody to cover their eyes.

When I was sure the raccoon was dead, I grabbed a shovel from the garage. I scooped up the animal and somberly walked it across my yard. As I looked down at the raccoon's inert body, its haggard fur and lolled-out tongue, George Bernard Shaw's words revisited me. "Life is a disease and the only difference between one another is the stage of the disease at which he lives."

Here we were, two mammals bound for the same inevitable end in the sod. This was but a brief moment—albeit a symbolic one—in a relentless, unending cycle. One diseased creature returning another back into the earth.

16
A Shot in the Dark
Hunting and Collecting

"When cornered, desperate, or isolated, man reverts to those instincts that aim straight at survival. Quick and just."
—Delia Owens, *Where the Crawdads Sing*

L ions belong in dens. Wild dens are preferable, but cozy, book-lined dens make good habitat for them, too. A lion commands mine, a full-maned male I photographed out in the Gol kopjes of Serengeti. A lion adorns my dad's den, too, perched above the mantle. My regal lion, whose reign was scrupulously scrutinized by the Serengeti Lion Project, is the king of beasts at the apex of his power, governor of a large pride and many offspring. His visage is one of beauty, power, and might.

My dad's lion looks stoned and strung out, like it's hung out one too many summers with Jerry Garcia. The stylized cat vapidly stares off into the middle distance, muzzle to muzzle with an equally half-baked ox. The lion and his ox buddy aren't alone. They're flanked by goats, a leopard, a bear, some doughy, sour cream-colored people, and a "fatling," which my dictionary assures me is a young farm animal fattened up for slaughter. While my lion is majestic, it's also cliché and forgettable. My dad's is not.

Other people thought so too. The painting, *The Peaceable King-dom*, was liked well enough to be painted sixty-two times, by a destitute Quaker minister named Edward Hicks. Although his animal depictions need help, Hicks is hard not to like. His mother died when he was eighteen months old, and his teenage years were spent trying to help his family monetarily by painting horse-drawn coaches. For seven years, Hicks faithfully painted buggies, handing his money over. But finally, sometime in his twenties, he cracked. Specifics aren't recorded. The only clue turns up in his memoirs, where Hicks describes himself as "a weak, wayward young man...exceedingly fond of singing, dancing, vain amusements, and the company of young people, and too often profanely swearing."

While many of us wouldn't bat an eye at such coming-of-age frivolity, Hicks saw teleological emptiness. So he joined the Quaker church, got married, and began preaching. Though he found purpose, steady income proved elusive. By the birth of his fifth child, Hicks was penniless. A friend suggested he return to decorative painting, something he'd dabbled in earlier. Hicks consented, soon completing *The Peaceable Kingdom* in 1820.

Every creature in his masterwork was intentional. A lion with an ox, leopards with children, sleeping bears, and, in some versions, Pennsylvania's eponymous William Penn forging a treaty with Native Americans. Born into the upheaval that followed the American Revolution, Hicks craved peace—especially the peaceful coexistence depicted in Isaiah 11:6. Everywhere he looked, he saw discord in the colonists' relationships: to England, Native Americans, and nature. As a response, Hicks fixated on redemption.

This is why I love him. And why I've even grown to love my dad's creepy painting that hung above our fireplace. In Hicks's preaching and painting, the redeemed soul was his central interest.

We don't know the full extent of the discord Hicks saw. But he did leave us hints. In the darkened background of one *Peaceable Kingdom* version, he included a shattered tree trunk. While an ecologist like me would overlook it as a nice snag for an owl nest, its real intent was to represent a rift that had formed within Hicks's Society of Friends.

Aside from the rabid raccoon and some garden-saving, annual groundhog harvesting, I like to think I live in a peaceable kingdom, too. Our unexceptional house with perpetually flaking paint sits under seven red pines, which whistle during winter gales. So we've christened our postage-stamp-sized property "Whistling Pines," while Willow insists it's the "White House."

Ravines flank two sides, one of which a previous owner used as their personal dump. Bedsprings, sinks, shower curtains, paint cans, tires, and even an old commode poke out of the ravine's side like bleached mammoth tusks. While I've managed to remove the most egregious detritus, the rest I've opted to entomb, transforming it into a brush pile worthy of wildlife royalty. I've planted trees, built nature trails, and, on many winter mornings, fed chickadees from my hand a la Saint Francis.

Yes, I hunt poorly, kill groundhogs, and harbor a murderous cat. Whistling Pines certainly isn't an ecological utopia. But if we're judged by our works, I like to think the environmental pearly gates are in view. That if my life had been symbolized in the background of one of Hicks's paintings, I'd pass for a healthy tree. Or at least a decent one with only a few fungal cankers.

But alas, a deranged raccoon isn't the only confused quadruped that has lunged at the backdoor. We have black bears, too. And unlike the bears in Hicks's painting, they haven't been curled up in a cute little ball. A few years ago, at dinner time, a bear shuffled onto our back deck. All five of us were seated around the kitchen table for a later-than-usual meal, enjoying our typical, interruptive banter.

"A bear!" Linda whisper-yelled, pointing over my shoulder. Her eyes were saucers. We all turned toward the glass-paneled door, mouths agape. The bear sniffed around our grill and swung its large head in our direction. Two steps later it was an arm's length away, looking at us or studying its reflection in the plastic storm door I'd spent the previous weekend constructing to keep the coming winter's winds at bay.

For a long moment, we said nothing, absorbing the bruin's glistening muzzle, small ears, and brown beady eyes that stared back at us. Most striking was the round, anthropoid face.

• • • •

The humanlike face adds to the hard-to-define, magnetic aura bears have. Something about them prompts big-game hunters to shoot them and five-year-olds to dress them up in overalls for hosting tea parties. I chalk the pull bears have on us up to an abstruse concept known as the phylogeny of relatedness, which suggests that we're drawn to creatures that resemble us. Chimpanzees are the best example. Their opposable thumbs, forward-facing eyes, and expressive faces draw us to them. Fur and the ability to occasionally stand bipedally help, too. Disney and Pixar know this, hence why all their protagonists and lovable side-kicks—Flounder, Nemo, Maximus—look as much like us as possible, experiencing serious eye-socket adjustment along the way.

Bears have something else, too—predatory power. When we hike and camp, we're at their mercy. If hungry, surprised, or just plain old bored, they can shuck us like an ear of corn. When we're in bear country, we're pushed off our pedestal, at once both hypnotized and humbled. "We look on predators with fascination due to our evolutionary background as hunters," Hans Kruuk wrote in his book *Hunter and Hunted*. "We look on them as competition. And, because we were prey, with anti-carnivore loathing."

• • • •

For a long, adrenalized moment, we were spellbound at the dinner table. But it quickly turned to loathing. The bear crossed a line I hadn't known existed. For reasons I know not, the bear opened its mouth in what looked like a large yawn and then chomped down on my home-made storm door. The heavy-duty plastic popped like guitar strings on contact. When the bear opened its mouth again, there were four large punctures and a raggedy flap that hung like a turkey's beard. Now the previously taut storm door resembled a waterlogged diaper.

While the odd hermit up in Moose Jaw may be used to being van-dalized by bears, I wasn't. I had a family, some of them nugget-sized.

I utterly lost it. My peaceable kingdom had been breached.

• • • •

There was once a peaceable kingdom in East Africa's Serengeti, too. For hundreds of years, a smattering of herding and pastoralist peoples lightly used the fourteen-thousand-square-mile grassland and savanna ecosystem that is today the park, peacefully coexisting with the teeming herds around them. Once the park was established in 1951, however, locals were squeezed out, unable to utilize the park as they always had. As human populations steadily grew, pressures on the park—and on the people—mounted. Conflict between humans and wildlife mushroomed.

This is the cauldron I drove my rickety Land Rover into when I naively began my PhD research. As I built relationships with local people in hopes of understanding the context, it dawned on me right away that hunting and collecting, Soulé's eighteenth extinction factor, would play a central role. For the next five years, I focused my gaze on these primary interactions people had with the park, now illegal in the eyes of the national government.

I hung out in villages, learned Swahili, and slowly wormed my way in. Of all the world's people, East Africans are the friendliest: hospitable, generous, and forthcoming. And after building up an inch of trust, the hunters among them were, too. Under a sliver of shade in a nondescript patch of thorn scrub, I peered into the expressive faces of over one hundred such men—called poachers—and asked them matter-of-factly: "Why do you do it?"

Money, most replied. While there was no reason to disbelieve them, my hunch was that money was a proximate motivation, obfuscating a deeper truth. These poachers risked life and limb. They entered the park at night, in flip-flops, with a flickering flashlight and often an armload of wire for snares. They checked snare lines, removed dying animals strangled in them, and avoided hungry lions, leopards, and hyenas that were drawn to the very same traps.

Just getting to their snare lines was hazardous. Buffalos, elephants, and hippos stood belligerently upon thorn-ridden paths. Snakes lay unseen and motionless. Disease-carrying tsetse flies buzzed by day, malaria-riddled mosquitoes by night, and ranger patrols presented the constant threat of arrest, fine, and imprisonment.

"Do you sell the bushmeat you obtain?" I asked Juma, a fifty-something Tanzanian man with a wrinkled brow, calloused hands, and pencil-thin wrists. His tattered button-up shirt looked three sizes too big.

"I do."

"So, it's all for money?"

"Yes."

"Do you think of yourself as poor, middle class, or rich?" I asked, suspecting he'd say poor. Juma thought for a moment, looking out over my shoulder.

"Middle class."

"Really?" I was surprised.

He nodded.

"Can you live off the crops you grow?"

"If the elephants don't trample them," Juma replied. I sensed he knew what I was getting at: why poach wildlife if his needs were met?

"I sell bushmeat," he explained, "so I can send my kids to school."

This, I learned over the next several field seasons, is why the people living around Serengeti risk life and limb to earn a few hundred extra dollars each year. They're not starving. They simply lack freedom, or agency, to go where they want to in life. It's what renowned economist Amartya Sen calls "capability deprivation," an inability to climb life's ladder. While many Americans and Western Europeans flail about amid a pile of vocational choices, rural East Africans hope merely for one. Most just seek the ability to choose.

Without legal options for making money, young men default to hunting, the availability of bushmeat often just a half-day's walk from their home. It's easy to vilify these men. Easier still to label them poachers and unleash the avalanche of pejorative adjectives that accompany it, words like evil, greedy, heartless, and selfish. Many well-meaning conservation organizations never get beyond this label, regarding poachers as public enemy number one in the fight against extinction.

Michael Soulé, I'm pleased to report, didn't make this mistake. While too much hunting and collecting can certainly drive populations down, he understood that our lazy dichotomies that separate good guys and bad guys are often wrong and unhelpful. Soulé knew that context matters.

For one thing, labels, as we all should have learned in high school, can create unbreakable stereotypes that suffocate context and flatten nuance. To understand the context, envision yourself in a mud hut under a lone acacia tree. You have a hardworking wife, four kids, a goat, and a handful of scrawny chickens. Your food and income depend on whatever rain falls from the sky. This year, you've carefully prepared your fields, planted, weeded, and are a week away from harvesting what looks to be a good crop of maize and cassava. Sometime in the wee hours of the night, you hear crunching. Your mangy dog goes berserk and you follow it outside, a lump rising in your throat. A herd of elephants trundles off as you run toward them, shouting. Even in the moonlight, the carnage is clear. When the sun finally rises, it's confirmed: your lovely maize crop is reduced to a few stalks the elephants happened to miss.

Before the elephants, your subsistence-level life afforded few avenues for advancement. Now, you wonder how your family will survive the next month. Next door lies the vast Serengeti National Park, today a World Heritage Site, the place your grandpa used to hunt. You know the risks. You know it's illegal. You also know how the park just ruined you. Does hunting in the park mean you're an evil and greedy person? Or does it mean that you're rational and a good father?

This was the story I heard over and over. More than one hundred interviews later, I knew that if I were in my respondents' shoes—flip-flops, rather—I would hunt, too. Call me whatever you like. Why? Because the desire for agency isn't merely an American ideal. I'd hunt for food to send my kids to school and to buy a shirt that actually fits.

The men I talked to were courageous, not evil and greedy. They dared for a better life. And judging by some of the gruesome injuries they showed me, they suffered for it. If the hunters I interviewed are greedy for wanting money and basic human freedoms, then we all are. Bus drivers, artists, politicians, lawyers, even meddlesome researchers chasing a PhD.

• • • •

Yet I mustn't stereotype. Africa is big, and poaching differs vastly country by country, region by region. While those who shared with me pursued personal freedoms and livelihood options, hunters elsewhere have other motivations. The hunting and collecting that Soulé worried about involves avaricious profit seekers. Profit, of course, can only be made if there's demand. Unfortunately, demand for wildlife products is insatiable, which is why hunting and collecting factors prominently in extinction.

Some of the wildlife products people want you've heard about: ivory, turtle shells, tiger bones. Others you likely haven't: shahtoosh from Tibetan chiru, glandular secretions from civet cats, and ambergris—a fecal-smelling rock-like thing found in just 5 percent of sperm whales. As long as humans have been walking the earth, wildlife products have been sought and acquired. What's startling, however, is how valuable some have been. "Indeed, when the *Titanic* went down in 1912," Kirk Wallace Johnson wrote in *The Feather Thief*, "the most valuable and highly insured merchandise in its hold was forty crates of feathers, second only to diamonds in the commodities market."

Instead of lulling you to sleep with an exhaustive inventory, I'll whittle my examples down to two. One you're aware of—rhino horn— and another you probably aren't—bear bile. Admission: I still don't really understand bear bile. But I do know this: two examples are more than enough to convince you that the earth doesn't revolve around the sun, it revolves around consumption.

• • • •

While I was interviewing hunters in the Serengeti about the animals they killed, one thing quickly became clear: they didn't kill rhinoceros. There was a good reason for this: there weren't any rhinos to kill. There used to be plenty. For millennia, rhinos rumbled about the Serengeti's plains and woodlands like the prehistoric armored tanks they are. The famously nearsighted beasts browsed, wallowed, and created habitat for other species every time they walked through a thicket. Placid, they would have been an appropriate addition to Hicks's *Peaceable Kingdom*.

Up until recently, rhinos have done a terrific job avoiding extinction. The lineage is successful—rhino ancestors have bulldozed along the mammalian branch of life for over thirty-five million years. Unhorned, barrel-shaped rhinocerotoids bequeathed the five species we have today. One of these, the Sumatran rhino, has arguably been on earth longer than any other mammal. Look at it and you'll see why: it's basically Eeyore draped in a baggy trench coat.

Huge and horned, Africa's two rhino species have met all of life's age-old challenges—lions, disease, and drought—head-on. But evolution hasn't equipped white rhinos or black rhinos from a far more formidable foe: market demand. In an ironic twist, the very horns that historically helped them ward off what few enemies they had, have become their Achilles' heel. Fun fact: rhinos mate for longer than any other mammal. This doesn't include the time they spend wooing, batting eyelashes, and flirting; it is the actual duration of coitus. It's about thirty minutes of intromission without an intermission. You're welcome.

Hairsplitters might argue that lions enjoy sex for longer, doing the wild thing every fifteen minutes for forty-eight consecutive hours. Others might give the nod to the hyena, as their barbed penises get the males locked up when the females are knocked up. Titillating trivia aside, rhinos have a serious strike against them as far as humanity is concerned: they're just too darn horny.

The real problem isn't the rhino's horniness, it's ours. Remember Darwin, the peacock's extravagant train, and his contention that the world is driven by sex? Coupled with consumption brought on through capitalism, the desire for good, long-lasting sex has birthed demand for a lascivious beast more mythical than Nessie: the aphrodisiac.

Other than the rhino's mind-bending coitus and the phallic undertones of its horn, its correlation with enhanced human sex is spurious at best. Rhino horn is simply a mass of compressed keratins, the fibrous structural proteins that make up fingernails, hair, feathers, hooves, wool, epidermis, and more. To save the rhino, aphrodisiac seekers should just chew their fingernails. The effect on their sex life will be the same. Plus, they'll save a hundred grand or so.

Seriously. Rhino horn is more valuable gram-for-gram than gold, cocaine, and heroin. According to author Julian Rademeyer's bestseller, *Killing for Profit*, a kilogram of rhino horn can fetch $65,000 USD. An adult white rhino's horn weighs an average of four kilograms. Notwithstanding the fact that black-market numbers are always fuzzy and fluctuating, this means that the average rhino walks around with $260,000 USD perched above its nose. While a rhino is a far cry from a Lamborghini, it's worth noting that its horn could buy a spit-shined Lamborghini Huracán, with sixty grand left over for some beluga caviar. Outlandishly valued like this, it's no wonder rhinos are staring down extinction. What Africa produces, a sage once said, can never meet demand.

• • • •

Tanzania's rhinos are long gone, as are most of East Africa's rhinos. Had rhinos been around, I'm certain the hunters I talked to would have sought them. Not for themselves, but to meet the demand emanating mostly from the Far East. It's simple math. In the larger context of rhino hunting, the local guys pulling the trigger get the bad rep. But really, they're just pawns. Where illegal rhino hunting does happen, like Mozambique and South Africa, local hunters only get a fraction—perhaps $2,000 USD—compared to what the middlemen and kingpins get. But $2,000 is a windfall regardless, easily outweighing the risks involved. That much, at least, is black and white.

Another aspect of rhinos is black and white, too—their names. The black rhino has a hooked, finger-like mouth, which it uses to pluck vegetation. It's a shy, retiring browser. The white rhino, on the other hand, has a wide mouth, useful for grazing. Both rhinos, and a few sub-species, have been mercilessly poached. According to the International Union for Conservation of Nature, the black rhino population dropped 97.6 percent from 1960 to the 1990s. The white rhino didn't fare much better. But both species have hung on in isolated pockets, largely due to heightened public awareness, deep-pocketed benefactors, privatization, and militant, 24-7, armed surveillance.

Most rhinos today resemble incarcerated inmates. Despite Africa's immensity, they have to be secured behind electrified fences. If you spy one in the open, odds are you'll notice a beret-clad man touting a semi-automatic not far behind—the rhino's personal guard, not a poacher. In an effort to avoid this, to experience rhinos without the trappings of a prison cell, I recently visited Ol Pejeta, a progressive conservancy in central Kenya. I succeeded in finding rhinos, four of them in fact. They calmly grazed a high plateau amid a half dozen amiable warthogs. Larks fluttered by, their musical songs ascending to the pillowy clouds overhead. At Ol Pejeta, the rhino's kingdom was, in a word, peaceable.

But the real drama in Ol Pejeta was occurring well away from the public eye, in seven-hundred-acre enclosures. There, every rhino's move and mouthful was scrutinized and recorded. The action began in 2009 when Ol Pejeta received four northern white rhinos from a zoo in the Czech Republic. The quartet represented over half of the northern white rhinos left on earth. There were two females—Najin and Fatu—and two males, Suni and Sudan. With the rhinos came hope. Najin and Suni mated but for whatever reason, Najin didn't get pregnant. Sadly, not long later, Suni died of natural causes. That left poor Sudan as the world's last remaining male northern white rhino. Poor guy. Talk about performance pressure. If anybody needed an aphrodisiac, it was poor, old Sudan.

Whether it was the world's leering eye or a long list of infections that Sudan had, he caved to the pressure, dying in 2018. As this book goes to print, we're left with Najin and Fatu, two females both declared incapable of pregnancy. But hope remains in human ingenuity and stem cells stored in liquid nitrogen. The plan is to place the stem cells in a surrogate mother, likely a southern white rhino. I'm hopeful but scratch my head nonetheless. Whenever talk turns to gametes, surrogates, and pluripotent stem cells, I can't help but wonder how we let it come to this.

• • • ○

Rhinos aren't the only ones facing grim odds due to hunting and collecting. So are pangolins, tigers, casqued hornbills, and an armada of sea turtles and tortoises, to name but a few. Fortunately, several others on the most traded species list—leopards, serows, and bears—aren't yet reduced to liquid nitrogen lives. For now. For these species, I fear the meter's running. All share one thing in common: a particular body part the world covets. Skin, horns, and in the bear's case, bile. I can't bypass it—after all, the bear brought its bile to my doorstep, raising bile of my own. Of all the wonders I've discussed, bear bile is easily the most flabbergasting.

Had I known that the bear that had just mangled my storm door produced a magical substance capable of curing acne, colds, sore throats, rheumatism, poor eyesight, gall stones, hemorrhoids, conjunctivitis, and even cancer, I may not have acted as I did. I didn't know about it because, well, urso-deoxycholic acid rarely appears in conversation. Nor does its other name, bile, for that matter. But we certainly should talk about this substance.

Think about it: each year black bears in northern climes routinely go one hundred days without eating, drinking, urinating, defecating, or exercising. In case you skimmed that, let me reiterate: a large mammal, whose body temperature never drops below eighty-eight degrees Fahrenheit, goes three months without moistening its lips or taking a trip to the loo. And you thought your constipation was bad. To top it all off, black bears emerge in mint condition, no worse for the wear. Granted, they've lost a little weight and appear a little groggy. But if a freshly woken bear walked into a gym and started doing squat thrusts and bicep curls, they'd hoist as much weight as the previous autumn. If we awoke from a three-month hibernation, on the other hand, we'd be withered prunes and riddled with bedsores.

Metabolism is what prevents us from emulating a bear's hibernation. Like us, bears are composites of trillions of cells. Chemical reactions occur in every cell, the sum total of which we call metabolism. Water, the lifeblood of the world, is the medium for these reactions, hence why complex organisms like us are 70 percent water. We remove the waste products and excess salts through our urine. If we don't, lethal toxicity builds up. Again, black bears are no different, with one big exception: that mystical three-month spell in which they forgo water. No Nalgene, CamelBak, or Gatorade. Nada. Yet also—abracadabra—no dehydration.

The miracle of bear bile allows this metabolic sleight of hand. In ways that still perplex physiologists, bile enables bears to use urea, a chief component of urine, in ways humans can only dream of. If marooned on a desert island, our starving body will break down muscle and organ tissue to supply protein. If a fully stocked lifeboat were suddenly to appear in the midst of this—and we still had a pulse—the organ and tissue damage to our bodies would be irreparable. Not so for a stranded she-bear. She hops into the lifeboat after three waterless months, suckles her cubs she birthed in mid-hibernation, and at long last cracks open a well-deserved can of tuna.

Picture this: A six-year-old mother bear curled up in a small hollow at the base of an overturned oak. Her meager den offers little insulation to the sub-zero winds that nightly howl through the Saskatchewan forest. In the very center of her tight body ball rests her cub, kept alive by her mother's rich milk and belly warmth. A pinched but peaceable kingdom, right? Up until a mammalogist falls through the thin layer of snow atop the den, that is.

This very event happened. The guy, Lynn Rogers, fell atop a snuggling mother and cub. Like babies anywhere that are awakened in the night, the cub bawled. Rogers didn't scramble out of the den and run for his life. Rather, he lounged atop his ursine beanbags and methodically started his stopwatch. Exactly eight minutes later, Rogers recorded, the mother awoke.

Rogers was a brave and bona fide ursophile. Like many of us, he'd been mesmerized by bears his whole life. Wanting to unlock the secrets of hibernation and bile, he repeated the stunt a few years later, on a cold January day. This time he wiggled through a den's front entrance, coming alongside a comatose female. "I tried to hear the heartbeat of a soundly sleeping five-year-old female by pressing my ear against her chest," Rogers wrote. "I could hear nothing. Either the heart was beating so weakly that I could not hear it, or it was beating so slowly I didn't recognize it. After about two minutes, though, I suddenly heard a strong, rapid heartbeat. The bear was waking up. Within a few seconds she lifted her head as I tried to squeeze backward through the den entrance."

Showing nerves of steel, stolid Rogers again refused to run. With his stopwatch and clipboard, he loitered about the entrance like a sixteen-year-old outside a tattoo parlor. He added, "Outside, I could still hear the heartbeat, which I timed (after checking to make sure it wasn't my own) at approximately 175 beats per minute." Untrained in ursine cardiomyopathy, I don't know how Rogers heard the heartbeat while outside the den. Maybe his stethoscope had a really long cord. Or maybe the acoustics in bear dens are above average. Regardless, I believe him. His account was, after all, published in *Natural History*, a credible magazine. Even if it wasn't, it's easy to believe in bear bile.

• • • •

I'm not alone. At least half the world believes in bile, too. This is why bear bile farms have sprung up across China with a mere teaspoon selling for over twenty-five US dollars in China, Japan, and South Korea. As a depressing but obligatory aside, if you thought feed lots were bad, you've never seen a bile farm. Bears are kept in cages they can't stretch out in. Captives are sedated and undergo surgery to have a permanent passageway installed that connects their gallbladder to their abdomen. Bile is collected via a free drip from the bears, euphemistically referred to as "production units." Since poor nutrition causes a bear to produce more bile, captive bears are intentionally half-starved.

What concerns us and Soulé is that the two most intensively farmed species—Asiatic black bears and sun bears—have plummeting populations. It is more cost-effective to hunt down and collect more bears to be farmed than it is to breed bears for their bile, questions of humaneness aside. All of it, the farms and the threat to the bears' extinction the farms pose, is, in a word, bile.

• • • •

Perhaps what I did next was bile, too.

"My storm door!" I yelled, breaking the spell the black bear had cast upon my astonished family. "This must stop!" Pushing back from the kitchen table, I leapt to the door, now separated from the bear by just a quarter-inch of glass.

Unmindful of the example I was showing my kids, I uncurdled a primeval scream coupled with a Jackie Chan karate pose. Nonplussed, the bear didn't flinch. Time to take things up a notch. "Where's my gun?!" I yelled. The question was nonsensical—only I knew where I'd hidden my out-of-reach gun. While rummaging in the basement, it suddenly occurred to me that it was October, so bears could be legally hunted in western New York. Plus, the deer tag I'd recently purchased included one for bear. I wouldn't be calling animal control.

But a problem remained. Rifle season hadn't started yet, and only bows could be used in October. Maybe Iroquois hunters once shot bears with bows. But I doubted modern-day hunters did. My bow would have to do. I grabbed it, along with two arrows, the only two left over from last deer season.

Bow in hand, another dilemma remained. How could I shoot? If I went outside, I'd become a human hors d'oeuvre. No, I couldn't risk that. Since the bear had tried to storm the castle head-on, I'd defend it from the ramparts.

"Dad, there are two bears!" Ezra shouted. Indi hung behind Linda, who peered out a side window.

"Two? Are they still on the deck?"

"No, now they're by the garage! And one is humongous!" Ezra's intel left me two options. Open the side door of the garage and face the bruins on level ground or loose an arrow from our back window, from our very living room. Unnerved by the lead bear's bravado, I opted for the latter.

I opened the only window that afforded a shot and peered out. Twilight had fallen, casting shadows over the lawn. I could vaguely discern each bear's general shape. Both had noses to the ground, pawing at something in the grass. It was too dark to shoot. "Linda, can you turn off the lights?" I asked, hoping it'd help my eyes adjust to the outside darkness. Linda flicked them off but it didn't really help. That left me only one last option.

"Ez, shine this flashlight!" I instructed, thrusting a headlamp into his obliging hands. The beam whipped around the yard as he searched them out. Just thirty feet from my small open window, his beam found them. "Great! Now, stand well behind me!" Whoops. As Ezra stepped backward, his beam cast my shadow upon the yard, blotting out the bears. "Guess you'll have to come alongside me!" Ezra stepped forward. I drew back, my right arm quivering under the fifty-pound draw weight. In my bow's tiny peep sight, the bears were hazy and amorphous in the gloaming. My eyes started playing tricks on me.

"Ez, are they still there?"

"Yeah!"

"Both of them?"

"Yeah!"

I shot. *THUNK.* I knew that sound. It was the sound of an expensive broadhead arrow tip hitting dirt, a sound I'd sadly produced many times before. The bears, however, didn't recognize the sound. Or they chose to ignore it. Both kept their muzzles low, eating something off the ground. One arrow left. I nocked it, pulled back, and again squinted through my sight. A kaleidoscope of black and gray played across my retinas.

"I don't see them, Ez!"

"They're right there!"

"Where?"

"There!"

"Are you sure you see them?"

"I'm sure!"

I trusted his eyes more than mine. "Okay, here goes nothing!"

THWACK! This was a profoundly different sound than the earlier one. For a few seconds, nothing happened. Then a bellow from the pit of Mount Doom rang out across the yard.

"The death cry!" Linda whispered, flipping the lights back on. "You must have got it!" We stared at each other for a long moment. "But we need to shift gears. Tomorrow's a school day. Let's get the kids to bed."

Shaking, I hung up my bow in the garage and started the bedtime routine. While I might've hit one of the bears, there was no way I killed one. Had I used a howitzer or a hand grenade, maybe. Plus, even if I had somehow managed a lethal shot, bears were as tough as nails. A wounded bear would go miles before collapsing. Surrounded on all sides by head-high corn, the chances of tracking and finding it were nil. Nor was I about to track a wounded bear in the dark, or the day for that matter. Like Linda said, it was time to shift gears. It was better to get the kids to bed and get ready for class tomorrow.

A high-maintenance bedtime routine helped me forget about the bear. My dreams were free of bears, too. I slept soundly, awoke at dawn, and poured myself a bowl of cereal across from bleary-eyed Ezra. With my spoon midway to my mouth, I heard Linda yell from the top of the stairs. "The bear!"

My heart dropped into my feet, thinking the bear had returned to wreak more havoc. If it had, it wasn't on the back deck. "Eli, it's in the backyard! I think it's dead!"

My cereal went unfinished. I bounded up the stairs to join Linda at the window. "There!" she said, pointing to a black shape, spread-eagled at the edge of the yard. Above the right rear leg, sticking up like a white flag, was my arrow. "You did it!" she said, beaming at me. It was the look all husbands crave, capable of fueling many more years of futility. In Linda's eyes was pure, unfiltered admiration that momentarily deleted a long ledger of shortcomings. I'd seen it at the altar, and perhaps once after I unclogged the septic tank.

Two hours later, one class done for the day, I was in the backyard figuring out my newest problem, how to get nearly two hundred pounds of deadweight into the back of my truck. Unlike moving a wardrobe, the furry, floppy bear offered little purchase. Still powered by Linda's admiration and a few two-by-fours, I finally managed by yanking the carcass up a ramp by its stubby ears. I left my arrow embedded, fearful its removal would bring the bear back to life.

"Wowwee!" exclaimed my ponytailed meatcutter through his few remaining teeth. Together we dragged the bear out of my truck where it flopped heavily onto his driveway. "Don't do many o' these!" he said, standing back with his hands on his hips. A flock of scraggly chickens emerged from under a rusty car propped up on cinderblocks. A droopy-eyed basset hound sniffed the bear curiously. "Got 'er with a bow, did ya?"

I nodded, unwilling to admit I'd dispatched it from my living room window.

He bent down running his fingers along the arrow. Where it entered the bear's hide, he parted the fur and poked around. "How far'd this girl run?" he asked.

"Not far. Fifty yards max."

"I'd say yer pretty damn lucky, son."

"Why's that?" I said, though I knew he was right.

"Can't be sure till I skin 'er, but I do believe you got 'er in the one place that'll keep a bear from goin' far. Better even than the heart."

I looked at him, confused.

"That shaft looks sunk in the femoral artery. Needle in a haystack shot. Like I said, wowwee!"

· · · ·

We ate the bear for over a year. The rest we gave to very thankful folks at a local Salvation Army. I utilized every part I could. A tooth went to New York's Department of Environmental Conservation for analysis, the skull sits on my shelf, and the hide rests on my office floor. At the time, I knew nothing of bear bile, neither its wondrous effects nor the world's demand for it. If my butcher harvested it, he never said anything. I hope he instead tossed it out back with the offal, where it slowly oozed back into the earth, liberating its life-giving chemicals to nourish uncountable microorganisms.

I also hope to never shoot another bear, even one that eats my door. Not because of a newfound set of morals. Nor because black bears are threatened with extinction—they're not. Rather, I'd just prefer to learn how to live with them. To share the world with them, and at least occasionally, my yard.

Conservationists often talk about carrying capacity, a term used for describing the population size a given environment can sustain for a particular species. Turns out there's another term, even more alliterative and more relevant to today's extinction crisis—cultural carrying capacity. Cultural carrying capacity is about humanity's collective tolerance for wildlife—the number of animals we're willing to allow to tip over our garbage cans, raid our bird feeders, and munch our storm doors. It's not an easy question to answer in the United States. In other parts of the world, like the Serengeti, it's even harder. How many elephants will poor farmers let raid their fields? Can they afford to let any?

No matter how much we like wildlife, our valuation changes the moment they impose their will. The more animals the better, I always thought. But that changed when the bear wrecked my storm door, interrupting our dinner. Suddenly, my cultural carrying capacity sprang a leak. Vengeance, I declared, was mine. Africans living alongside Serengeti lose far more than storm doors to large mammals. Some lose their food supplies while others lose their very lives. Seeking vengeance and a little agency is a natural—and logical—response.

At the same time, population sizes of many species, especially our top predators, are shadows of their former selves. Every remaining lion, tiger, and bear matters. The integrity of our ecosystems and the vitality of our imaginations depend on them. Certainly, the larger and more charismatic animals the better. But context matters, and increasing the populations we have will come at a cost. Much more than a new sheet of plastic for a storm door. Decoupling the world's subsistence farmers from an elephant's whimsy and helping them reach higher on life's ladder of opportunity—this is the true cost of saving the world's remaining species.

• • • •

The Peaceable Kingdom is a pie-in-the-sky painting. This side of heaven, no lion is going to chill cheek to cheek with an ox. Leopards aren't going to cuddle lambs, and bears certainly won't sleep their entire lives away in happy little balls. But that's just it. *The Peaceable Kingdom* isn't meant to be realistic; it's meant to be aspirational. It reflected a desperate and destitute period of Edward Hicks's life, mired within a context of unrest with England, greedy subjugation of Native Americans, and domination of the natural world. All of which makes me wonder if anything has really changed.

The painting itself, like I've said, is creepy. The cupid-like people need vitamin D and a serious exercise regimen. The animals need to sober up and lay off the hashish. Even so, the painting went through sixty-two highly sought-after versions. I can think of only one reason for this: the people in Hicks's day weren't after perfection. Rather, like Hicks, they were seeking redemption.

When I think about our current relationship with the natural world, with rhinos living on liquid nitrogen and grotesque bear-bile farms, I can't help but think we should aim at the very same thing.

Even if we're shooting in the dark.

17

BATWOMAN
Habitat Disturbance

"Unless someone like you cares a whole awful lot,
nothing is going to get better. It's not."
—Dr. Seuss, *The Lorax*

Michael Soulé's penultimate extinction factor, habitat disturbance, is easy to understand piecemeal but difficult to comprehend as a whole. It's more multifaceted than his other factors, both good and bad for endangered species. I'm going to couch Soulé's concept in the context of Michigan, the pleasant state that boasts three great lakes, two peninsulas, and an advertising campaign touting "Pure Michigan." Michigan is our backdrop neither for its purity nor for an abnormal amount of disturbances it has suffered. It was merely where I recently taught a summer conservation biology course to a lovely bunch of undergraduates. But the state also happens to boast one of the rarest warblers in the country, some down-on-their-luck plovers, and a baby bat that showed me how, with love and care, most anything can be saved. We'll bookend our birds with the bat.

● ● ● ●

Before the bat disturbed us, we disturbed it. "What is that sound?" Hannah asked, imploring a local historian, appropriately named Ivy Groves.

"Bats," Ivy said, involuntarily shivering as she looked up into the dark-timbered rafters. "They moved in right after we closed the building to the public." We had just walked into Edward E. Hartwick

Memorial Building, which Ivy had generously offered to give my class a special tour of, following an informative session about Michigan's logging history. Dank mustiness hung in the air as our eyes adjusted to the dark interior.

"Watch your step!" Jonathan said, halting my forward progress with his arm. He pointed to the floor. A brown furry object not much larger than a grape was inches from my right foot.

"It's alive," I said, still unsure what it was. All six of my conservation biology students crouched down, faces close to the old hardwood floor. Ivy, I couldn't help but notice, hung back.

"Aw, it's a baby bat!" Hannah exclaimed. "Listen to those pitiful squeaks!" Three weeks into the five-week course, I had already learned that Hannah was different. Although she was the same age as my other students, she had a two-year-old. Instead of dropping out of college, here she was, taking summer classes, bringing her child along on field trips when not in the care of a friend. Despite so much responsibility at such a young age, Hannah was attentive, insightful, and, as I was about to find out, incredibly bighearted.

"This baby needs its mother!" Hannah said. "Do you folks have an animal rehabber here at Hartwick?" she asked hopefully, looking up at Ivy.

"I'm afraid not," Ivy answered, frowning. Still she stood well behind us.

"We can't just leave it!" Hannah said. "It's going to starve and freeze on this cold floor." She stood up and faced Ivy. "Do you mind if I take it to a rehabber?"

Ivy paused, unsure. Obviously state park employment didn't confer immunity to chiroptophobia. Unsettled, Ivy stuck her arms out as if halting traffic. "Just take it!" she said, heading toward the door.

Wow. Now this was a curveball. A park official allowing a visitor carte blanche to make off with a bat? What about rabies, Ebola, and Marburg? State park visitors were prohibited from bringing their own firewood and picking flowers, but they could walk out with moribund bats?

Having secured Ivy's terror-addled blessing, Hannah turned to me. Shoot. Now *I* had to pass judgment. I like bats. I also knew that the chances that this baby harbored a malevolent disease were small. Philosophically at least, I was fine with taking the bat. But logistically I wasn't. This was our second-to-last week of the course. I had tests to write and papers to grade. Spare time didn't exist for the provision of infant bat care. Not to mention the fact that I'd have a better chance of skipping a stone across Lake Huron than this pathetic creature had at surviving the night. "Hannah, I simply don't have time to care for a bat right now," I said as gently as I could.

"Not you," Hannah replied. "Me!"

"Wait, *you* want to take it?"

"Yeah, I'll hunt down a rehabber."

"Hannah, I'd feel better if…"

"I'll find somebody this very evening!" she interrupted. I paused, which gave Hannah the opportunity she needed. "Does somebody have an envelope?" she asked, turning to the other students.

"How about a piece of paper?" Jonathan offered, ripping a page from his field journal.

"Perfect," Hannah said, folding the paper once and gently sliding it under the bat. Groaning, I looked at Ivy, who smiled weakly. Oh well, Hannah would get the bat to a rehabber and it'd be over by tonight. I fished my keys out of my pocket and walked toward the van. What a pushover I was.

• • • •

When ecologists think about Soulé's seventeenth extinction factor— habitat disturbance—they tend to think about it only in one direction: the disturbance that humans exact on wildlife habitats. It's well justified to think about it like this, as humanity's ever-growing population does exactly that. Clearly, that should be our focus. But our relationship with nature is messy. As my class learned from Ivy, nearly the entire state of Michigan was logged, for example, which posed a pretty serious disturbance for animals dependent on mature forests. At Hartwick Pines

State Park, a few forward-thinking people had the presence of mind to preserve a few groves, providing what are now the park's hallmark hiking trails. Like all places people frequent, however, infrastructure went up to accommodate visitors—roads, bathrooms, administrative buildings, and the memorial building, of course. Bats took to it. They overlooked our transgressions and adapted to the new conditions. Some species, like chimney swifts, have adapted so well that they've nearly become dependent on humanity's artifices. But other species, like spotted owls and loggerhead turtles, haven't been able to. These are some of the many wrinkles of habitat disturbance.

Habitat disturbances happen when temporary changes in environmental conditions cause large, often long-lasting, changes in ecosystems. They can be caused by virtually anything: fires, floods, earthquakes, droughts, invasive species, climate change, disease. It is even thought that the great flocks of the now extinct passenger pigeon caused routine habitat disturbance. Communal roosting thinned canopies by breaking branches while the thick carpet of guano they produced suffocated plants below. Billions of these birds, thinking goes, created patchwork environments and more heterogenous habitat types, shaping the great eastern forests they lived in.

Disturbances can whip through an ecosystem quickly, like a flock of pigeons, or take their precious time, like the cankers that marched across America chestnut tree by chestnut tree. A disturbance, Soulé well knew, also has an unsettling habit of begetting another and another, like an Old Testament lineage of kings. The interactions of varying nested disturbances have emergent properties with difficult-to-predict consequences for endangered species. And, if all that nuance isn't bad enough, there's another plot twist: many species actually depend on habitat disturbances, even some of the most endangered. Lest too much abstraction endanger us, let's narrow our focus to particular species. We'll swoop away from bats to focus on two birds that nobody reviles: piping plovers and Kirtland's warblers.

Piping plovers, which we'll begin with, are the definition of cute. They have Disney-sized eyes and a stubby beak atop a dumpy little body and impossibly twiggy legs; peeping, cream-colored Koosh balls that skitter about the sand. The fluffy, gangly chicks are even cuter. Want to watch somebody's heart melt like an ice cube on hot asphalt? Hand them a baby piping plover.

• • • •

The day after Hannah adopted the baby bat, my class traveled across the mitten to Sleeping Bear Dunes National Lakeshore on Michigan's west coast. We were there to hunt for the rare Lake Huron tansy, study some dune ecology, and discuss appropriate conservation initiatives for fragile ecosystems. We didn't go to the beach for piping plovers. But they were there for us.

"Would you folks mind going around?" a khaki-clad woman asked, dark hair spilling out from under her full-brimmed hat. It was a false pretense of diplomacy; annoyance oozed out of her expressionless face. A spiffy spotting scope stood next to her.

"Piping plovers?" I asked, hoping to soften her abrasiveness.

"Yes," she answered, peering back into her scope.

"They doing okay here?"

"They were," she replied, implying that our momentary appearance on the beach had halted that progress.

Of friends and fiends, this lady was definitely the latter. From her vantage point, we were likely just another band of numbskulls who would further disturb her birds. But I hadn't been rude. Yet. I decided to take one more stab.

"We're a conservation biology class," I offered, "trying to learn about some of the threats facing Michigan's wildlife. Can you tell us anything about this population?"

The lady looked up and forced a smile. "We have five active nests here," she said, holding up her left hand. "And twelve on Dimock Point."

"That's not a lot," I said fatuously.

She stared at me, unwilling to suffer fools.

"How does that compare to previous years?" I added, hoping to sound less moronic.

"Our all-time low was 1990. Twelve pairs total. A few years back we recorded seventy-six pairs."

"What's your goal?"

"One hundred fifty pairs," she stated flatly. "Tough to do with all the predators though. Not to mention the beach traffic."

I looked at the ground. We, my happy-go-lucky class trying to save the planet, were clearly the beach traffic she had in mind. Sensing tension, my students wisely remained silent. For a moment we all were. The only sounds were gulls and Lake Michigan's gentle waves washing up on the pebbly beach. Though we'd not transgressed, my heart felt heavy. Guilt-giving, I realized, may be the first thing the conservation community has to change. It's a terrible motivator, evidence lying in the number of New Year's resolutions abandoned well before February.

I hesitated to ask Piping Plover Lady more. My students loved the natural world. All of them sought careers in environmentally-related fields, hence why they'd sacrificed a beautiful summer for a conservation course when they could have been sailing. I worried this encounter would demotivate them, giving inroads to conservation fatigue. What my students needed was inspiration and a path to follow, not more blame.

They also needed to see the piping plovers the lady was looking at. Perhaps I could build more rapport and win them the chance. "What are their main predators?" I asked, raising my binoculars in the direction her scope pointed.

"Let's see, where to start?" she asked rhetorically. "Try dogs, cats, gulls, rats, fox, raccoons, weasels, skunks, crows, and ravens, to name a few." Okay, so maybe her militaristic approach was justified. "And you should see the merlins," she said. "They pick the plovers off the beach like popcorn."

"Aside from the dogs and cats," I said, "have the piping plovers always had this many predators?"

"Well, some semblance of this predatory guild has always been around but not in these numbers. Dogs off the leash are the real problem."

The lady's mention of a predatory guild reminded me of an important ecological idea called mesopredator release. It happens when larger top predators are removed from an ecosystem, relieving top-down pressure on the smaller, medium-sized predators underneath them. This allows the smaller predators—raccoons, foxes, weasels—to increase in number, assume new roles, and exert greater influence. For prey, mesopredator release isn't just a bummer to shrug off. It can create serious, wholesale structural change—habitat disturbance—that can decrease biodiversity. Awareness of mesopredator release contributed to the push to reintroduce wolves into Yellowstone. With skyrocketing populations of foxes, coyotes, and raccoons masquerading as the big bad wolf, it's doomsday for smaller mammals and birds. For piping plovers on a Lake Michigan beach, it can cause an absolute meltdown.

Before the onslaught of dogs, cats, and a phalanx of mesopredators, piping plovers survived well enough with indomitable crypsis. While other animals rely on thick vegetation to disappear, piping plovers vanish in plain sight. They simply hold still, their beach-toned coverts blending perfectly with the sand and debris around them. Their nests, just a half-inch deep and strewn with pebbles just above the water line, are equally invisible. This makes their camouflaged eggs remarkably easy for a beachgoer to step on, or zoom over in an ATV.

"Do you ever think you'll hit 150 breeding pairs?" I asked, sensing the lady was slowly softening.

"Gonna be hard," she said, scribbling something onto her clipboard. "The lake's come way up. And development is pressing in from the other side."

I cringed at the word "development." It's the ultimate habitat disturbance, a force no piping plover can hide from and the one most of humanity is complicit in. As a macro-level, far-reaching force, development is the form of habitat disturbance Soulé was most concerned with. Species have long adapted to habitat disturbance's other forms, like floods and forest fires. But few species, outside of starlings, house sparrows, and rock doves, have adapted to the inexorable tide of development and all the concrete, asphalt, and altered landscapes it entails.

As a conservationist who cut my teeth in rural Africa, development has long been a thorn in my side, too. The trouble is, development—at least in the form of livelihood opportunity—is exactly what poor people need in many countries. It's what the hunters I hung out with need to decouple them from their poaching lifestyle. But in other places, like Lake Michigan's ever-crowded coastline, development constitutes the ultimate shape-shifting disturbance. When it happens heedless of creatures, like a poorly planned golf course or a reckless oil pipeline, it can irrevocably destroy critically needed habitats. Even well-intended development, like increasing the number of eco-conscious safari camps in Serengeti, can exacerbate problems. Camps need staff and staff will often bring their families. In a roundabout way, this inadvertently draws outsiders into a region, increasing human-wildlife conflict. More camps can also mean more park-goers, suffocating cheetah with paparazzi tour buses.

"I'm Eli, by the way," I said, extending my hand.

"Janet," she answered, shaking my hand, "with the University of Minnesota."

"How often do you monitor these nests?" I asked.

"Every day. But there's a coalition of us that does it every summer."

I glanced at my students, hoping they'd pick up on this critical aspect of conservation: dedication. A few of them were indeed scribbling notes in their journals. At the same time, I couldn't help but wonder if Janet's coalition was merely a lifeboat. Could it really keep piping plovers alive for the long haul? Holding off frisbee-catching Fido was one thing. Holding off the steady advance of beach condos was another.

"Would your students like to look through my scope?" Janet finally offered.

"They'd love to!" I replied enthusiastically. Janet's initial abrasiveness had turned 180 degrees.

Unsurprisingly, Hannah stepped first to the spotting scope. "You guys have to see this!" she squealed. "The babies are adorable!" One by one, my students peered through Janet's scope, affirming the piping plovers' adorability. Each one, I hoped, had new fluffy inspiration to guide their next vocational steps.

• • • •

Equally threatened, but a little less cute, was another species I took my class to visit in the northern part of Michigan's Lower Peninsula—the Kirtland's warbler. As Neotropical warblers go, Kirtland's warblers are pretty standard, sporting blue-gray backs, lemon-yellow underparts, and white crescents above and below their eyes. During the winter months, they have the good sense to lounge about the Bahamas. Come summer, they migrate north, opting to bypass the deciduous forests of the East for the coniferous forests of Michigan. Not just any old forest; only jack and red pine forests suffice, preferably with a rich understory of blueberries.

Even that isn't good enough for the Kirtland's warbler's highly specific tastes. The jack pine the bird prefers best are those that stand between five and twenty feet tall, falling between the ages of six and twenty-two years old. Stands of at least eighty acres are sufficient, but three to four hundred is better. Fastidiousness notwithstanding, there's a method behind the Kirtland's madness. Unlike most warblers, Kirtland's nest on the ground. Unable to hide in plain sight like the piping plover, the warbler wants trees young enough to allow an under-story of vegetation yet old enough to hide its nest with a layer of lower branches. Mesopredators aren't just at the beach.

With such fastidious habitat requirements, it's no wonder it took people a while to figure out where the bird nested. First documented in 1851 in Cleveland, Ohio, it wasn't until 1903 that its nesting site was discovered in Michigan. Since specific habitat requirements like this aren't widespread, Kirtland's has always had a limited distribution. But as the nineteenth century gave way to the twentieth and logging increased, it became even smaller. Where trees weren't cut, fires were suppressed, slowing growth and aging the trees out of the range of suit-ability that the warblers needed. According to the US Fish and Wildlife Service, the loss of warblers mirrored the loss of suitable jack pine. By

1961, the total number of males and females amounted to one thousand individuals. Ten years later, it had dropped to four hundred.

Fortunately, awareness of the warblers' decline grew and, under the Endangered Species Preservation Act, the bird was officially placed on the endangered species list in 1967. As often happens with rare species, the public's interest in the bird grew as its population declined. Many federal and state organizations threw in their support and a Kirtland's Warbler Recovery Team was assembled. Jack pine forests became managed to enhance the Kirtland's habitat. As birding grew as a hobby, people flocked to see the bird. A Kirtland's Warbler Festival even sprang up. Unsurprisingly, I journeyed from New York to see the bird for myself during my college years.

Now, I wanted my students to see the Kirtland's warbler. The bird had rebounded fantastically since its brush with extinction, to the point of being officially removed from the endangered species list in 2020. I wanted them to celebrate this recovery, and see firsthand how federal, state, and local support can bring a species back from the dead. But at the same time, I wanted to show them why Soulé's habitat disturbance factor can't be overgeneralized.

At Hartwick Pines State Park, Ivy had educated my class about Michigan's long history of wildfires. Fires, she'd said, used to be a common summer occurrence in the state, especially the north-central forests of predominantly jack pine. Accustomed to the periodic disturbance, the trees had adapted to the point of dependency. Like the cones of western trees that have evolved with routine wildfire, jack pine cones are serotinous, meaning they only completely release their seeds when subjected to fire. Though fires regularly destroyed large swaths of jack pine, the trees readily responded with a new crop of seedlings. Kirtland's warblers, meanwhile, responded to the ever-shifting mosaic by selecting whichever stand suited their specific nesting requirements.

Native Americans knew all this and let fires burn, sometimes even setting fires of their own. European colonists, however, didn't see fire's promise. Rather, they viewed it as a competitor, stealing trees from their own future harvests. While this story is grossly simplified, the result was over a century of fire suppression, exactly the opposite of what Kirtland's warblers needed to survive. The bird, you see, depends on habitat disturbance.

• • • •

How a species responds to disturbance is known as resilience. I made this critical quality the studs of my dissertation in grad school, using it to describe how the people I studied responded to things like drought, livestock losses, or elephant raids on their maize fields. It was especially pertinent to the illegal hunters I interviewed, who, in the language of the Resilience Alliance, were able to "absorb or withstand perturbations and other stressors such that the system remains within the same regime, essentially maintaining its structure and function."

I forgive you for skimming that. In other words, I wanted to see how hunters responded to livelihood setbacks and how the ecosystem responded to their hunting. Resilience is critical to any discussion of habitat disturbance because it determines how much an ecosystem—or a species—can endure before cracking. How many beaches, for example, can you open to the public and maintain piping plovers? How long can you withhold fire from jack pine forests and maintain Kirtland's warblers? What is the resilience of these respective species? If we don't assess it accurately, we risk losing them to extinction.

The concept is far more fun to demonstrate than define. In class, I try to conceal my malicious smile while filling a paper cup to the brim with water. Then, I ask my most self-assured student to come up front, hand them the cup, and casually lean back against the chalkboard. "Walk from one end of the room to the other," I stoically instruct. "Most importantly, don't spill."

Students always succeed, rarely sloshing a drop. "Great job," I say. "But can you do it twice?" This time, right at the point when the student passes me, I release my most earsplitting, bloodcurdling yell. I throw in a wild-eyed jumping jack for good measure. It's disturbing. The student jumps and the water sloshes, sometimes dousing the front row. When that happens, the hooded, phone-absorbed kid in the back row stops texting, glances up, and smirks. Sometimes, however, a student senses my antics and braces for it, losing hardly any water at all.

The point is this: animals respond differently to disturbance. For some, any disturbance is stressful. Others, like starlings, hardly bat an eye. This is the great riddle of habitat disturbance: we don't always know how sensitive species are until it's too late. Too much of it threatens the piping plover. Too little of it threatens the Kirtland's warbler. Can humanity strike the right balance? It's a tall order. But two people in Michigan, Janet and Hannah, gave me hope. Janet, through her angsty dedication to the piping plover. And Hannah through her dedication to the baby bat. Neither did it perfectly, but they both tried. Both tried something I'd blow off as inconvenient, too labor-intensive, or impossible. So we return again to Hannah's bat. Trust me, it's worth it.

Five days after promising to take the bat to a rehabber "that very evening," Hannah came to class and casually sat down amid the five other students. Three sentences into a lecture about our national wildlife refuge system, squeaking sounds erupted. By now, all heads instinctively swiveled toward Hannah. Frowning, she looked down, seemingly into her shirt. The squeaking intensified. Turning in her chair to shield us from seeing, she fumbled around in her blouse. We couldn't help but stare. What on earth was happening?

Seconds later Hannah turned back around with a wide smile. "Fred's here," she said, holding the little bat she'd scooped up at Hartwick in her hands.

"He's alive?" I asked, astounded. "Was he in your pocket?"

"My bra," she replied matter-of-factly. "He likes to feel snug."

Several students gasped. Eyebrows shot up amid nervous side glances. Hannah's news was shocking on many levels. That Fred was alive, that she'd brought him to class, and that the two of them were bosom buddies.

"Do you mind if I feed him?" she asked, grinning. Nobody moved. "He likes kitty formula," she added, sensing our worry. Everybody noticeably relaxed before Hannah continued. "The kitty bottle nipple is too big so I have to put this coffee filter on it for him to suck on."

Needless to say, the appearance of little Fred overshadowed the rest of my lecture. For five minutes, everybody crowded around Hannah as she took out a medicine dropper and a vial of milk. "It's a rat with wings!" Emily exclaimed, as Fred eagerly lapped up the milk, inky eyes very much alert. The hungry bat drank and drank, ending his kitty-formula Slurpee with a downward-facing dog yoga pose, a sure sign of his renewed vigor.

"Do you think I can take him to Texas?" Hannah asked.

"Why Texas?" I asked, no longer surprised by anything Hannah said.

"I'm heading to Texas this coming weekend to see my boyfriend and I'd rather not leave Fred behind."

"But you said you were going to give the bat to a rehabber," I said, still annoyed that Hannah hadn't kept her word.

"I did try," Hannah said, screwing the cap back on her milk vial. "I called a bunch of places. But nobody would take him in. They just won't do bats. It's currently illegal in Michigan to rehabilitate rabies vector species—bats and skunks. But there is a place in Texas that will."

I had to give Hannah credit. In addition to her unlimited empathy, she had certainly been proactive on the bat's behalf.

My course ended just before Hannah's Texas trip, which mercifully brought an end to the complicity I felt. Curious as to Fred the bat's fate, I couldn't resist sending Hannah a follow-up email. I received a return email in short order, bursting with smiley-face emojis, exclamation marks, and best of all, photos of Fred hanging upside down in a little mesh enclosure on a window sill with the Chicago skyline behind him. Hannah's play-by-play was both improbable and hilarious.

So Hannah, together with her fiancé, Fred the bat, and her two-year-old in the back, eventually drove to Texas. "We were able to sneak Fred into a hotel under a pile of dirty clothes. We almost died laughing when he started squeaking in the lobby and we just looked around as if we didn't know where the sound was coming from. Luckily nobody was in the elevator with us. We set his cage in the windowsill with a nice view."

Once in Texas, Hannah found a rehabber who agreed to take Fred in long-term. On the way there, however, she and Fred had grown attached. So much so that Hannah debated keeping him upon arriving in Texas. She thought better of it, "even though having a pet dragon creature would be sooooooo cool." Hannah has kept in touch with Fred's new caretakers, and related their latest update: "His name is Angus now and he's bossing them all around and complaining bitterly if he isn't the first to be fed. They say he has more personality than any bat they have ever met."

• • • •

We disturbed Fred's habitat and then he, in turn, disturbed ours. Such is life when we share the planet with untold species. Habitat disturbances are messy and multifaceted. Most important are the disturbances that humanity imposes on habitats, like putting up beach condos near piping plover nesting grounds or suppressing wildfire in Kirtland's warbler locales. It's complicated: Our disturbances may push some species toward extinction. But a lack thereof may do the very same thing. While it's often unclear how best to manage disturbance, this much is clear: it will take a whole lot of care and dedication. We need more Hannahs and Janets. Though they can rankle and their methods aren't perfect, we need at least a pinch of their zeal to rub off on the rest of us.

Sometime later yet another email popped up from Hannah. "Would you be willing to write me a recommendation letter?" she asked.

"Of course," I wrote back immediately. If Hannah was going to pursue further opportunities to work with wildlife and conservation, I was certainly going to help her along. Her never-say-die attitude and deep empathy could only help the cause. So, I described Hannah's many positive qualities but opted against mentioning her adoption of the bat. Besides, if she got the job, Hannah's true colors would show through soon enough. And when they did, everybody would be better for it. Perhaps a bat would, too.

18
MELTDOWN
Habitat Destruction

*"But most of all I love them because they
make me feel alive in a way nothing else can."*
—Christina Baal, *When Birds Are Near*

Since the year 1600, eighteen mammals, thirty-four birds, and nine fish have gone extinct in America. These species, notes author Dan Flores in *Coyote America*, merely had the misfortune of occupying too narrow a niche. "They disappeared not because of direct attack," Flores writes, "but because their habitat got logged." Or, in the case of the fish, their habitat became altered. This brings us to the final leg of our slog through Soulé—habitat destruction. Soulé listed habitat destruction as just one of his eighteen factors that cause extinction. He didn't rank them. But perhaps he should have; habitat destruction has a ring of ultimacy to it.

Soulé didn't, I think, because he wanted to emphasize the particularity of each threat, how they differ significantly in time and space. Plus, habitat destruction isn't always the leading threat. Black rhinos, for example, are far more threatened by illegal hunting than they are by habitat destruction. For Kirtland's warbler, the trouble is the age and structure of their habitat, not necessarily the removal of it. Nonetheless, habitat destruction is the right factor to end on because its wide reach affects many of the others in nontrivial ways.

"I believe our biggest issue is the same biggest issue that the whole world is facing," said the late, great Steve Irwin regarding his native

Australia, "and that's habitat destruction." What Irwin meant is that if so many of the world's habitats weren't already destroyed, we wouldn't have experienced the spate of extinctions that we have. In a way, all seventeen of Soulé's other factors are more proximate, their effects exacerbated by the destruction of habitats. Give cheetah the space they need, for example, and their inbreeding problems melt away.

Whenever habitat destruction is broached, a lot of terminological rubble is cast about. Some equate habitat disturbance to destruction. I'd rather not. I prefer to see a disturbance as a temporary state of an ecosystem, something the flora and fauna can plausibly recover from. Destruction, on the other hand, has a finality to it, like filling in a wetland with a Walmart parking lot. Other terms, like habitat degradation and habitat fragmentation, can also muddy the waters. Like a disturbance, degradation and fragmentation can certainly destroy habitats. But let's agree to view them as obstacles species can possibly overcome, perhaps with some luck, management, and adaptability. As for Soulé's last factor—habitat destruction—consider it the sickle in the Grim Reaper's bony hands. When it falls, it's over folks.

While you're surely antsy to get to the finish line, relax, we're going to meander down this old, winding river one last time. Our journey will be framed by a two-year study I took part in that focused on the disappearance of salmon from a small creek outside Sacramento. The project formed the heart of my master's degree, so we'll make a fitting detour to Chernobyl, as both events led to meltdowns. To lighten the carnage along the way, I'll make a final, obligatory digression to beavers. Mostly because, if we insist on destroying habitats, it'd be wise to follow the beaver's lead. Better than any other creature, beavers have taught me the meaning of creative destruction. They've shown me that habitat destruction is lodged—pun intended—in the eye of the beholder. But before we encounter any rodents of unusual size, dammit, let's head to balmy Santa Barbara.

● ● ● ●

"This is our conceptual model," I said, glancing up at the large screen above my head. I prayed the sweat trickling down the sides of my torso hadn't soaked through my tucked-in, button-up shirt. To hide my shaking frame, I stood statuesque behind a podium, at the bottom of an auditorium packed with at least three hundred expectant faces. While professional athletes may be used to being gazed at from above, I wasn't. In this Roman coliseum my demise felt imminent.

Many faces, fellow students and professors, were familiar. Others, outside professionals we'd partnered with, weren't. In dry-cleaned suits, they nodded stoically and looked on, making notes in their steno pads. "Don't hire this kid," I imagined them writing. To make our work more relevant, each thesis had been a joint effort of student groups, outside professionals, and overseeing faculty, all assigned to work on actual environmental problems California faced.

Despite my interest in birds, I'd committed to a project to improve the prospects of Chinook salmon. The fish intrigued me, the way they split their lives between tiny streams and the Pacific Ocean. It mirrored my own life, a student by day and cartooning and working in a coffee shop in whatever time remained. For two years, my group and I drummed up ways to improve salmon spawning in Secret Ravine, a polluted and sluggish creek that ran through Sacramento, narrow enough for a decent college long-jumper to clear. Salmon were worth it, I figured, and I longed to watch huge fish return to their little natal streams in the autumn in their herculean efforts to procreate. After spawning, the exhausted fish died.

Our project made me feel like I was going to die, too. At the outset, we'd split up the work. Dimly, I agreed to create our group's conceptual model. What could be easier, I thought, than whipping up a simple box-and-arrow diagram? It'd be easy to produce a spiffy little schematic with salmon, Secret Ravine, and a handful of obstacles the salmon faced. As I researched conceptual models, I ran across an ominous line by statistician George Box, in a book dryly titled *Empirical Model-Building and Response Surfaces*. "All models are wrong," Box wrote, "but some are useful." No problem, I assured myself. Nobody was better equipped than me to make a faulty model. But Box elaborated:

"The practical question is how wrong do they have to be to not be useful?"

Regarding the endless models I created, my group couldn't agree. Kirk liked simplicity, a clean model with just a handful of stressors. Suzanne, the realist, wanted more. Julie wanted the arrows to point both directions. Kirk didn't. Suzanne wanted dotted lines. Julie wanted them straight. Liz wanted a box around everything. Kirk didn't. Liz wanted life stages distinguished by color. Julie didn't. Kirk wanted links between the physical and biological stressors. Liz didn't. Suzanne thought the chemical stressors should be linked with the others. Julie didn't.

Nothing I did was right. Barbara, our outside consultant, said just enough to get us jousting again. Bruce, our faculty advisor, smirked, chortled, and refused to take sides.

By the time our big final presentation rolled around, I had produced a model that, as George Box predicted, was horribly wrong. And it was not useful. Scores of variables were squeezed into tiny boxes in microscopic font. Arrows pointed in every compass direction. A hodgepodge of dotted lines and solid lines linked disjointed ideas, and a kaleidoscope of colors highlighted everything in such a way that nothing stood out. It was ugly, cluttered, and unintelligible. And now, as I stood before my peers and a collection of professionals, it reared its ugly head, covering the theater-sized screen behind me.

"I've heard it said," I began, leaning into the microphone, "that all models are wrong, but some are useful." I pointed up at the screen. "The same," I continued, "can be said of grad students." I paused, hoping my joke would defuse the tension I felt. Crickets. I glanced at my group, sitting off to the side. Eyes darted around awkwardly. Before I could proceed, a voice rang out from the middle of the auditorium.

"Looks like the wiring plan of our building!"

The place exploded. Everything went blurry after that. I don't remember anything else about our presentation. But I pushed through it because I had to, kind of like how the plants and animals did following the worst nuclear disaster in the history of the world.

• • • •

Chernobyl is the ultimate example of Soulé's ultimate factor of extinction. It spewed thousands of tons of radioactive waste into the atmosphere, forced 116,000 people to evacuate, and killed uncounted thousands via cancer and other radiation-related illnesses. For comparison, the disaster emitted four hundred times more radiation than the atomic bomb dropped on Hiroshima.

I was eight years old at the time—1986—too buried in birdwatching and baseball cards to understand the magnitude of the event. While the destruction it caused was unprecedented, how ecosystems responded was even more so. Wildlife's response to Chernobyl displays wild hope better than anything else I've ever seen in nature.

The meltdown lasted ten days. As radiation fell out of the sky, pine trees for miles around reddened and died. Insects died instantly by the millions. Animals sickened. Soil absorbed radioactive fallout and became contaminated. In the immediate area of the fallout zone, food webs collapsed. Pripyat, a bustling city of fifty thousand before the accident, was abandoned. Dishes, card games, and sewing projects were all left unfinished. Bowls left on counters, toys strewn about floors, sock drawers wide open, utterly apocalyptic. For safety, a thirty-kilometer exclusion zone was set up along the border of Ukraine and Belarus. The entire zone immediately became a ghost town, houses and buildings left open and accessible. Not long later, things began to get interesting.

Overnight, Chernobyl became the equivalent of Iceland's Surtsey, a natural laboratory to watch the imperialism and resilience of living things sans *Homo sapiens*. Chernobyl granted scientists another opportunity, too: to witness firsthand how wildlife responds to one of the gravest forms of habitat destruction. What was worse for wildlife? Sharing space with people before the nuclear disaster? Or moving into a destroyed habitat with high levels of radioactivity? The answer is unsettling.

Despite the radioactivity, wildlife was quickly drawn to the exclusion zone, almost entirely because it was free of people. In just a few decades, all its original inhabitants returned: red deer, roe deer,

European bison, lynx, elk, moose, beaver, fox, badger, and a weird creature called a raccoon dog, which I'd forgive you for assuming was a newfangled hybrid. More impressively, apex predators that hadn't been recorded in the region for over a century also returned: brown bears and wolves. Finding houses deserted, the wolves set up dens in them, like a family of squirrels moving into your attic.

Other animals that have galloped across these pages have flourished in the exclusion zone. Four years after the meltdown, thirty-six Przewalski's horses, the endangered Mongolian horses with an odd number of chromosomes and an equine mullet, were released into the exclusion zone. In the absence of poaching and competition for grazing, the horses thrived, more than doubling their population. European boar, the same species hanging above my dining room table, have made a happy home snuffling about the zone. The boars' hardiness is on full display. Much of the food they eat is laced with significant levels of cesium 137, meaning the Belarusian boars are radioactive, too. It also means—hee, hee—that they leave a trail of radioactive dung everywhere their muddy hooves go.

Just think: all these species thriving amid nuclear fallout for one reason alone—people aren't there. Though we may like to think of ourselves as neighborly, most species heartily disagree. To the largest and most charismatic species, we're plain old stressful. We trap, shoot, build, pave, poison, mow, suppress, run over, chop, contaminate, excavate, honk, blockade, and otherwise mangle habitats to a point they're unlivable. What habitat does a wolf prefer? Studies comparing wolf density in the radioactive exclusion zone to the peopled areas around it have shown wolves to be nineteen times more abundant in the exclusion zone. While Chernobyl certainly destroyed habitats, mere human presence seems to be worse.

• • • •

Unsettling human presence became clear to me during my study of Chinook salmon, too, and not just during the meltdown I suffered during our final presentation. In the process of making our conceptual model, I realized how difficult we've made the lives of the great fish that swim up our little streams. No matter how many lines, arrows, and boxes I used, I couldn't begin to adequately show the stressors humanity has imposed on the fish. Noxious chemicals from landscape maintenance, runoff from impervious surfaces, channelization from construction and development, altered flow regimes and nutrient loading from water treatment plants, poisonous slurries from old mining operations, destruction of riparian vegetation, encroaching orchards, competition from introduced fish, erosion from off-road vehicles, siphoned water for irrigation, and dams, which we'll get to soon enough.

Each of these is a habitat disturbance. Combined, they constitute destruction. Their interactive effects caused an avalanche of physical, chemical, and biological stressors, all of which I felt compelled to cram into the model. These included increased sediment, altered flow regime, altered stream morphology, high water temperature, altered riparian vegetation, reduced access, hydrocarbons, pesticides, excessive nutrients, metals, depleted food supply and predation. How badly the salmon were affected depended on the life stage they were in—the young were more affected by contaminants, for example, while older and larger fish suffered more from stream blockages and reduced access.

Secret Ravine didn't have a lot of salmon in the water, hence why we were studying it. But a few hardy, brave Chinook were still trying. Their habitat was mostly destroyed, but not entirely. This is the key point—for where we are today with our extinction crisis: the fate of many species isn't yet sealed. It's preventable. The Grim Reaper's sickle is dropping fast, but if we act quickly and shrewdly, perhaps we can wrest it from his deathly hands. Sullied Secret Ravine continues flowing. But how much more engine coolant, faded flip-flops, pop cans, submerged shopping carts, and water diverted for agriculture can the little creek take? How much can the beleaguered salmon take?

If Chernobyl is our guide, quite a lot. The wildlife of the exclusion zone showed us they can survive everything we throw at them, including the kitchen sink. They survived, however, because humans left and gave them the opportunity to do so. This isn't realistic everywhere else. If anything, in much of the world's remaining habitats, humans are only going to become more populous. How can wildlife survive the coming habitat destruction that will surely accompany this? Well, our destruction has to be more creative, for one thing. That's why we'll close with the beaver.

• • • •

"One of the penalties of an ecological education is that one lives alone in a world of wounds," Aldo Leopold once wrote, before adding, "Much of the damage inflicted on land is quite invisible to laymen." My experience supports Leopold's assertion, though dams—all ninety-some thousand in the United States alone—don't fall into his invisible category. Unlike pesticide use and climate change, they're big and obvious. Dams have pushed some species, like the pikeminnow and the razorback sucker, to the brink of extinction, making them what John McPhee unequivocally declares, the "absolute epicenter of hell on earth."

While I could kill our joie de vivre with a discussion about the merits and demerits of hydropower, flood control, and humanity's dams, here's why beavers will paddle us home instead. They provide an example when we need it most: they're used to swimming upstream, their dams increase biodiversity, and they'll stop at nothing to accomplish their goals—one hard-up beaver was apprehended in a department store in Charlotte Hall, Maryland, after attempting to procure plastic-wrapped Christmas trees. More seriously, we're wise to follow the beavers' lead because we already share a lot in common with them. They are the ultimate keystone species and a continental-scale force of nature. They even shaped us. According to Ben Goldfarb in his magisterial account, *Eager*, beavers "shaped North America's ecosystems, its human history, its geology."

Our commonality isn't lost on ecologist Tom Wessels either. "Beavers are the only animals, other than humans," he writes, "that will create entirely new ecosystems for their own use. And often, like humans, once they have depleted an area's resources, they will abandon their holdings and move on." Through their dam building, beavers destroy habitats. Once clear-flowing streams swell into stagnant, mucky ponds. Surrounding trees suffocate and die. Other trees are systematically gnawed down for dams and fodder. Sharpened stumps litter the ground, waiting to impale the clumsy hiker, and fallen trees lie scattershot. It's awful country for kayaking, fly fishing, swimming, and I can only assume, nude sunbathing.

Goldfarb, who has investigated far more beaver dams than I, describes the transition of a pellucid stream to beaver wreckage like this: "It's a sluggish, murky swamp, backed up several acres by a messy concatenation of woody dams. Gnawed stumps ring the marsh like punji sticks; dead and dying trees stand aslant in the chest-deep pond. When you step into the water, you feel not rocks underfoot but sludge. The musty stink of decomposition wafts into your nostrils. If there's a fisherman here, he's thrashing angrily in the willows, his fly caught in a tree."

Eventually, beavers eat themselves out of dam and lodge. When food runs too low, they move on and destroy anew. The dams they leave behind inevitably fail, ponds drain, and new tree species—willow, aspen, red maple—soon invade and take over. This, you may recall, is the predictable ecological process of beaver-caused succession—forested streams to ponds, which give way to wet meadows and, eventually, forested streams again.

But there are two key differences. First, beaver destruction—the ponds they create—are actually more diverse than the original habitat. In the intermountain West, Goldfarb reports that wetlands compose just 2 percent of the total land area yet support 80 percent of the biodiversity. And second, unlike people, beavers have the wisdom to move on and let the habitats they mangle recover. People tend to destroy habitats and stay put, unless they're forced out by the worst nuclear disaster in the history of the world.

So while humans and beavers both devour habitats greedily and predictably, beavers do it auspiciously. In a beaver pond, ornithologist and entomologist alike have all the birds and the bees they can handle. "An almost unfathomable seventy-three bugs per square meter" were found in beaver ponds, Goldfarb reports, "up to five times more invertebrates than open channels." This critical cog in the food chain lures bigger creatures, too: moose, mink, deer, bobcat, coyote, fox, and bear, to name a few. In the West, beaver ponds also attract salmon.

A dam, you might think, would harm salmon rather than help them. But in fact, beaver ponds provide salmon ideal summer rearing habitat for their young and generate oodles of fish food. Plus, the dams trap sediment that can smother spawning grounds, and the vast amount of woody debris creates refugia to help the fish survive droughts and floods. And while the dams can pose temporary obstacles to migrating fish, Goldfarb reports that salmon rarely have much trouble, bypassing them via side channels, biding their time in plunge pools as they await high flows, or simply soaring over the barriers straightaway.

Herein is the crux of the beaver: their destruction is creative, begetting abundant life. Entire biological communities depend on their avarice. "No other creature," Wessels writes, "fashions such an array of habitats on which so many other species are dependent. How poor our countryside would become," he adds, "if this species were again to be lost." Hence the beaver's keystone status, a label of importance it has shared with elephants in Africa, otters in the Pacific Northwest, and bison in the Great Plains, among a few others. It's like an all-star team, critical bits of mammalian masonry upholding their fellow creation.

Some fish, like the Chinook salmon I studied, are considered keystones, too. History details how they supported Native Americans of the Northwest for millennia, not to mention bears, eagles, and other scavengers. Salmon may have indirectly kept spotted owls and marbled murrelets alive, too, birds that nest in large, old-growth forests. Not as a food source, as one might think, but rather as fertilizer. Upon spawning, salmon die and bears and eagles feast on them, scattering the fishy remains about the ecosystem. It's one last posthumous gift of the salmon: a nitrogen-rich offering in a nutrient-poor place, just the thing embryonic trees need to get started. "When one tugs at a single thing in nature," John Muir famously wrote, "he finds it attached to the rest of the world." It's crazy but true: fish feed forests.

The keystone species concept is hotly debated in ecological circles. Since we don't know species' true interdependence, trumpeting one's value over another may not be wise. As I discovered when designing a conceptual model, the web of life is unknowable in its entirety. But we do know this: certain species do cause disproportionate effects on ecosystems.

So, does that make us—*Homo sapiens*—keystones, too?

Absolutely not. That's where humans and beavers part ways in a yellow, hopefully marshy, wood. Our destruction, in its contemporary form, simply isn't that creative. The landscapes we alter are too rarely an integrated part of the functioning system. Subdivisions, parking lots, and strip malls don't beget life. "A thing is right when it tends to preserve the integrity, stability, and beauty of the biotic community," Aldo Leopold wrote. "It is wrong when it tends otherwise." Despite a brain the size of a walnut, beavers have fully comprehended Leopold's sentiment.

● ● ● ●

And yet our hope should remain buoyant. For one thing, the human brain is larger than a walnut. For another, creativity oozes out of its 1,400-cubic-centimeter-average capacity. Although we mindlessly destroy habitats, we can creatively rehabilitate them too. Goats, I promise, will be our final digression.

In the late 1950s, a few shortsighted fishermen living on the Galápagos decided to create a quick and dirty, labor-free farm. So, in their spare time, they released a few goats on some of the smaller islands around which they fished. The goats happily went along with the plan and ate and bred like crazy. On Pinta Island, they consumed every scrap of vegetation, which pushed several tree species to near extinction. As trees died, soil erosion sped up, hurting other plants and accelerating the ecosystem's decay. Worse yet, the Pinta giant tortoise—

offspring of those that had survived a trans-Pacific journey—now had a greedy new competitor, meaning slow but certain extinction.

This final story is to offer hope, not to add another log of guilt to the fire. Not because we succeeded in restoring Pinta's tortoise; we didn't. But we did exhibit some rarefied creativity in ridding Pinta of goats, a final arrow of hope to tuck in your quiver.

Eradicating goats on offshore islands is tough, akin to making origami cranes with your toes. Topography presented the biggest challenge on Pinta Island. Vertiginous, ridge- and ravine-laden land besmeared in whatever thorny, shin-slicing vegetation the goats couldn't eat. Nabbing a few goats with high-powered rifles wasn't hard. But nabbing every last one, all the napping ones, the panicky ones, and the hidden ones, was. After two furious but failed attempts in the 1990s, a light bulb went on. How about radio collars? If a few bellwethers were trapped and affixed with collars, perhaps they could do the dirty work, betraying their kin to the rifle-toting park officials. Perhaps we could make them "Judas goats"?

The plan was enacted. The Judas goats weren't as insidious as Judas Iscariot; they didn't betray their brethren intentionally. They just did what goats do—herded together with their friends. Systematically, the park service visited Pinta Island at varying intervals and shot every goat they saw. Except for the Judas goats, that is. As Henry Nicholls wrote in *Lonesome George*, "it must be pretty disconcerting to be a Judas goat. Just when you think you've made a new friend, bang! It slumps to the ground."

The Judas goat method of invasive species removal worked marvelously. Without goats, the island's vegetation bounced back and with it a healthier, more complete ecosystem. But like I said, it was a hair too late for the Pinta tortoise. Which makes me unable to shake a niggling doubt: Are we Judas goats ourselves, blithely standing pat while our scaly, furry, and feathered friends fall around us? In the end, it's worth remembering that the Judas goats succumbed as well.

• • • •

It's too late to "keep every cog and wheel," as Leopold advised for humanity's first step in intelligent tinkering. But there's still a whole lot left, approximately 1.7 million species (over 80 percent of which remain undescribed), give or take a few hundred thousand. While all of Soulé's extinction factors are critical, nothing we do will matter unless we stop destroying habitats.

In *The Atlantic*, Scott Frank, a professor at Case Western Reserve University's School of Medicine, suggested there are three ways to think about the causes of a person's death: the medical cause, the actual cause, and the "actual actual" cause. The medical cause is the most proximate cause of death, the diagnosable cancer or heart disease. Less proximate—and thus, more ultimate—is the actual cause, habits and behaviors that over time contributed to the medical cause. This might be a lifetime of inactivity, cigarettes, or in my case, too many Pop-Tarts. Lastly is the "actual actual" cause, the ultimate reason. Such factors are bigger, society-wide forces that shaped these habits. For this example, it may be forces like poverty, low levels of education, or racial inequality.

What is the actual actual cause of extinction? Is there a factor even beyond habitat destruction? I think there is. Consider this my last—and appropriately obscure—word: *finitude*. Though this word may rarely roll off your tongue, I'm convinced you know it: the state of having limits or bounds. We know it and must face it: we are finite. No matter how much we cram into our brains, our knowledge is limited.

In *Beyond Stewardship*, ecologist James Skillen documents egregious examples of finitude in the lives of scientists and governmental agencies. He also sees it in us, too, giving the following example: "In a globalized economy, we buy coffee from Indonesia, bananas from Ecuador, oil from Saudi Arabia, shoes from China, wine from France, chocolate from Belgium, vanilla from Madagascar, and so forth." This vast network of relationships—and their impacts on native species—is invisible and indecipherable. It's the dizzying conceptual model—the wiring plan—that caused me heartache in my final presentation. Dizzying but real, and its impacts on the world's species are rarely innocuous. "As the market economy grows in space and complexity, so does consumer ignorance," Skillen soberly concludes.

Homo sapiens is many things. Creative, industrious, intelligent, but also, and perhaps most importantly, finite. If we could accept our finitude, perhaps it wouldn't result in habitat destruction and extinction. Regarding Leopold's dictum, we don't always know when a thing is right. We can't always predict when our actions will "preserve the integrity, stability, and beauty of the biotic community." Even when we do, we have human lives to think about, too.

That's why I studied salmon. It's why, regardless of my flawed model and a subpar presentation, I gravitate to them still. For two years, they were a mirror. Outsized organisms in a stressful world. Forging ever onward, forced into finitude, inexorably driven by a larger goal. Will my life, like theirs, nourish others? Will I sustain mammals and birds and help grow forests?

My motivation to keep trying comes from the mouth of a child. At the time, former Secretary of the Interior Bruce Babbitt was seeking justification for pushing his conservation agenda forward. Data, experts, and well-articulated philosophic arguments were at his disposal. But Babbitt turned to children, asking them why we should save our fellow species. One ten-year-old's answer stood out from the rest. We should save our fellow species, the child reasoned, because we can.

The child was dead serious.

Conclusion

I began this book with a promise I'd tell the truth. I lied. Just one little prevarication. I withheld one critical statement Michael Soulé made about his *Table 1*, the list of "Possible Factors Contributing to the Extinction of Local Populations" that we've used to guide our journey. Before I rectify my sin of omission, pass your eyes one last time over Soulé's list:

1. Rarity – Low Density
2. Rarity – Small, Infrequent Patches
3. Limited Dispersal Ability
4. Inbreeding
5. Loss of Heterozygosity
6. Founder Effects
7. Hybridization
8. Successional Loss of Habitat
9. Environmental Variation
10. Long-Term Environmental Trends
11. Catastrophe
12. Extinction of Mutualist Populations
13. Competition
14. Predation
15. Disease

16. Hunting and Collecting
17. Habitat Disturbance
18. Habitat Destruction

Hopefully, Soulé's concepts have gone from a collection of dusty taxidermy mounts to living ideas eager to follow you outside. Anyway, here's what I conveniently omitted, Soulé's sentiment about his list of extinction factors: "One-dimensional lists such as that given in *Table 1* are of limited use because they contain no information on the interaction of the threatening factors. Some of the factors listed in *Table 1* do not become operative until one or more of the other factors have reduced the local population to a very small size." Soulé followed up these statements with a cluttered *Table 2* and a "Domino Flowchart of Ecological Disintegration." Both *Table 2* and the flowchart were Soulé's quick and dirty stab at showing how his eighteen concepts interacted.

In case Soulé's jargon dulled you, allow me to paraphrase: don't waste your time with my list because the factors themselves are trivial; it's how they *interact* that matters.

Wait a minute, let's get this straight: In what many consider to be one of the most important conservation papers ever published, Michael Soulé downplayed his own list? Yes. Hence my trepidation. Had you known this a priori, I feared you might have slammed *Dead Serious* shut. But unless you're one of those weirdos I've met who read books backwards, you suffered through eighteen chapters only to get duped now. So, I've got some explaining to do. In both senses of the word, consider this apology.

Here's the truth: I see more value in Soulé's list than he does. While he's undoubtedly right about the importance of factorial interaction, he's wrong about the uselessness of his reductionism. Sometimes, simple lists are what's needed most. Whether it's a trip to the grocery or outlining Millennium Development Goals, the truth is—lists help. Consider the list created by the Endangered Species Act, enacted to rally federal and state agencies to the cause of some of the most iconic species in the United States. In the midst of DDT being sprayed, wetlands being drained, and subdivisions going up, the act helped us get our collective act together and prioritize. While the process of listing a species isn't simple, the list itself is. Since its inception in 1973, nearly fifty species have recovered and been taken off the list. Fifty!

Critics are quick to point out that this number pales in comparison to the almost two thousand species that have appeared on the list, alongside the eleven that have gone extinct. It's true, the ratio of listed-to-recovered species is remarkably low, and we've lost eleven species to date. But without the list, we would have lost more. Plus, delisting isn't the best way to judge the Endangered Species Act. Extinction prevention is. If we focus on the species that have improved or stabilized their populations—though short of the threshold for delisting—the statistics are much better—over 40 percent. If the act is evaluated on its success rate for safeguarding plants and animals from extinction, it increases to 99 percent effective. Species like grizzlies, eagles, condors, alligators, and peregrine falcons likely owe their iconic lives to the act.

But the critics are right. There's lots of work to be done. Not enough species have recovered sufficiently to be delisted, and nearly a third of the list's species still lack active recovery plans. The act's equivalent on the global level—the Red List established by the International Union for Conservation of Nature (IUCN)—reveals an equally unsettling task: over twenty-eight thousand species are considered at risk of extinction because of human activity.

These lists have obvious merit. Soulé's list does, too, especially because it goes beyond the Endangered Species Act's list and the IUCN's Red List. Soulé's list is a vital complement to these, showing the reasons why species are listed in the first place and the challenges that remain in recovery efforts. Its value lies in its simplicity. As I learned when making a conceptual model for salmon in a simple little creek, it's difficult to show how factors interact. Perhaps harder still to write a book about them. There are too many connections, too many emergent properties, and too much unpredictability to reliably depict reality. Soulé's calming list unclutters all that. It's a rare case in conservation where less is more.

So I disagree with Soulé—I don't think he should have down-played his list at all. Plus, in case you missed it, it was impossible to discuss the predicament of any creature—pika, panthers, Przewalski's horses—without alluding to other extinction factors, too. Regardless of how many times I straightened the horse's blinders, we still routinely veered off path. One factor was tied to another and another. Even if I wasn't a sucker for ecological digressions, it's the reality of ecosystem complexity. While no one factor pushes a species off a cliff by itself, they're best understood apart from the others, one by one. Soulé's clear-eyed list is as good a place to start as any.

It's also good to start—and finish—with what most ecologists consider the two most important words in the discipline: *it depends*. That's effectively what Soulé said about his list; all eighteen factors of extinction depend. One upon another, and all upon us. That's the only thing Soulé was unequivocal about: our role in causing extinction. "Now the disease appears to be spreading to the continents," he wrote forebodingly. "You already know the pathogen—it is man."

Here I'll step away from Soulé at last and plant my own flag. Whether he's right or wrong in his assessment, I don't think the public needs any more guilt or name-calling. For a final bit of wild hope amid the sixth extinction, I think we need two things: more owls and one last list.

• • • •

I found the list when I was looking for owls. This past Christmas, my family stayed in a small rental house in a nondescript subdivision in Cape Coral, Florida. On our first morning there, Linda and Ezra came back from a grocery run with a report of burrowing owls poking out of a series of holes outside a nearby community baseball complex. Ezra was breathless with excitement and demanded we go see them. I was startled on two fronts. One, that burrowing owls had shacked up so close by in the city. And two, that Ezra wanted to drop everything to go see them.

Granted, Ezra has always loved owls. Since his days in diapers,

I've taken him to see owls whenever and wherever I've found them. But since he'd become a teenager, I'd backed off dragging him along on my birding forays, worried they'd bore him and drive him away. As the adage advises: if you love someone, set them free.

In Cape Coral, Ezra was free. And since he wanted to see the owls, I decided to take him. We awoke early the next morning and headed over to the baseball complex. Sure enough, Ezra's burrowing owls were exactly where he said they'd be. Quietly, we watched them from the sidewalk as the sun crested rooftops and lit up their symmetrical faces and perceptive, yellow eyes. We were hardly alone: a mother walked by us pushing a baby stroller, joggers trotted by with a wave, and cars zoomed past. Within spitting distance of the sidewalk, the owls, hardly bigger than soda cans, were visible to all. The residents of Cape Coral passed us by with knowing smiles. They'd granted them ground for a while.

It's a good thing, too, because the owls can use all the ground they can get, no stranger to lists themselves. In Canada, they're listed as endangered, and in Mexico, as threatened. In Florida, they've waffled between "a bird of concern" and "threatened" status, largely because their burrows are destroyed during the development process. Understanding this, the local Cape Coral community rallied to their cause, developing a volunteer "owl prowl" that dedicated time to posting stakes and signs to prevent mowers from hurting them and clipping weeds that clog up burrow entrances. Concern has turned to citywide pride in the unique ground-dwelling birds. City leaders made burrowing owls their official bird in 2005, which they followed up with two mascots—Owliver and Owlivia—and "Ground Owl Day," which the locals use to predict, like the groundhog, whether there will be six more weeks of winter.

"Dad, let's see how many owls we can count!" Ezra suggested once we'd finished our vigil with the owls at the baseball complex.

"Okay," I consented, "we'll drive around a couple of blocks. But we need to get back for breakfast." Slowly, we wove through sleepy subdivisions, many of them laden with more owls. Their rounded heads poked out of front yards, backyards, vacant lots, church fronts, ditches, and even a driveway culvert. Cape Coral, we realized, was owl-infested.

"Let's head back, Ez," I said, my empty stomach rumbling.

"We have to break twenty-five," Ezra replied. "Let's just circle that school." The school turned out to be Pelican Elementary, which turned out to be poorly named. Parliament Elementary would have fit better, because the schoolgrounds were encircled by owls, most just outside a short chain-link fence. On the fence at fifty-yard intervals were one-word qualities, which the administration obviously hoped to impart to its students.

"Can you stop here for a minute, Dad?" Ezra requested, pointing out his window. "I can't tell whether that burrow is occupied." I pulled over and stopped while Ezra hopped out and approached. One owl popped up and perched atop the fence while Ezra counted the burrow's other occupants. On the fence just below the owl was the word *courage*. For a long moment I stared at the owl and the word, realizing how apt the juxtaposition was for Cape Coral's treatment of its owls, and for our response to the sixth extinction more generally. For the rest of our circuit around the school, the words diverted my attention from the adorable owls. There were nine altogether. Here they are, the last list I'll give you:

Courage

Honesty

Integrity

Responsibility

Kindness

Respect

Self-control

Commitment

Citizenship

Herein is the key to ending the sixth extinction. Simple qualities needed to solve complex realities. Soulé's list is longer than Pelican Elementary's and its factors are more complicated, the interactions between them even more so. But the solution to extinction isn't. As the mouth-to-beak resuscitators, Boy Scouts, summit stewards, and many others showed, it's rooted in basic human concern, calling for the same qualities we learn in elementary school. The endurance of these qualities in people around me explain my stubborn wild hope amid the sixth extinction.

Cape Coral's two hundred thousand residents are squeezed between the Gulf of Mexico on one side and mushrooming Fort Myers on the other. The city's challenges are the same humanity faces everywhere—human encroachment and habitat destruction. Yet amid all this sprawling development, a threatened owl, one that has appeared on a few lists itself, is thriving. It has found a place where people give way, cheer, and embrace it as their mascot.

Ezra found twenty-six owls that morning. I found hope.

ACKNOWLEDGMENTS

Last spring, I put a birdhouse just outside my office window while putting the finishing touches on *Dead Serious*. By the sixth of May, a house wren was jamming every stick it could find into the house, much like I've jammed everything into this book. Mostly the wren succeeded. But every fifth time or so, the bird tried inserting a twig into the entrance hole while holding it horizontally in his bill, like a person trying to walk through a door cradling skis. Each time, the twig fell haplessly to the ground and each time the wren flew off for a new one.

Writing this book felt like this. Smooth periods followed by short-sightedness, blind hope, and what seemed like an unending search for another twig. I never would have succeeded without Torrey House Press and the vision, flexibility, and encouragement they provided. First and foremost, I thank Kirsten Johanna Allen, for providing inspiration at my very first utterance of the idea so many moons ago in Salt Lake City's Tracy Aviary. Kirsten saw something in nothing, provided scaffolding, and wiggled deadlines amid a pandemic. Soon after, munificent Anne Terashima came alongside and managed the rare feat of graciously driving a road grader down a very rough manuscript. Anne pointed me toward fresher and better twigs and filled me with the confidence to insert them the right way. Kathleen Metcalf, artistic wizard that she is, provided steadfast amenability and technical skill I've grown accustomed to. I thank Kathleen for seeing how conservation importance and high comedy come together in a piping plover chick. Without the timeliness of Rachel Buck-Cockayne, I would have missed half a dozen deadlines and never reached this point. Thanks to Rachel, as well, for designing the book's beautiful interior. I thank Michelle Wentling for her tireless behind-the-scenes work and thoughtful coordination of events and publicity. The same goes to Maya Kobe-Rundio. Thanks for giving *Dead Serious* a chance to shine.

If Torrey House Press provided the house to nest in, my brother Andrew Knapp gave me the lift I needed to keep flying. While it's hard to yield dominance to a younger brother, I have to do it here, for Andrew improved my work immeasurably and kept his pleasure in exposing my ignorance in check. It was immensely fun to send chapters to him, endure each tongue-in-cheek rebuke, and learn that a woyote is a portmanteau. While I'm indebted to Andrew and acknowledge his intellectual chops, I'm buoyed by the fact that my yard will always yield more bird species than his. I thank my brother Ethan, too, for keeping me current with his steady diet of fascinating tidbits and YouTube clips about the creatures I pursued. As usual, I thank my children, Ezra, Indigo, and Willow, for providing me fodder, listening to my chapters, proofreading the manuscript, and helping me realize there's more important things than finishing a thought.

A medley of others are also due thanks: Matthew Reitnour, for his steady cheerleading over the years, getting me out on the Appalachian Trail, and his unflagging interest in living well with the wild things; my students at Houghton College and Au Sable Institute of Environmental Studies, for helping me see the world in fascinating ways; sidekick Nathan Peace, for his dependability, selflessness, and willingness to loiter indefinitely in my life; Paul Shea, for being my personal champion; Douglas Bassett and Matthew Nusstein, for filling my head with botanical and zoological information; the Letchworth regulars, who throw snowballs, lend me hand lenses, and get equally excited by fuzzy foot fungus; Silas Miller, for reminding me of the importance of living like Indiana Jones; Ransom Poythress, for late-stage fact checking; Java House in Naivasha, Kenya, for fortifying me with endless coffee and sorely needed Wi-Fi; the half-baked good Samaritan, who preserved my mind and body in Maui; and all the sweet librarians who helped me along the way. Especially the one in New Caledonia public library who draped a shawl over my shoulders to ward off the early spring chill.

Not everybody adores house wrens, of course. For all their ebullience, they are stubborn, selfish, and when their nest is falling apart, obstreperous. That's me with a book project. Nobody knows this better than my wife, Linda. Back when we exchanged vows, I should have inserted the clause: "In sickness and in health, and in long, sequestered periods of contemplative thought." That's been the reality of our lives as I've so often holed up in my aerie and written. Words can't express my gratitude for corralling kids, overlooking undone tasks, and enduring my faraway looks and general ineptitude. Even more so, thanks to Linda for the many hours she spent giving the creatures in this book new life with her lovely illustrations. Collaboration with her counts as my greatest joy.

Lastly, I thank the late Michael Soulé. Without his paper and critical insight, *Dead Serious* would be extinct as well.

ABOUT THE AUTHOR

ELI J. KNAPP, PhD, has had a fascination with wildlife ever since the days he obsessively counted deer on his bus rides to school. His wildlife interests have put him into dugout canoes, hot air balloons, paragliders, Land Rovers, and his faithful 1993 Toyota pickup increasingly held together by bumper stickers. When not watching birds, Eli teaches conservation biology, ornithology, wildlife behavior, environmental science, and human ecology at Houghton College in western New York, where he is an associate professor of biology. For fifteen years, Eli directed or assisted the Houghton East Africa program, which spawned out of a three–year stint in Serengeti National Park studying the coexistence of people and wildlife around protected areas. Eli's work has appeared in a variety of technical journals and other outlets including *Conservation & Society*, *Development in Practice*, *Oryx*, *Birdwatcher's Digest*, *New York State Conservationist*, *Arizona Wildlife Views*, *Sisyphus*, *River Hills Traveler*, and many others. His first book, *The Delightful Horror of Family Birding: Sharing Nature with the Next Generation*, was published by Torrey House Press. Today, Eli enjoys sharing nature with his wife and three kids on a three-acre patch christened "Whistling Pines" that certainly feels like more than a lot.

ABOUT THE COVER IMAGE

Dennis Goodman's photographs have been published in *Gulfshore Life Magazine, Portfolio Magazine, Life in Naples, Naples Scene, Marco Scene, Island Scene, Kiplinger Magazine, Connection Magazine,* and *Views Magazine.* This includes feature articles as well as over twenty-two covers of magazines. His accolades include Nature's Best Photography Awards, National Audubon Photography Awards, Epson Pano Awards, and various art show awards.

For Further Reading

Here is a list of sources I drew upon for statistics, quotes, and general information and inspiration. It is a blend of technical articles, trade books, news articles, and reputable websites—all helpful and illuminating. Each chapter's sources are listed as they sequentially appear in the text.

—*Eli J. Knapp*

Introduction

Otieno, Nickson E., Chirchir Shadrack, Naliayana Nicodemus, and Mitei Barnabus. "Effect of habitat alteration on density and distribution of Turner's Eremomela, Eremomela Turneri, in South Nandi Forest, Kenya." *Ibis* 153, no. 2, (March 2011): 436-437.

Pollan, Michael. *A Place of My Own: The Architecture of Daydreams.* New York: Penguin Books, 2008.

Rosling, Hans. *Factfulness: Ten Reasons We're Wrong About the World—and Why Things are Better Than You Think.* New York: Flatiron Books, 2020.

Teal, Edwin Way. *A Walk Through the Year.* New York: Dodd, Mead, 1978.

Soulé, Michael. "What Do We Really Know About Extinction?" In *Genetics and conservation: a reference for managing wild animal and plant populations*, edited by CM Schonewald-Cox, SM Chambers, B MacBryde, W Lawrence Thomas, 111–124. Menlo Park: Benjamin/Cummings, 1983.

Quammen, David. *The Song of the Dodo: Island Biogeography in an Age of Extinction.* New York: Scribner, 1997.

Wilson, Edward O. "A Biologist's Manifesto for Preserving Life on Earth." *Sierra Club Magazine*, December 2016.

Chapter One

Hollars, B. J. "The Resurrection of the Lord God Bird." *Wisconsin People & Ideas*, Spring/Summer 2015.

Gordon-Reed, Annette. *The Hemingses of Monticello: An American Family*. New York: W. W. Norton & Company, 2009.

Wilcove, David S. "Rediscovery of the Ivory-billed Woodpecker." *Science*. 308, no. 5727 (June 2005): 1422–1423

Gaston, Kevin J., and Tim M. Blackburn. "Who is Rare? Artefacts and complexities of rarity determination." In *The Biology of Rarity: Causes and consequences of rare—common differences.* Population and Community Biology Series, vol. 17. edited by W. E. Kunin and K. J. Gaston. Berlin: Springer, Dordrecht, 1997.

Sauer, J. R., D. K. Niven, J. E. Hines, D. J. Ziolkowski Jr., K. L. Pardieck, J. E. Fallon, and W. A. Link (2017). The North American Breeding Bird Survey, Results and Analysis 1966-2015. Version 2.07.2017. USGS Patuxent Wildlife Research Center, Laurel, MD, USA.

Rosenberg, Kenneth, V., Dokter, Adriann M., Blancher, Peter J., Sauer, John R., Smith, Adam C., Smith, Paul, A. Stanton, Jessica C., Panjabi, Arvind., Helft, Laura., Parr, Michael., Marra, Peter P. "Decline of the North American avifauna." *Science* 366 no. 6461 (October 2019): 120–124.

CHAPTER TWO

Brinkley, Douglas. (2010). *The Wilderness Warrior: Theodore Roosevelt and the Crusade for America. Harper Perennial.*

Walters, MacKenzie. (2020). "Conservationists say more than 17,000 rare Nevada wildflowers dug up and destroyed." https://mynews4.com/news/local/more-than-17000-rare-nevada-wildflowers-dug-up-and-destroyed

Slack, Nancy G. (2007). *Adirondack Alpine Summits: An Ecological Field Guide*, Adirondack Mountain Club.

Minton Jr., Sherman A. (1969). "The Feeding Strike of the Timber Rattlesnake," *Journal of Herpetology* 3(3/4):121-124.

CHAPTER THREE

Abad-Santos, Alexander. (2012). "This College Student's 'Turtle Project' Proves Humans Are Jerks," *The Atlantic*, December 27.

Herzog, Hal. (2011). *Some We Love, Some We Hate, Some We Eat: Why It's So Hard to Think Straight About Animals*, Harper Perennial;

Reprint edition.

Caccone, Adalgisa; Gentile, Gabriele; Gibbs, James P; Frirts, Thomas H.; Snell, Howard L.; Betts, Jessica; and Jeffrey R. Powell. (2002). "Phylogeography and history of giant Galapagos tortoises," *Evolution* 56(10):2052-2066.

MacArthur, Robert H; and Edward O. Wilson. (1967). *The Theory of Island Biogeography*, Princeton University Press.

Fridriksson, Sturla. (1987). Plant Colonization of A Volcanic Island, Surtsey, Iceland, *Arctic and Alpine Research* 19(4):425-431.

Magnusson, Borgthor, Sigurbur Magnusson, Erling Olafsson, Bjarni D. Sigurdsson (2014). "Plant colonization, succession and ecosystem development on Surtsey with reference to neighboring islands." *Biogeosciences Discussions* 11(6).

Chapter Four

International Crane Foundation. www.savingcranes.org/species-field-guide/whooping-crane/

Pearse, Aaron T.; Metzger, Kristine L.; Brandt, David A.; Bidwell, Mark T.; Harner, Mary J.; Baasch, David M.; and Wade Harrell. (2020). "Heterogeneity in migration strategies of Whooping Cranes," *The Condor*, 122(1).

Hughes, David; Hughes, Carol. (2002). "Snake Killers: Honey Badgers of the Kalahari," *National Geographic.*

Cheetah Conservation Fund. www.cheetah.org

O'Brien, Stephen J. (2005). *Tears of the Cheetah: The Genetic Secrets of Our Animal Ancestors*, St. Martin's Griffin; First edition.

O'Brien, Stephen J.; Johnson, Warren E.; Driscoll, Carlos A.; Dobrynin, Pavel; and Laurie Marker. (2017). "Conservation Genetics of the Cheetah: Lessons Learned and New Opportunities," *Journal of Heredity* 108(6):671-677.

Leopold, Aldo. (1968). *A Sand County Almanac and Sketches from Here and There*, Oxford University Press, 2nd edition.

Chapter Five

Haskell, George. (2013). *The Forest Unseen: A Year's Watch in Nature*, Penguin Books, Reprint edition.

Merrill, Arch. (1953). *Land of the Senecas*, American Book-Stratford Press; Second Printing edition.

Rue III, Leonard Lee. (1997). *The Deer of North America*, Lyons Press, 1st edition.

Pimm, S.L.; Dollar, L.; Bass Jr., O.L. (2006). "The genetic rescue of the Florida Panther," *Animal Conservation*.

Lanham, J. Drew. (2017). *The Home Place: Memoirs of a Colored Man's Love Affair with Nature*, Milkweed Editions; Reprint edition.

Chapter Six

Oliver, Mary. (1986). *Dream Work*. The Atlantic Monthly Press.

Forsdick, Natalie, J. Ilina, Cubrinovska, Massaro, Melanie, and Marie L. Hale. (2017). "Genetic diversity and population differentiation within and between island populations of two sympatric Petroica robins, the Chatham Island black robin and tomtit." *Conservation Genetics*, 18: 275-285.

Paxinos, Ellen E., James, Helen F., Olson, Storrs L., Leonard, Jennifer A., Fleischer, Robert C., and Jonathan D. Ballou. (2002). "Prehistoric Decline of Genetic Diversity in the Nene." *Science*, 296(5574): 1827.

Chapter Seven

Monzon, Javier, Kays, Roland, and D.E. Dykhuizen. (2014). "Assessment of coyote-wolf-dog admixture using ancestry-informative diagnostic SNPs." *Molecular Ecology*, 23(1): 182-197.

Wilkens, John S. (2009). *Species: A History of the Idea*. University of California Press, Berkeley.

Packer, Craig. (2015). *Lions in the Balance: Man-eaters, Manes, and Men with Guns*, University of Chicago Press, Illustrated edition.

Lau, Allison N., Peng, Lei, Goto, Hiroki, Chemnick, Leona, Ryder, Oliver A., and Kateryna D. Makova. (2009). "Horse Domestication and Conservation Genetics of Przewalski's Horse Inferred from Sex Chromosomal and Autosomal Sequences," *Molecular Biology and Evolution* 26(1):199-206.

Berry, Wendell. (2015). *The Unsettling of America: Culture and Agriculture*, Counterpoint, Reprint edition.

Flores, Dan. (2016). *Coyote America: A Natural and Supernatural History*, Basic Books, First Edition.

CHAPTER EIGHT

Brinkley, Douglas. (2010). *The Wilderness Warrior: Theodore Roosevelt and the Crusade for America*, Harper Perennial.

Mississippi State Univerity (2012). "Ecology & Management of the Northern Bobwhite."

Millard, Candice (2006). *The River of Doubt: Theodore Roosevelt's Darkest Journey*, Broadway Books, 1st edition.

North American Breeding Bird Survey. www.usgs.gov/centers/pwrc/science/north-american-breeding-bird-survey?qt-science_center_objects=0#qt-science-center_objects

CHAPTER NINE

Babine, Karen. *Water and What We Know*. University of Minnesota Press, 2015.

Kahneman, Daniel. *Thinking Fast and Slow*. Farrar, Straus and Giroux, 2013.

Benton, Michael J. *When Life Nearly Died: The Greatest Mass Extinction of All Time*. Thames & Hudson, 2015.

Beever, Erik A., Brussard, Peter F., and Joel Berger. (2003). "Patterns of apparent extirpation among isolated populations of pikas (Ochotona princeps) in the Great Basin." *Journal of Mammalogy*, 84(1):37-54.

Mote, Philip; Lettenmaier, Dennis, P.; Li, Sihan; Xiao, Mu; and Ruth Engel. (2018). "Dramatic declines in snowpack in the western US," *Climate and Atmospheric Science*, 1(1).

Angier, Natalie. (2012). "Warm and Furry but They Pack a Toxic Punch." *The New York Times*.

Weinberg, Samantha. (2001). *A Fish Caught in Time: The Search for the Coelacanth*. Harper Perennial; First Edition.

Pickett, Steward. 2013. "Introduction to Ecosystems: Science, Values, and Action." In: Rozzi R., Pickett, S., Palmer, C., Armesto J., Callicott J. (eds). *Linking Ecology and Ethics for a Changing World*. Ecology and Ethics, vol. 1, Springer.

Chapter Ten

Rubenstein, Madeleine. (2017). "Migratory bird phenology in a changing climate," *The Wildlife Society*. Feb 10.

Jefferson, Thomas. (1799). *A Memoir on the Discovery of Certain Bones of a Quadruped of the Clawed Kind in the Western Parts of Virginia*, Transactions of the American Philosophical Society, American Philosophical Society, pp. 246-260.

Dugatkin, Lee Alan. (2019). "Buffon, Jefferson and the theory of the New World degeneracy," *Evolution: Education and Outreach*, 12(15).

Wilson, Douglas L. (2004). "The Evolution of Jefferson's Notes on the State of Virginia," *Virginia Magazine of History and Biography*, 112: pp. 98-133.

Ambrose, Stephen. (1997). *Undaunted Courage: Meriwether Lewis, Thomas Jefferson, and the Opening of the American West*, Simon & Schuster, 1st edition.

Nagaoka, Lisa, Torben, Rick, and Steve Wolverton. (2018). "The overkill model and its impact on environmental research," *Ecology and Evolution*, 19: 9683-9696.

Global Monitoring Laboratory. https://gml.noaa.gov/ccgg/trends/

Chapter Eleven

Quammen, David. (2009). *Natural Acts: A Sidelong View of Science and Nature*, W.W. Norton & Company; Revised, Expanded ed. Edition.

Benton, Michael J. (2015). *When Life Nearly Died: The Greatest Mass Extinction of All Time*, Thames & Hudson; Revised edition.

Lyell, Charles. (1990). *Principles of Geology*, University of Chicago Press, 1st edition.

Ayanda, Opeyemi, I., Ajayi, Tolulope, and Femi P. Asuwaju. (2020). "Eichornia crassipes (Mart.) Solms: Uses, Challenges, Threats, and Prospects," *Scientific World Journal*.

Greene, Dan. (2020). "Swine Country: How Feral Pigs Took Over the U.S." *Sports Illustrated*, Feb.

Chapter Twelve

McKee, Jeffrey K. (2005). *Sparing Nature: The Conflict between Human*

Population Growth and Earth's Biodiversity, Rutgers University Press.

Darwin, Charles. (1862). "On the Various Contrivances by Which British and Foreign Orchids are Fertilized by Insects, and on the Good Effects of Intercrossing," Cambridge University Press.

Wulf, Andrea. (2016). *The Invention of Nature: Alexander von Humboldt's New World.* Vintage; Illustrated Edition.

Abrahamczyk, S., Souto-Vilaros, D., and S.S. Renner. (2014). "Escape from Extreme Specialization: passionflowers, bats, and the sword-billed hummingbird." Proceedings of the Royal Society.

Valauskas, J. Edward. "Darwin's orchids, moths, and evolutionary serendipity." Chicago Botanic Garden. Feb 2014. www.chicagobotanic.org/library/stories/darwins_orchids

Chapter Thirteen

Tudge, Colin. (2010). *The Bird: A Natural History of Who Birds Are, Where They Came From, and How They Live*, Crown, Annotated edition.

MacArthur, Robert H. (1958). "Population Ecology of Some Warblers of Northeastern Coniferous Forests," *Ecology* 39(4):599-619.

Berry, Wendell. (1987). *Home Economics.* North Point Press.

Chapter Fourteen

Hewitt, Gordon. (1921). *The Conservation of the Wild Life of Canada*, Charles Scribner's Sons, New York

Malthus, Thomas R. (2007). *An Essay on the Principle of Population*, Dover Publications.

Marra, Peter P., and Chris Santella. (2016). *Cat Wars: The Devastating Consequences of a Cuddly Killer*, Princeton University Press, Illustrated edition.

L'Amour, Louis. (1981). *The Sacketts*, Book 4, Bantam.

Miller, Charles. (2015). *The Lunatic Express*, Head of Zeus.

Sheriff, Michael J., Krebs, Charles, J., and Rudy Boonstra. (2009). "The sensitive hare: sublethal effects of predator stress on reproduction in snowshoe hares," *Journal of Animal Ecology*, 78:1249-1258.

Chapter Fifteen

Quammen, David. (2013). *Spillover: Animal Infections and the Next Human Pandemic*, W.W. Norton & Company; Illustrated edition.

The American Chestnut Foundation. www.acf.org

Gray, J.S. (1996). "The ecology of Lyme borreliosis vector ticks," *Ecology and Evolution of the Acari*, Proceedings of the 3rd Symposium of the European Association of Acarologists 1-5, July 1996, Amsterdam, The Netherlands.

Chapter Sixteen

Kruuk, Hans. (2002). *Hunter and Hunted: Relationships between Carnivores and People*, Cambridge University Press; 1st edition.

Knapp, E.J.; Peace, Nathan; and Lauren Bechtel. (2017). "Poachers and Poverty: Assessing Objective and Subjective Measures of Poverty among Illegal Hunters Outside Ruaha National Park, Tanzania," *Conservation and Society* 15(1):24-32.

Johnson, Kirk Wallace. (2019). *The Feather Thief: Beauty, Obsession, and the Natural History Heist of the Century*, Penguin Books; Illustrated edition.

Rademeyer, Julian. (2012). *Killing for Profit: Exposing the Illegal Rhino Horn Trade*, Zebra Press, 1st edition.

Rogers, Lynn L. (1981). "A bear in its lair," *Natural History*, 90(10):64-70.

Chapter Seventeen

Novak, Ben Jacob. (2016). "Deciphering the ecological impact of the Passenger Pigeon: a synthesis of paleogenetics, paleoecology, physiology, and morphology." Masters Thesis, Advisors: James A. Estes, Beth Shapiro.

Gratto-Trevor, C.L., and S. Abbott. (2011). "Conservation of Piping Plover (*Charadrius melodus*) in North America: Science, successes, and challenges," *Canadian Journal of Zoology*, 89(5):401-418.

Prugh, Laura R.; Stoner, Chantal J.; Epps, Clinton, W.; Bean, William T.; Ripple, William J.; Laliberte, Andrea S.; and Justin S. Brashares. (2009). "The Rise of the Mesopredator," *Bioscience* 59(9): 779-791.

Donner, Deahn M.; Brown, Donald J.; Ribic, Christine A.; Nelson, Mark; and Tim Greco. (2018). "Managing forest habitat for conservation-reliant species in a changing climate: The case of the endangered Kirtland's warbler," Forest Ecology and Management, 430:265-279.

Resiliance Alliance. www.resalliance.org

CHAPTER EIGHTEEN

Flores, Dan. (2016). *Coyote America: A Natural and Supernatural History*, Basic Books; First Edition.

Knapp, Eli; Ayres, Elizabeth; Lieberman, Suzanne; Love, Julie; and Kirk Vodopals. (2003). "Assessment of Stressors on Fall-Run Chinook Salmon in Secret Ravine (Placer County, CA)." Masters Thesis, Donald Bren School of Environmental Science and Management, University of California, Santa Barbara.

Wendell, John. (2016). "Animals Rule Chernobyl Three Decades After Nuclear Disaster," *National Geographic*, April 18.

Goldfarb, Ben. (2019). *Eager: The Surprising, Secret Life of Beavers and Why They Matter*. Chelsea Green Publishing; Reprint edition.

Wessells, Tom. (2005). *Reading the Forested Landscape: A Natural History of New England*, Countryman Press; 1st edition.

Nicholls, Henry. (2007). *Lonesome George: The Life and Loves of the World's Most Famous Tortoise*, Pan Macmillan.

Pinsker, Joe. (2020). "The Pandemic Will Cleave America in Two," *The Atlantic*, April 10.

Skillen, James. (2019). "Stewardship and the Kingdom of God." In *Beyond Stewardship: New Approaches to Creation Care*. David Paul Warners and Matthew Kuperur Heun (eds). Calvin College Press.

Babbitt, Bruce. (1995). "Between the Flood and the Rainbow." A speech to the National Press Club, December 13.

CONCLUSION

Soule, Michael E. (1983). "What Do We Really Know About Extinction?" In *Genetics and Conservation: a reference for managing wild animal and plant populations*, Christine M. Schonewald-Cox, Steven M. Chambers, Bruce MacBryde, W. Lawrence Thomas (eds.),

The Benjamin/Cummings Publishing Company, Inc. Chapter 7, pp. 111-124.

The IUCN Red List of Threatened Species, www.iucnredlist.org

Greenwald, Noah; Suckling, Kieran F.; Hartl, Brett; and Loyal A. Mehrhoff. (2019). "Extinction and the Endangered Species Act," *PeerJ*. Vol. 7.

TORREY HOUSE PRESS
Voices for the Land

The economy is a wholly owned subsidiary of the environment, not the other way around.
—Senator Gaylord Nelson, founder of Earth Day

Torrey House Press publishes books at the intersection of the literary arts and environmental advocacy. THP authors explore the diversity of human experiences with the environment and engage community in conversations about landscape, literature, and the future of our ever-changing planet, inspiring action toward a more just world. We believe that lively, contemporary literature is at the cutting edge of social change. We seek to inform, expand, and reshape the dialogue on environmental justice and stewardship for the human and more-than-human world by elevating literary excellence from diverse voices.

Visit www.torreyhouse.org for reading group discussion guides, author interviews, and more.

As a 501(c)(3) nonprofit publisher, our work is made possible by generous donations from readers like you.

This book was made possible by a generous gift from the Sam and Diane Stewart Family Foundation. Torrey House Press is supported by Back of Beyond Books, the King's English Bookshop, Maria's Bookshop, the Jeffrey S. and Helen H. Cardon Foundation, the Barker Foundation, Diana Allison, Klaus Bielefeldt, Laurie Hilyer, Shelby Tisdale, Kirtly Parker Jones, Robert Aagard & Camille Bailey Aagard, Kif Augustine Adams & Stirling Adams, Rose Chilcoat & Mark Franklin, Jerome Cooney & Laura Storjohann, Linc Cornell & Lois Cornell, Susan Cushman & Charlie Quimby, Don Gomes & Annie Holt, Donaree Neville & Doug Neville, Betsy Gaines Quammen & David Quammen, the Utah Division of Arts & Museums, Utah Humanities, the National Endowment for the Humanities, the National Endowment for the Arts, and Salt Lake County Zoo, Arts & Parks. Our thanks to individual donors, members, and the Torrey House Press board of directors for their valued support.

Join the Torrey House Press family and give today at
www.torreyhouse.org/give.